# LATIN FOR GCSE

# Fred Pragnell

First Edition 2014

ISBN 978-0-9573829-6-1

**By the same author**

*A Week in the Middle East* An Arabic Language Reader, with CDs 1984, revised 2003 ISBN 095446062-6

*Arabic in Action* A Basic Course in Spoken Arabic 1992 with CDs ISBN 0-9544606-4-2

*London Times* EFL course combining grammar with historical themes and the main attractions of London, 2001 revised and reprinted 2011 ISBN 0-9549538-4-3

*The Arab News* Arabic-English Reader for Intermediate Students, with CDs 2003 ISBN 0-9544606-0-X

*Palestine Chronicle 1880 - 1950 Extracts from the Arabic press tracing the main political and social developments* 2005, revised with a set of translations and word list on CD 2008 ISBN 0-9549538-0-0

*Preparatory Arabic, A Basic Course in Arabic for Schools* 2010 ISBN 0-9549538-4-3

*The Odyssey The Story in Basic Latin* 2012 ISBN 0-9549538-8-6
*The Odyssey The Story in Very Basic Latin* 2014 ISBN 978-0-9573829-5-4

*The Adventures of Odysseus, A Basic Greek Reader* 2012 ISBN 0-9549538-7-8

*Cambridge Latin Course Conversion Vocabulary* 2012 ISBN 0-9549538-6-X

*An Introduction to Classical Greek* with Kris Waite, Galore Park 2012 ISBN 978-1-905735-88-4

*Latin for Common Entrance Level 1* 2013 ISBN 978-0-9573829-0-9
*Latin for Common Entrance Level 2* 2013 ISBN 978-0-9573829-1-6
*Latin for Common Entrance Levels 3 & Scholarship* 2013 ISBN 978-0-9573829-2-3
*Latin for Common Entrance Levels 1&2 Workbook* 2013 ISBN 978-0-9573829-3-0

*Arabic-English Word List to accompany GCSE Arabic Companion* by Chawki Nacef 2014 ISBN 978-0-9573829-4-7

Series Editor of *Translating Arabic Literature*:

*Modern Iraqi Short Stories 1* Sayyab Books 2009 ISBN 978-1-906228-125
*Ten Stories from Iraq 3* Sayyab Books 2011 ISBN 978 1 90 6228 989
*The Scent of Winter* by Mahmoud Abdul Wahab Sayyab Books 2012 ISBN 978-1-906228-37-8
*The Train Heading up to Baghdad* A dual language Arabic-English Reader, based on the short story by Mahmoud Abdul Wahab, with notes, exercises and CD 2013 ISBN 0-9549538-9-4

Printed in Great Britain by **four point printing**

# Preface

## Aims

This course book aims to prepare students for both the Foundation and Higher Tiers of the OCR GCSE. Chapters 43 and 44 have extended passages of Latin to help GCSE candidates improve their reading fluency and also to introduce the vocabulary prescribed for AS level.

## Basis

It is not a beginners' course. Familiarity with Levels 1 and 2 of the Common Entrance syllabus, or equivalent, is assumed. There are some fifty CE words used in this course which are not on the prescribed GCSE syllabus. These are marked with an asterisk in the vocabulary list at the end of the book. The book follows a grammar-based approach and there is abundant practice for translating both from and into Latin. In this way students will learn to analyze with confidence and precision both the Latin and the English they meet.  At the rate of three hours per chapter, the core material can be covered in some 120 hours. So, together with the 120 hours for levels 1 and 2 of *Latin for Common Entrance*, the complete syllabus covering the Higher Tier will require some 240 hours of guided learning.

## Audience

Each chapter has both core and extra exercises, marked 'E'. They are designed and presented so as to be used by a number of overlapping groups:

(i)      As a comprehensive revision of the prescribed vocabulary and constructions for GCSE. For this group the core exercises will suffice. With constant repetition of the vocabulary, reading fluency will be developed and the underlying structures reinforced.

(ii)     Students who have completed CE level 2 can choose which extra exercises are necessary in each chapter to master the materials.

(iii)    Those with CE level 3 can skip over Chapters 4, 5, 6, 7, 8, 9, 10, 12, 14, 15, 23 and 25, though the new vocabulary should be practised. The same will apply for those who have covered the CE Scholarship syllabus, which is covered in chapters 17, 19, 20, 23, 25, 26, 36 and 40.

(iv)     Any of the above who intend carrying on to AS or A2. The English-Latin sentences are especially important as they encourage proper understanding of the basic structures so indispensable for further study. Chapter 45 has a number of extended passages of English for translation into Latin.

## Materials

The Foundation Tier is covered by chapters 1 -30, while chapters 31 - 45 contain the material for the Higher Tier. There is a summary of the vocabulary introduced in each chapter on page 155 for reference so that learning of the new words can be systematic and gradual. Students learning classical Greek may well find the presentation of materials reassuringly familiar. This should be of mutual benefit.

The cartoons with the multiple choice answers will provide additional practice for directed 'reading for a purpose' to encourage reading fluency. The word searches, done quickly and competitively, will encourage consolidation of new vocabulary and grammar.

Reading fluency is encouraged by having, as far as possible, meaningful discrete sentences. The occasional gap-filling exercises test not only vocabulary but also an understanding of the grammar – a kind of quick check for those with limited time.

In chapter 42 there is practice of conversational Latin which, while not on the syllabus, may well interest those who would like to practise spoken Latin. With the addition of a small amount of vocabulary, students should be able to make a presentation similar to one that is used in the oral part of modern languages GCSE.

In chapter 43 a series of passages, adapted from Ritchie's *Fabulae Latinae*, based on the Odyssey, followed by some more sentences, should develop help develop reading fluency. The new vocabulary glossed in the passages and sentences is listed in the word list on page 135 and covers all the extra vocabulary prescribed for AS level. By reading these passages and sentences a number of times, students can familiarize themselves with the words in advance.

In Chapter 44 there is the original version of the Odyssey stories from Ritchie's *Fabulae Latinae*, followed by a second list of some two hundred further new words. By the very gradual addition of vocabulary into the familiar story of the Odyssey that had already been met in Books 1 and 2 of *Latin for Common Entrance*, students will retain and develop their confidence and reading fluency.

In chapter 45 there is a series of passages to practise translation into Latin for those going on to AS and A2 . These can be tackled once chapter 43 is finished.

Since the materials are on CD, teachers can add to and adapt them as required.

Translations of the Latin into English exercises are given on page 160 to allow immediate feedback and resolve any problems in the translation. Once the students have mastery of these basic sentences they will have the confidence to progress to adapted Latin texts and thence onto 'real' Latin. Short-cutting at this stage can lead to unwelcome rote-learning of passages of English as students prepare their set texts for GCSE and beyond.

Fred Pragnell

July 2014

# Contents

**Continued**

## Higher Level

# Chapter 1  Review of tenses and some new verbs

Perhaps it is some time since you last saw any Latin, so we shall start with a review of the four **conjugations** of verbs in the **tenses** needed for GCSE.

| | 1 | 2 | 3 | 4 | 3½ | irregular |
|---|---|---|---|---|---|---|
| **present** | | | | | | |
| I | amo | moneo | rego | audio | capio | sum |
| you *(sing.)* | amas | mones | regis | audis | capis | es |
| he, she, it | amat | monet | regit | audit | capit | est |
| we | amamus | monemus | regimus | audimus | capimus | sumus |
| you *(pl.)* | amatis | monetis | regitis | auditis | capitis | estis |
| they | amant | monent | regunt | audiunt | capiunt | sunt |
| **future** | | | | | | |
| I | amabo | monebo | regam | audiam | capiam | ero |
| you *(sing.)* | amabis | monebis | reges | audies | capies | eris |
| he, she, it | amabit | monebit | reget | audiet | capiet | erit |
| we | amabimus | monebimus | regemus | audiemus | capiemus | erimus |
| you *(pl.)* | amabitis | monebitis | regetis | audietis | capietis | eritis |
| they | amabunt | monebunt | regent | audient | capient | erunt |
| **imperfect** | | | | | | |
| I | amabam | monebam | regebam | audiebam | capiebam | eram |
| you *(sing.)* | amabas | monebas | regebas | audiebas | capiebas | eras |
| he, she, it | amabat | monebat | regebat | audiebat | capiebat | erat |
| we | amabamus | monebamus | regebamus | audiebamus | capiebamus | eramus |
| you *(pl.)* | amabatis | monebatis | regebatis | audiebatis | capiebatis | eratis |
| they | amabant | monebant | regebant | audiebant | capiebant | erant |
| **perfect** | | | | | | |
| I | amavi | monui | rexi | audivi | cepi | fui |
| you *(sing.)* | amavisti | monuisti | rexisti | audivisti | cepisti | fuisti |
| he, she, it | amavit | monuit | rexit | audivit | cepit | fuit |
| we | amavimus | monuimus | reximus | audivimus | cepimus | fuimus |
| you *(pl.)* | amavistis | monuistis | rexistis | audivistis | cepistis | fuistis |
| they | amaverunt | monuerunt | rexerunt | audiverunt | ceperunt | fuerunt |
| **pluperfect** | | | | | | |
| I | amaveram | monueram | rexeram | audiveram | ceperam | fueram |
| you *(sing.)* | amaveras | monueras | rexeras | audiveras | ceperas | fueras |
| he, she, it | amaverat | monuerat | rexerat | audiverat | ceperat | fuerat |
| we | amaveramus | monueramus | rexeramus | audiveramus | ceperamus | fueramus |
| you *(pl.)* | amaveratis | monueratis | rexeratis | audiveratis | ceperatis | fueratis |
| they | amaverant | monuerant | rexerant | audiverant | ceperant | fuerant |
| **infinitive** | amare | monēre | regĕre | audire | capĕre | esse |
| **imperatives** | | | | | | |
| *sing.* | ama | mone | rege | audi | cape | es |
| *pl.* | amate | monete | regite | audite | capite | este |

You will remember that Latin verbs are given in a dictionary in their principal parts. So far we have met three of the four; this fourth part we shall be meeting in Chapter 8.

For a regular verb the three principal parts are:

**present tense** (1ˢᵗ person singular)        **infinitive**        **perfect tense** (1ˢᵗ person singular)

Note that we need **all** these parts for complete information for writing a verb. For example, -*o* ending could be both 1ˢᵗ and 3ʳᵈ conjugation and the infinitive -*ere* is both 2ⁿᵈ and 3ʳᵈ, though pronounced differently. Some books distinguish between the 2ⁿᵈ conjugation long e (ē) and 3ʳᵈ conjugation short e (ĕ). In addition, the number of the conjugation is sometimes put instead of the infinitive. Modern textbooks call the *capio* verbs of the 3ʳᵈ conjugation either 3½ or mixed conjugation. Dictionaries usually put the English meaning in the infinitive form: '**to** warn'.

We shall revise the tenses using some new verbs, listing in their principal parts:

| present | infinitive | perfect | conjugation | meaning |
|---------|-----------|---------|-------------|---------|
| invito | invitare | invitavi | 1 | to invite |
| saluto | salutare | salutavi | 1 | to greet |
| doceo | docēre | docui | 2 | to teach |
| ago | agĕre | egi | 3 | to do, act, drive |
| emo | emĕre | emi | 3 | to buy |
| traho | trahĕre | traxi | 3 | to drag |
| vendo | vendĕre | vendidi | 3 | to sell |
| vivo | vivĕre | vixi | 3 | to live |

The **present tense** is used to describe an action happening now

ventus navem ad insulam agit.
The wind is driving the ship to the island.

It is also used for a repeated action:

senem saepe saluto.
I often greet the old man.

Note the uses of *doceo*:

hic vir Graecum docet.
This man teaches Greek.

hic vir puellam Graecum docet.
This man is teaching the girl Greek (Note double accusative)

hic vir puellam scribere docet.
This man is teaching the girl (how) to write.

1 femina puerum legere docet.
2 dominus ad villam ancillam trahit.
3 puella a villa nautam agit.
4 femina pulchra ad cenam nautam invitat.
5 miles tristis feminam salutat.

Note the use of the infinitive.

Note that in Latin the present tense is also often used to give vividness to an action in a story that is set in the past. This so-called **historic present** is used colloquially in English when we are telling a joke or, for example, reporting on an event in a football match: 'then he shoots...'

## Exercise 1.1     Translate into English

1. dominus meus amicum numquam invitat.
2. venti saevi nautas miseros ab insula agunt.
3. soror mea aurum numquam emit.
4. miles validus corpus ducis e proelio iam trahit.
5. senex omne aurum hodie vendit.
6. pater filium parvum in agro currere docet.
7. ille senex prope mare iam vivit.
8. dominus malus equum mortuum vendere cupit.
9. nemo illum iuvenem miserum invitat.
10. 'quid tu in agro agis?' inquit dominus iratus. 'ego laboro', respondet servus perterritus.

The **imperfect tense** is used to describe an uncompleted action, that is, an action that was going on when something interrupted it.

ubi venti navem ab insula agebant, subito nauta in mare se iecit.
As the winds were driving the ship from the island, a sailor suddenly threw himself into the sea.

The imperfect is also used to express a repeated action in the past, translated by 'used to' 'continued to' or even 'tried to', 'intended to'. English often uses the simple past tense to translate the Latin imperfect.

mater filiam parvam diu docebat.
The mother continued to teach / taught her small daughter for a long time.

## Exercise 1.2     Translate into English

1. nonne dominus tuus comitem semper salutabat?
2. venti saevi omnes naves ab insula forte agebant.
3. 'mi amice, servosne Graecos emebas?'
4. miles fessus corpus ducis e proelio iam trahebat.
5. senex omnia arma amico vendebat.
6. 'comitemne gladio pugnare docebas?'
7. nemo hunc equum fessum emere cupiebat.
8. 'num hunc equum mortuum vendebas?'
9. mei amici hanc iuvenem pulcherrimam invitabant.
10. 'quid vos in villa agebatis?' inquit dominus iratus. 'nos laborabamus', responderunt servi.

The **future tense** is normally translated by *'I shall'* and *'we shall'* and *'will'* for the other persons.

Note that there are two different patterns for the future: *-bo, -bis, -bit* etc. for 1st and 2nd conjugations and *-am, -es, -et* etc. for 3rd and 4th conjugations. Note also that except for the 1st person singular, the endings of the future tense of the 3rd conjugation are very similar to those of the present tense of the 2nd conjugation.

## Exercise 1.3    Translate into English

1. cras mei amici has iuvenes pulchras invitabunt.
2. nonne tu in hac insula vives?
3. ventusne saevus naves nostras ab insula aget?
4. vir tres e libris comiti mox vendet.
5. num hunc cibum malum seni vendes?
6. mi amici, illosne servos Graecos emetis?
7. nonne frater tuus comites suos invitabit?
8. num puerum parvum gladio pugnare docebis?
9. Troianine equum ingentem in oppidum trahent?
10. illumne virum malum in via salutabis?

1 magister pueros ad cenam invitat.
2 magister historiam pueros docet.
3 magister discipulos ad forum trahit.
4 pueri magistrum salutat.
5 pueri magistrum dormire docent.

With a few exceptions, the **perfect tense** of all the 1st conjugation are regular; so the perfect of *invito* is *invitavi* and the perfect of *saluto* is *salutavi*. Whilst there are patterns for the verbs in the others conjugations, it is advisable to learn them as they are met:

| doceo | docēre | docui | 2 | to teach |
|-------|--------|-------|---|----------|
| ago | agĕre | egi | 3 | to do, act, drive |
| emo | emĕre | emi | 3 | to buy |
| traho | trahĕre | traxi | 3 | to drag |
| vendo | vendĕre | vendidi | 3 | to sell |
| vivo | vivĕre | vixi | 3 | to live |

The perfect tense is translated by e.g. 'taught', 'has taught' or 'did teach' depending on context.

## Exercise 1.4    Translate into English

1. heri mei amici comites caros invitaverunt.
2. quis hunc equum ferocem emit?
3. ventus saevissimus omnes naves nostras ab insula egit.
4. vir decem libros comiti vendidit.
5. agricola miser et filii sui cibo malo diu vivere debebant.
6. mi comes, cur hos libros malos emisti?
7. frater diu in illa insula laete vixit.
8. num illos servos gladio pugnare docuisti?
9. deinde Troiani equum ingentem in oppidum traxerunt.
10. illam mulierem in via non salutavi.

The **pluperfect tense** is formed by taking off the ending -*i* from the perfect and then adding the imperfect tense of the verb *to be* -*eram* etc. The pluperfect refers to something that had happened before something else. English always translates using 'had'. Great attention must be paid to verb endings, especially the pluperfect.

puer, quod librum non acceperat, miserrimus erat.
The boy was very unhappy because he had not received the book.

4

**Exercise 1.5    Translate into English**

1. ante bellum mei amici me Romam iam invitaverant.
2. vir quod illum equum malum emerat tristis erat.
3. venti omnes naves nostras ad insulam egerant.
4. vir, ubi decem libros iam vendidit, statim discessit.
5. arma mala ante proelium vendideramus.
6. antequam ad villam meam heri discessi, etiam comitem meum invitaveram.
7. cur fratrem tuum non invitaveras?
8. dominus illos servos gladiis pugnare numquam docuerat.
9. antequam Graeci redierunt, Troiani equum ingentem in oppidum iam traxerant.
10. illas mulieres in via numquam salutaveram.

**Exercise 1.6E    Translate the following verbs into Latin and find them in the wordsearch**

```
A I S D N A G E S S U
G D U O V E N D U N T
O I M C P O T M M R B
T D E E E I E J A U P
Q N H B G M P X T E K
L E A A E R E V I Y M
Z V R T R R Z P V H M
X R T N U M E V N W B
V V M N N L L B I G C
I Q T B T R A H U N T
H C M G Q J U S D W L
```

we invite, they greet, he used to teach, she is driving, they buy, we drive, they are selling, they have driven, we shall buy, they dragged, I sold, they are dragging

**Exercise 1.7E    Review          Complete the following and translate into English**

1. num haec arm_ mala sen_ misero vendidisti?
2. mi amici, illosne serv__ Graec__ emetis?
3. senex omnia arm_ amico vendid__ .
4. antequam ego ad vill__ meam heri discess_ , comitem iam invitaveram.
5. vent_ saevi quattuor naves ab insul_ forte egerunt.
6. num hunc puer__ parvum gladio pugn___ docebis?
7. Troianine equum ingent__ in oppid__ trahent?
8. quis h___ equum emere cupit?
9. heri mei amic_ comites car__ invitaverunt.
10. 'quid tu in agro agis' inquit dominus irat__ . 'ego laboro', respondit serv__ perterritus.

# Chapter 2  Review of cases of nouns in first three declensions

| declension | 1 | 2 | 2 | 2 | 2 |
|---|---|---|---|---|---|
| gender | feminine | masculine | masculine | masculine | neuter |
| **singular** | | | | | |
| nominative | puella | servus | puer | ager | bellum |
| vocative | puella | serve | puer | ager | bellum |
| accusative | puellam | servum | puerum | agrum | bellum |
| genitive | puellae | servi | pueri | agri | belli |
| dative | puellae | servo | puero | agro | bello |
| ablative | puella | servo | puero | agro | bello |
| **plural** | | | | | |
| nominative | puellae | servi | pueri | agri | bella |
| vocative | puellae | servi | pueri | agri | bella |
| accusative | puellas | servos | pueros | agros | bella |
| genitive | puellarum | servorum | puerorum | agrorum | bellorum |
| dative | puellis | servis | pueris | agris | bellis |
| ablative | puellis | servis | pueris | agris | bellis |

| declension | 3 | 3 | 3 neuter |
|---|---|---|---|
| **singular** | | | |
| nominative | rex | civis | nomen |
| vocative | rex | civis | nomen |
| accusative | regem | civem | nomen |
| genitive | regis | civis | nominis |
| dative | regi | civi | nomini |
| ablative | rege | cive | nomine |
| **plural** | | | |
| nominative | reges | cives | nomina |
| vocative | reges | cives | nomina |
| accusative | reges | cives | nomina |
| genitive | regum | civium | nominum |
| dative | regibus | civibus | nominibus |
| ablative | regibus | civibus | nominibus |

Remember that nouns **decline** and verbs **conjugate**. Dictionaries give the nominative and genitive singular, the declension and the gender of a noun. For 3rd declension nouns, the genitive singular gives us the stem on to which we put the appropriate ending.

# New nouns

| | | | | |
|---|---|---|---|---|
| cena | cenae | 1 | f. | dinner, meal |
| domina | dominae | 1 | f. | mistress |
| epistula | epistulae | 1 | f. | letter |
| ianua | ianuae | 1 | f. | door |
| silva | silvae | 1 | f. | forest, wood |
| taberna | tabernae | 1 | f. | shop, inn |
| vita | vitae | 1 | f. | life |
| | | | | |
| hortus | horti | 2 | m. | garden |
| libertus | liberti | 2 | m. | freedman |
| | | | | |
| consilium | consilii | 2 | n. | plan, idea, advice |
| forum | fori | 2 | n. | forum, market-place |
| | | | | |
| ars | artis | 3 | f. | art, skill |
| canis | canis | 3 | c. * | dog |
| leo | leonis | 3 | m. | lion |
| mercator | mercatoris | 3 | m. | merchant |

\* c. = common i.e. the gender of the noun will depend on the particular person or animal

## Exercise 2.1     Translate into English

1. in vita mea mulierem pulchriorem numquam vidi.
2. libertus omnes comites ad cenam heri invitavit.
3. iuvenis tristis ad dominam iratam multas epistulas misit.
4. mercator multas artes Graecas in foro vendebat.
5. canis ingens et ferox ante ianuam tabernae stabat.
6. vir uxori consilium dedit, sed frustra, nam ea non audiebat.
7. incola fortis leonem ferocem gladio occidit.
8. duo canes in horto liberti dormiebant.
9. mercator artes notas emebat et vendebat.
10. incolas leones in silva conspexerunt.

## Exercise 2.2E     Translate the following nouns into Latin and find them in the wordsearch

```
F E J U R H Q K K C O
F R X S H O R T O S N
L O W G V U B N I E E
M T R D C U S A Y N P
A A X O Y I A N U A I
N C T M L C N A R C S
E R L I B E R T U M T
C E U N V V E U B C U
A M D A G M B X W I L
E N O E L Y A K V C A
W F V C D Y T O O D S
```

life *(acc.)*, dinner *(acc.)*, mistress *(gen.)*, letters *(acc.)*, door *(nom.)*, shops *(acc.)*, gardens *(acc.)*, freedman *(acc.)*, plan *(acc.)*, forum *(abl.)*, art *(acc.)*, dogs *(acc.)*, lion *(abl.)*, merchant *(abl.)*

| cura | curae | 1 | f | care, worry |
|------|-------|---|---|-------------|
| porta | portae | 1 | f | gate |
| victoria | victoriae | 1 | f | victory |
| | | | | |
| animus | animi | 2 | m | spirit, soul, mind |
| | | | | |
| castra | castrorum *(pl.)* | 2 | n | camp |
| signum | signi | 2 | n | sign, seal, standard |
| | | | | |
| amor | amoris | 3 | m | love |
| consul | consulis | 3 | m | consul |
| imperator | imperatoris | 3 | m | emperor, general, leader |
| pax | pacis | 3 | f | peace |
| senator | senatoris | 3 | m | senator |
| caput | capitis | 3 | n | head |
| tempus | temporis | 3 | n | time |

## Exercise 2.3    Translate into English

1. dux miser caput canis ad hostes misit.
2. iuvenis maxima cum cura epistulam amoris scribebat.
3. senator omnibus amicis cenam dedit.
4. senatores signum victoriae tandem dederunt.
5. dux signum videre cupivit.
6. domina ad libertum epistulam non misit, nam tempus non habebat.
7. imperator milites suos inire per portam castrorum iussit.
8. canem meum vendere in animo habeo.
9. tandem fuit pax per omnes terras.
10. dominus omne tempus et in agris suis consumpsit.

## Exercise 2.4E    Translate the following nouns into Latin and find them in the wordsearch

```
C S S W E M L L T A A
O T I E F I T N H I N
M E G T N W B H R Z Y
I M P E R A T O R I M
N P J R M O T B C J U
A O M O M C P O U H N
S R R I I A N O R O G
P E Y V C S F I A E I
M O L E U T U Q M O S
U W M L G R M G H Y W
V P E H C A P I T A F
```

care *(acc.)*, gates *(abl.)*, victory *(abl.)*, mind *(abl.)*, camp *(nom.)*, sign *(acc.)*, love *(acc.)*, consul *(abl.)*, emperor *(abl.)*, peace *(acc.)*, senators *(nom.)*, heads *(nom.)*, time *(abl.)*

**Exercise 2.5E    Translate into English**

1. mercator multas artes Graecas in animo vendere habuit.
2. imperator audax leonem ferocem gladio occidit.
3. senatores imperatorem ad cenam heri invitaverunt.
4. post proelium  multi milites signum tandem reliquerunt *(deserted)*.
5. imperator victoriam claram in animo habuit.
6. dux magna cum cura consilium paravit.
7. tres canes feroces prope ianuam tabernae stabant.
8. 'iam servi caput cenae *(main course)* portant' inquit senator.
9. in vita sua dux oppidum maius numquam viderat.
10. hostes castra Romanorum subito oppugnaverunt.

**Exercise 2.6E    Review         Complete the following and translate into English**

1. mercator fili__ parvum in for_ currere docebat.
2. quis hunc can__ em___ cupit?
3. domin__ meus illam tabern__ vendere cupit.
4. nonne hi senator__ imperatorem semper salutabant?
5. venti saev_ quinque naves ab insul_ forte agebant.
6. 'mi amice, quid in anim_ fac___ habes?
7. antequam domum heri discessit, libertus duo sign_ emit.
8. serv_ boni magna cum cur_ cenam imperatori parav_____ .
9. can__ ingens et ferox per viam curr____ .
10. magister iratus ad patrem huius puer_ multas epistul__ misit.

1 senator ancillam ad tabernam ire iubet.
2 imperator nautae pecuniam dat.
3 libertus agricolam in horto laborare iubet
4 senator filiam ad forum ire iubet.
5 rex servum artes Graecas docet.

1 ancilla in taberna dormit
2 mercator cibum et vinum vendit.
3 libertus vinum et aquam emit.
4 domina vinum et aquam portat.
5 puella per hortum ambulat.

# Chapter 3  Direct questions

You have already met questions beginning with

| | |
|---|---|
| cur? = why? | quid? = what? |
| quis = who? | ubi? = where? |
| -ne? = question | nonne? = surely? |
| num? = surely not? | |

**Exercise 3.1     Translate into English**

1. cur imperator canem vendidit?
2. quid mercator emit?
3. quid consulem terruit?
4. nonne comitem invitare tempus habes?
5. leonisne corpus in forum viri traxerunt?
6. o serve, num canes feroces in villam egisti?
7. ubi sunt tabernae optimae vini?
8. 'ubi est cena mea?' uxori perterritae clamavit vir.
9. 'cur milites signum reliquerunt?' rogavit imperator.
10. 'ubi est canis?' rogavit vir. 'ante ianuam dormit' respondit filius.

1 'quot fratres habes?'
2 'quo hoc traho?'
3 'quo modo fugere possumus?'
4 'salve, imperator?'
5 'quot epistulas scripsisti?'

Further words introducing questions

| | |
|---|---|
| qualis? quale? = what sort of? | quantus -a -um = how big? how much? |
| quo? = to where? | quo modo? = how? |
| quot? = how many? | |

Examples:

> 'qualis est ille miles?' rogavit imperator. 'optimus' respondit dux.
> 'What kind of soldier is he?' asked the emperor. 'Very good' replied the general.

> 'quale est hoc aurum?' rogavit mulier. 'pessimum' respondit mercator.
> 'What type of gold is this?' asked the woman. 'Very bad' replied the merchant.
> Note that *quale* is neuter, agreeing with *aurum*.

> 'quantum est forum Romanum?' rogavit miles. 'maximum' respondit imperator.
> 'How large is the Roman forum' asked the soldier. 'Very large' replied the emperor.

> 'quo festinas?' rogavit dominus. 'ad forum' respondit servus.
> 'Where are you hurrying to?' asked the master. 'To the forum' replied the slave.

> 'quo modo leo incolam occidit?'
> 'How did the lion kill the inhabitant?'
> *quo modo* = literally *In what way*?

> 'quot naves ad insulam festinant?' rogavit mulier. 'plurimae' respondit vir.

'How many ships are hurrying to the island?' asked the woman. 'Very many' answered the man.

*quot* is indeclinable, that is, it does not change, whether the noun is singular or plural.

## New words used in conversation

| | |
|---|---|
| ecce! = look! | minime = very little, least, no |
| satis = enough | salve! = hello! |
| vale! = goodbye, farewell | umquam = ever |

### Exercise 3.2    Translate into English

1. 'quot canes habet dominus?' 'quinque.'
2. 'o serve, unde cucurristi?' 'ab oppido.'
3. 'salve, o nauta, quo modo ad insulam venisti?' 'in illa nave.'
4. 'o liberte, maius forum umquam vidisti?' 'numquam.'
5. 'o miles, qualis est dux tuus?' 'fortissimus.'
6. 'quale est illud flumen?' 'altissimum.'
7. numquam dux plura verba dicebat quam satis erant.
8. 'mi fili, satisne temporis habes?' 'minime.'
9. 'quanta sunt castra hostium?' 'maxima.'
10. 'satis vidi; nunc vale!' inquit imperator.
11. 'ecce, hoc est forum Romanum. maiusne umquam vidisti?
12. 'quo pater tuus it?' 'domum.'

### Exercise 3.3    Translate into Latin

1. 'How many dogs do you have?' 'Four.'
2. 'What is your teacher like?' 'Very good.'
3. 'Have you ever seen a larger dog?' 'Never.'
4. The general had seen enough.
5. 'How did this young man cross the river?' 'In that ship.'
6. 'Why are you running to the forest?' 'Because I am afraid.'
7. 'Where are you hurrying to?' 'To the forest.'
8. 'Do you like the dinner?' ' No.'
9. 'Have the soldiers eaten enough food?' 'No.'

1 'bibistine satis vini, imperator?'
2 'vale, agricola!'
3 'quo is, senator?'
4 'quot libros habes, mercator?'
5 'salve, nauta!'

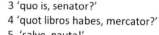

### Exercise 3.4E   Review       Complete the following and translate into English

1. 'quo tu festin__ ?' 'ad mare, mi amice'
2. mercator senatori epistulam non mis__ , nam temp__ non habebat.
3. 'mi fili, tune satis cibi hab__ ?' 'minime.'
4. mercatores multas art__ Graecas in illa tabern_ vendebant.
5. in vita sua senator muliere__ pulchriorem numquam viderat.
6. imperator victori__ claram in anim_ habuit.
7. omnes can__ meos vend___ in animo habebam.
8. dux audax leonem fero___ gladi_ suo occidit.
9. dux milites su__ inire per portam castr____ iussit.
10. libert__ hos comites ad cenam saepe invit__ .

# Chapter 4  The passive voice present tense

So far, the verbs you have met have all been in the active voice. Examples:

The soldier is warning the general. We send the messenger. They throw the spears. You are punishing the slave.

We can put these sentences into the passive voice thus:

The general is being warned by the soldier. The messenger is sent by us. The spears are thrown by them. The slave is being punished by you.

Since the passive voice occurs most commonly in the 3$^{rd}$ person, singular and plural, it is these that need to be learned and recognised.

| | | conjugation | | |
|---|---|---|---|---|
| 1$^{st}$ | 2$^{nd}$ | 3$^{rd}$ | 4$^{th}$ | 3½ |
| amor | moneor | regor | audior | capior |
| amaris | moneris | regeris | audiris | caperis |
| amatur | monetur | regitur | auditur | capitur |
| amamur | monemur | regimur | audimur | capimur |
| amamini | monemini | regimini | audimini | capimini |
| amantur | monentur | reguntur | audiuntur | capiuntur |

amor = I am loved, or I am being loved
monemur = we are warned, we are being warned
non reguntur = they are not ruled, they are not being ruled
auditur = (s)he, it is heard, (s)he, it is being heard
capimini = you are taken, you are being taken

Note that in English there is no direct passive of e.g. *he doesn't send the messenger.*


There is **no** present, imperfect or future passive of facio


**Exercise 4.1**      **Translate into English, giving just one version**

1. amantur      2. moneris      3. regitur      4. non audimur 5. non caperis

**Exercise 4.2E**   **Translate into English, giving just one version**

1. amatur      2. monemini   3. regeris      4. non audiuntur      5. non capimini

**Exercise 4.3**      **Translate into Latin**

1. He is loved           2. They are warned      3. We are ruled         4. They are being heard
5. She is captured

**Exercise 4.4E    Translate into Latin**

1. They are loved        2. He isn't warned        3. You *(sing.)* are ruled
4. We are being heard        5. We are captured

## Review of transitive verbs

### Exercise 4.5    Translate the following verbs into English

accipio, aedifico, ago, bibo, colligo, conspicio, constituo, consumo, defendo, deleo, duco, emo, expecto, gero, iacio, invenio, invito, iubeo, laudo, lego, libero, mitto, moveo, narro, neco, nuntio, occido, occupo, oppugno, ostendo, paro, pono, porto, reduco, saluto, servo, specto, supero, teneo, terreo, trado, traho, voco, vulnero

### Exercise 4.6    Translate the following verbs into English

accipiunt, aedificat, agit, bibit, colligunt, conspicit, constituit, consumit, defendunt, delent, ducunt, emit, gerit, iaciunt, invenit, invitat, iubent, laudat, legit, liberamus, mittimus, moves, necant, occidit, occupat, oppugnat, ostendit, parat, ponunt, portamus, reducit, salutat, servatis, spectant, superas, tenes, terret, tradit, trahit, vocat, vulneratis

### Exercise 4.7    Put the verbs in Exercise 4.6 into the passive

### Exercise 4.8    Translate into Latin

1. It is being built        2. They are defended        3. It is not being destroyed
4. We are being led        5. They are thrown        6. She is praised
7. You *(sing.)* are being sent        8. They are moved        9. It is bought

### Exercise 4.9E    Translate into Latin

1. They are invited        2. It is attacked        3. They are shown
4. It is being dragged        5. They are being carried        6. You *(pl.)* are led back
7. He is overcome        8. She is handed over        9. They are driven

To translate **by** + a person we use a/ab + ablative

urbs ab hostibus oppugnatur.        The city is being attacked by the enemy.

To translate **by** + a thing we use ablative only

urbs hastis oppugnatur.        The city is being attacked with spears.

## New vocabulary

| | |
|---|---|
| ac, atque   = and | interea = meanwhile, in the meantime |
| lente       = slowly | nec …. nec / neque … neque = neither … nor |
| paene      = nearly, almost | centum = hundred |
| mille *pl.* milia = thousand | |

**Exercise 4.10    Translate into English**

1. hi pueri miseri a canibus saevis vulnerantur.
2. paene omnes pueri ac puellae a magistro laudantur.
3. quot epistulae a domina leguntur?
4. interea ceterae naves ventis saevis ad insulam aguntur.
5. pauci servi a domino malo saepe puniuntur.
6. hoc vinum optimum a nautis novis lente bibitur.
7. quo modo nautae Graeci a centum militibus Romanis vincuntur?
8. ille miles a duce numquam legitur.
9. castra hostium a mille Romanis diu oppugnantur.
10. nos a militibus iratis nec capimur nec vulneramur.

**Exercise 4.11E   Translate into English**

1. Helena pulcherrima a Paride capitur.
2. haec urbs magna a mille Troianis fortiter defenditur.
3. hi viri fortes a Graecis nec occiduntur nec vulnerantur.
4. hic equus ingens a Troianis ad medium oppidum trahitur.
5. Helena miserrima a Menelao fortissimo tandem liberatur.
6. Troiani fessi ab his Graecis fortissimis facile superantur.
7. quo modo aurum ab illis Graecis felicibus capitur?
8. centum naves Graecorum iam delentur.
9. quantum vinum a Graecis fessis bibitur?
10. paene omnia castra ab hostibus crudelibus delentur.

**Exercise 4.12    Rewrite Exercise 4.10 putting the verbs into the active voice**

**Exercise 4.13 E  Rewrite Exercise 4.11E putting the verbs into the active voice**

**Exercise 4.14    Translate into Latin**

1. Those huge walls are being defended for a long time by the Trojans.
2. That bad pupil is always punished by the angry teacher.
3. The new ship is being driven towards the island by the fierce winds.
4. This wine is never bought by that merchant.
5. The soldiers are neither killed nor injured by the Romans.
6. This very good book is being read by the wise teacher.
7. The gate of the camp is being destroyed by the enemy.
8. Almost all the soldiers are being wounded in the fierce battle.
9. This cruel king is being warned by his slaves.
10. These soldiers are never praised by the emperor.

**Exercise 4.15E  Translate into Latin**

1. This large city is being destroyed by the Greeks.
2. Those good pupils are never punished by the teacher.
3. That small town is being attacked by the enemy for a second time.
4. The best food is taken by the angry king.
5. The rest of the soldiers are wounded by the cruel Greeks.
6. Meanwhile this very good wine is being drunk by the teacher.

7. The rest of the young men are being led back by the soldiers.
8. These young men are never invited to dinner by the senators.
9. That wretched leader is not being warned by his soldiers.
10. This proud old man is being slowly led to the villa by his companion.

**Exercise 4.16E   Translate the following words into Latin and find them in the wordsearch**

```
A C M K M H M X T A N
X K G H A L K I X E Z
K P H T O U Q E W R L
G M P F M I N I M E U
K Q N Q O Q H R N T V
Z U U G C C Y T S N S
F A P A E N E G O I P
M N E N L L X C T R M
Q T T T L I K A L K L
G U B J I R S N T Y X
M S G S M Z L A K A L
```

meanwhile, enough, how big? slowly, ever, scarcely,
how many? a hundred, what sort of? a thousand, not at all

1 murus ingens a sene misero lente deletur.
2 villa parva ab uxore laeta celeriter aedificatur.
3 corpus magnum ab agricola subito ostenditur.
4 murus parvus a servo iam aedificatur.
5 templum parvum a duce tandem invenitur.

1 servus miser ab ancilla pulchra spectatur.
2 rex iratus a regina necatur.
3 ancilla pulchra a nauta laeto spectatur.
4 ancilla laeta a sene sapienti laudatur.
5 femina crudelis a filio audaci auditur.

**Exercise 4.17E   Review          Complete the following and translate into English**

1. hic puer a cane saev_ vulner____ .
2. o serve, num can__ feroces in villam egisti?
3. quot epistul__ a duc_ nostro leguntur?
4. 'comites, quo vos festin___?' 'ad mare'
5. interea quattuor naves vent__ saevis ad insulam ag_____ .
6. 'ubi sunt serv_ ?' rogavit pater. 'ante ianuam dorm____ ' respondit filius.
7. 'ubi sunt libri me_ ?' uxori perterrit__ clamavit senator.
8. cives fess_ ab his militibus valid_____ facile superantur.
9. multae nav__ ventis saev__ iam delentur.
10. paene omnia castr_ ab host____ crudelibus delentur.

# Chapter 5  The passive voice imperfect tense

The imperfect passive is translated by 'used to be' or 'was/were being'

| 1st | 2nd | 3rd | 4th | 3½ |
|---|---|---|---|---|
| amabar | monebar | regebar | audiebar | capiebar |
| amabaris | monebaris | regebaris | audiebaris | capiebaris |
| amabatur | monebatur | regebatur | audiebatur | capiebatur |
| amabamur | monebamur | regebamur | audiebamur | capiebamur |
| amabamini | monebamini | regebamini | audiebamini | capiebamini |
| amabantur | monebantur | regebantur | audiebantur | capiebantur |

Thus  amabar = I used to be loved / I was being loved

monebar = I used to be warned / I was being warned

regebar = I used to be ruled / I was being ruled

audiebar = I used to be heard / I was being heard

capiebar = I used to be taken / I was being taken

**Exercise 5.1**  **Translate the following verbs into English using either *was / were being* or *used to be***

accipiebantur, aedificabatur, agebatur, bibebatur, colligebantur, conspiciebantur, constituebatur, consumebatur, defendebantur, delebantur, ducebatur, gerebatur, iaciebantur, inveniebatur, invitabatur, iubebantur, laudabatur, legebatur, liberabamur, mittebamur, movebaris, necabantur, occidebatur, occupabatur, oppugnabatur, ostendebatur, parabatur, ponebantur, portabamur, reducebatur, salutabatur, servabamini, spectabantur, superabaris, tenebaris, terrebaris, tradebatur, trahebantur, vocabatur, vulnerabantur

**Exercise 5.2E**  **Translate the following verbs into English using either *was / were being* or *used to be***

accipiebatur, aedificabatur, agebar, bibebantur, colligebamini, conspiciebaris, constituebantur, consumebantur, defendebaris, delebatur, ducebar, emebatur, gerebantur, iaciebatur, inveniebar, iubebamini, laudabar, legebantur, liberabar, mittebamini, movebamini, necabatur, occidebantur, occupabantur, oppugnabantur, ostendebantur, parabantur, ponebar, portabamini, reducebar, servabantur, spectabatur, superabamini, tenebamini, terrebamini, tradebantur, trahebar, vocabar, vulnerabatur

1 servus crudelis ab ancilla misera spectabatur.
2 rex iratus a regina tristi necabatur.
3 femina laeta a nauta pulchro spectabatur.
4 ancilla laeta a sene sapienti laudabatur.
5 femina crudelis a filio audaci vulnerabatur.

**Exercise 5.3**  **Translate into English**

1. Helena pulcherrima a Paride capiebatur.
2. urbs parva a centum civibus fortiter defendebatur.
3. milites Romani ab hostibus fessis non vincebantur.
4. quo modo equus ingens a Troianis trahebatur?
5. uxor felix a coniuge forti tandem liberabatur.
6. Troiani a Graecis audacibus vincebantur.

7.  quale vinum a Graecis felicibus capiebatur?
8.  terra a nautis laetis tandem conspiciebatur.
9.  post proelium cibus a militibus nostris consumebatur.
10. quot canes ab urbe a civibus saevis agebantur?

### Exercise 5.4E    Translate into English

1.  servus a domino saepe puniebatur.
2.  omnes discipuli a magistris sapientibus laudabantur.
3.  paene omnes libri ab omnibus pueris legebantur.
4.  quot naves vento saevo agebantur?
5.  quo modo servi a regina puniebantur?
6.  optimum vinum a nautis semper bibebatur.
7.  nautae Graeci a militibus audacibus vincebantur.
8.  quo equus mortuus a servis ac pueris trahebatur?
9.  omnes hostes a militibus crudelibus occidebantur.
10. servi a domino nobili nec puniebantur nec laudabantur.

### Exercise 5.5    Translate into Latin

1.  The large city was being destroyed by those cruel Greeks.
2.  What kind of food used to be bought by the king?
3.  To where were the soldiers being led by the Greeks?
4.  These bad pupils often used to be punished by the savage teacher.
5.  The small shops were being destroyed by the wild young men.
6.  The freedman was being greeted by his companion.
7.  The rest of the merchants were being driven from the forum.
8.  How many brave lions were being killed by spears and arrows?
9.  The wretched emperor was not being warned by the senators.
10. This sad old man was being led to the country-house by his companion.

1 aqua a comitibus tristibus bibebatur.
2 vinum sacrum ab uxoribus bibebatur.
3 vinum optimum a nautis bibebatur.
4 a senibus aqua diu bibebatur.
5 a patre et filio vinum regi tradebatur.

### Exercise 5.6E    Translate into Latin

1.  The gate of the camp was being defended by a few soldiers.
2.  This good pupil never used to be punished by the teacher.
3.  How many ships were being destroyed by the fierce wind?
4.  How many merchants used to be invited to dinner by the consul?
5.  The rest of the maids were being praised by the queen.
6.  Those very bad books were being read by the naughty pupil.
7.  How were the dead dogs being dragged out of the camp by the young men?
8.  How were the soldiers being captured in the war?
9.  Why was the emperor never warned about the danger by the senators?
10. The general was neither praised nor punished by the emperor.

### Exercise 5.7E    Review          Complete the following and translate into English

1. Helena pulcherrim_ a Paride capieb____ .
2. urbs parva a civ____ defendebatur.
3. milites Romani ab hostibus fessis non vincebantur.
4. quo modo equ__ ingens trahebatur?
5. uxor felix a coniuge forti tandem liberabatur.
6. vinum a nautis semper bibeb____ .
7. nautae Graeci a militibus audacibus vincebantur.
8. quo equus mortuus a serv__ trahebatur?
9. omnes hostes a militibus crudelibus occidebantur.
10. servi nec puniebantur nec laudab_____ .

# Chapter 6  The passive voice future tense; 5<sup>th</sup> declension nouns

The future passive is not very common, and is mostly found in the 3<sup>rd</sup> person

| 1<sup>st</sup> | 2<sup>nd</sup> | 3<sup>rd</sup> | 4<sup>th</sup> | Mixed |
|---|---|---|---|---|
| amabor | monebor | regar | audiar | capiar |
| amaberis | moneberis | regeris | audieris | capieris |
| amabitur | monebitur | regetur | audietur | capietur |
| amabimur | monebimur | regemur | audiemur | capiemur |
| amabimini | monebimini | regemini | audiemini | capiemini |
| amabuntur | monebuntur | regentur | audientur | capientur |

Thus     amabor = I shall be loved
         moneberis = you will be warned
         regetur = (s)he, it will be ruled
         audiemur = we shall be heard
         capiemini = you will be taken

## Exercise 6.1  Translate the following verbs into English

accipientur, aedificabitur, agentur, bibetur, colligetur,
conspicientur, constituetur, consumetur, defendetur,
delebuntur, ducetur, gerentur, iacientur, invenietur,
invitabitur, iubebitur, laudabitur, legetur, liberabimur, mittemur,
moveberis, necabuntur, occidetur, occupabitur, oppugnabitur,
ostendetur, parabitur, ponentur, portabimur, reducetur,
salutabuntur, servabimini, spectabuntur, superaberis, teneberis,
terreberis, tradetur, trahetur, vocabitur, vulnerabuntur

1 scuta a senibus crudelibus mox iacientur.
2 hastae a mulieribus laetis tandem vendentur.
3 sagittae magnae ab uxoribus iam emuntur.
4 sagittae magnae a nautis mox iacientur.
5 sagittae parvae a pueris audacibus trahentur.

## Exercise 6.2E    Translate the following verbs into English

accipietur, aedificabuntur, agetur, bibentur, colligemini, conspicieris, constituentur, consumentur,
defenderis, deletur, ducar, gerentur, iacietur, inveniar, iubebimini, laudabor, legentur, liberabor,
mittemini, movebimur, necabitur, occidentur, occupabuntur, oppugnabuntur, ostendentur,
parabuntur, ponar, portabimini, reducar, servabuntur, spectabitur, superabimini, tenebimini,
terrebimini, tradentur, trahentur, vocabor, vulnerabitur

## Fifth declension nouns

This declension has very few nouns; the most common are **res** = thing, matter f., **dies** = day m. and
**res publica** = the public interest, the republic, the state, often written as one word

|      | sing. | pl.     |
|------|-------|---------|
| nom. | dies  | dies    |
| voc. | dies  | dies    |
| acc. | diem  | dies    |
| gen. | diei  | dierum  |
| dat. | diei  | diebus  |
| abl. | die   | diebus  |

|      | sing. | pl.    |
|------|-------|--------|
| nom. | res   | res    |
| voc. | res   | res    |
| acc. | rem   | res    |
| gen. | rei   | rerum  |
| dat. | rei   | rebus  |
| abl. | re    | rebus  |

|      | sing.      | pl.            |
|------|------------|----------------|
| nom. | respublica | respublicae    |
| voc. | respublica | respublicae    |
| acc. | rempublicam| respublicas    |
| gen. | reipublicae| rerumpublicarum|
| dat. | reipublicae| rebuspublicis  |
| abl. | republica  | rebuspublicis  |

## Two & three, all cases

|      | masc.      | fem.   | neut.   | m.&f. | neut. |
|------|------------|--------|---------|-------|-------|
| nom. | duo        | duae   | duo     | tres  | tria  |
| acc. | duo,duos   | duas   | duo     | tres  | tria  |
| gen. | duorum     | duarum | duorum  | trium | trium |
| dat. | duobus     | duabus | duobus  | tribus| tribus|
| abl. | duobus     | duabus | duobus  | tribus| tribus|

## Time
Periods of time

hora  horae 1 f. = hour
dies diei  5 m.   = day
nox noctis 3 f.   = night
mensis mensis 3 m. = month
annus anni  2 m. = year

**New words used in the pictures**

aquila -ae 1 f  = eagle
equa -ae 1 f   = mare
capra -ae 1 f  = goat
phoca -ae 1 f  = seal

**To express time 'how long' Latin uses the accusative case**

Ulixes viginti annos afuit.              Odysseus was away for twenty years.
senex omnem noctem dormivit.             The old man slept all night.

sometimes **per** is put before the accusative of time. Thus,

hostes per multos dies in illo loco manserunt.
The enemy remained in that place for many days

**To express time 'when' Latin uses the ablative case**

Graeci decimo anno belli equum aedificaverunt.
The Greeks built a horse in the tenth year of the war.
secunda hora discesserunt.
They left at the second hour *(after dawn)*.

The Roman 'day' from dawn to dusk was divided into
twelve equal parts. Hence the length of the 'day' would
depend on the season of the year and latitude.

**To express time 'within which' Latin uses the ablative case**

dux tribus horis redibit.  The general will return within three hours

Note the common usage

multis post annis Romani vicerunt
After many years the Romans were victorious.

Here *post* is not a preposition but is used instead of the
adverb *postea = afterwards*; so here, literally *afterwards
by many years*.

1 aquila a phoca ingenti mox occidetur.
2 phoca ab iuvene irato tandem vulnerabitur.
3 equa ab aquila parva mox occidetur.
4 phoca perterrita ab aquila iam monebitur.
5 phoca misera ab aquila mox occidetur.

**Place**

|  | in / at | to / towards | from |
|---|---|---|---|
| **normal nouns** | in + abl. | ad + acc. | ab / ex + abl. |
|  | in agro | ad agrum | ex agro |
| **cities** | 'locative' | acc. only | abl. only |
|  | Romae | Romam | Roma |
|  | in Rome | to Rome | from Rome |
| **domus** | domi | domum | domo |
|  | at home | to home | from home |

Note:   *domus* f  is an irregular noun of 4<sup>th</sup> declension, to be learnt later
        Prepositions are not used with towns

**Exercise 6.3      Translate into English**

1. num dominae miserae a militibus saevis vulnerabuntur?
2. discipuli a magistris sapientibus cras laudabuntur.
3. quot libri a mercatoribus ementur?
4. ceterae naves ventis saevis quinque diebus delebuntur.
5. pauci servi a regina mala tertio die punientur.
6. quot horas ante portam castrorum manebunt?
7. nautae Graeci a militibus audacibus duabus horis vincentur.
8. nonne incolae miseri a leonibus mox occidentur?
9. custodes a militibus crudelibus in foro tribus horis occidentur.
10. milites Romani ab hostibus fessis nec vincentur nec vulnerabuntur.

**Exercise 6.4E    Translate into English**

1.  quot diebus servi Romam reducentur?
2.  urbs parva a civibus fortibus duos dies defendetur.
3.  servi boni ab imperatore nobili non punientur.
4.  equus ingens a Graecis sex diebus aedificabitur.
5.  uxor felix a coniuge forti liberabitur.
6.  Troiani a Graecis audacibus secunda nocte vincentur.
7.  multum auri a Graecis felicibus capietur.
8.  quo modo ianua tabernae ab iuvenibus delebitur?
9.  omnis cibus a mercatore cras emetur.
10. sagittae atque hastae ab his mercatoribus ementur.

**Exercise 6.5    Translate into Latin**

1.  The camp gate will be destroyed by the enemy within two hours.
2.  This bad pupil will be punished by the teacher tomorrow.
3.  The bravest soldiers will be killed in the war.
4.  The Roman standard will not be captured by the enemy.
5.  When will those consuls be praised by the citizens?
6.  Those enemy camp will be destroyed by the Romans within three days.
7.  How will these dogs be driven from our forum?
8.  That huge ship will be destroyed by fierce winds within three months.
9.  When will the emperor be warned about the danger?
10. Surely that bad pupil will not be praised by all the teachers?

**Exercise 6.6E    Translate into Latin**

1.  This large city will be attacked for three months.
2.  Surely these good pupils will not be punished by that teacher?
3.  The small town will be destroyed by the enemy within ten days.
4.  Almost all the best food will be eaten with seven days.
5.  Very many soldiers will be wounded in the battle tomorrow.
6.  The dinner will be prepared by the mistress within two hours..
7.  How will the rest of the soldiers be led back to the camp?
8.  These brave soldiers will be killed immediately by the spears and arrows of the enemy.
9.  How will the king be warned of *(= de)* the danger of war?
10. This sad old man will be taken back to his villa on the fifth day.

**Exercise 6.7E    Review        Complete the following and translate into English**

1.  num puell__    miserae a can_____    saevis vulnerabantur?
2.  pueri a magistro sapient_   heri laud_____  .
3.  quantum aurum a mercator_   cras em_____  ?
4.  nonne illa nav__    tempestate saeva tr_____    diebus delebitur?
5.  serv__ miser a regina mal_    saepe punitur.
6.  quot hor__    ante ianuam tabern__    canes manebant?
6.  incolae a Roman__    audacibus terti_   nocte vincentur.
7.  multum pecuni__    ab incol__    felicibus capiebatur.
8.  quo modo porta castr_____    ab illis milit_____    delebatur?
9.  hic cibus mal__    a mercator_    numquam emetur.
10. sagitt__    atque hastae a duc_    capiebantur.

# Chapter 7  Two irregular verbs: volo and nolo

## volo velle volui = I want

| present | imperfect | future | perfect | pluperfect |
|---------|-----------|--------|---------|------------|
| volo | volebam | volam | volui | volueram |
| vis | volebas | voles | voluisti | volueras |
| vult | volebat | volet | voluit | voluerat |
| volumus | volebamus | volemus | voluimus | volueramus |
| vultis | volebatis | voletis | voluistis | volueratis |
| volunt | volebant | volent | voluerunt | voluerant |

## nolo nolle nolui = I don't want

| present | imperfect | future | perfect | pluperfect |
|---------|-----------|--------|---------|------------|
| nolo | nolebam | nolam | nolui | nolueram |
| non vis | nolebas | noles | noluisti | nolueras |
| non vult | nolebat | nolet | noluit | noluerat |
| nolumus | nolebamus | nolemus | noluimus | nolueramus |
| non vultis | nolebatis | noletis | noluistis | nolueratis |
| nolunt | nolebant | nolent | noluerunt | noluerant |

Like **possum**, these two verbs are often followed by the infinitive

discedere volunt. They want to leave.

discipuli scribere nolebant.      The pupils were not wanting to write.

### Exercise 7.1      Translate into English

1. accipere vult
2. agere volunt
3. bibere volebat
4. colligere volui
5. consumere volueramus
6. defendere voluimus
7. delere non vis
8. docere nolebant
9. exspectare nolemus
10. gerere nolueratis
11. iacere vult
12. invenire volebat
13. iubere nolumus
14. laudare vultis
15. visne legere?
16. vultisne eos liberare?
17. mittere noluerunt
18. movere volent
19. narrare nolent
20. necare volet
21. nuntiare volumus
22. occidere volet
23. occupare voluistis
24. oppugnare nolo
25. ostendere noluimus
26. parare non vult
27. ponere nolebant
28. portare noluit
29. reducere nolebatis
30. visne servare?
31. vultisne spectare?
32. superare voluit
33. tenere volebat
34. terrere nolo
35. trahere nolent
36. vendere vultis

**Exercise 7.2E    Translate into English**

1. accipere volam
2. aedificare voluerunt
3. bibere volebamus
4. colligere voluerunt
5. consumere volueram
6. defendere voluistis
7. docere non vultis
8. ducere volebant
9. exspectare volemus
10. gerere noluimus
11. iacere volebant
12. invitare volebant
13. iubere volumus
14. laudare vult
15. vultisne legere?
16. voluntne eam liberare?
17. mittere nolet
18. movere voletis
19. narrare nolunt
20. necare voluerunt
21. nuntiare volo
22. occidere volent
23. occupare voluisti
24. oppugnare non vis
25. ostendere noluerunt
26. parare nolemus
27. ponere nolebat
28. portare nolebamus
29. reducere nolebant
30. voluntne servarene?
31. visne spectare?
32. superare voluerunt
33. tenere volebant
34. terrere volo
35. tradere noluerat
36. vendere voluerunt

**Exercise 7.3    Translate into English**

1. nonne hos libros legere vultis?
2. ille libertus cum uxore vitam laetam prope silvam agere volebat.
3. cur tu hoc facere nolebas?
4. quot milites flumen transire et castra hostium intrare voluerunt?
5. vultisne hunc hominem deum facere?
6. hic vir agricola esse nolebat.
7. quo modo Romam ire vis?
8. umquamne ad illam urbem ire voluisti?
9. poeta Romae vivere diu volebat.
10. cur epistulam scribere non vis?

# New adjectives

lentus -a -um = slow
stultus -a -um = stupid, foolish
summus = highest, greatest, top (of)

ferox -ocis = fierce, ferocious
fidelis -e = faithful, loyal
gravis -e = heavy, serious

# New noun

custos custodis 3 c. = guard

# Note

fidelis and gravis are declined like tristis -e,
with the ablative singular ending in -i

summus, like medius, functions as an adjective

ad summam urbem
to the highest part of the city

1 aquila equam spectare vult.
2 phoca misera fugere nolebat.
3 aquila saeva comitem occidere voluit.
4 aquila magna phocam occidere vult.
5 phoca fortis effugere noluit.

23

a summo monte
from the top of the hill

gravis can have a range of meanings:

| | |
|---|---|
| vir gravis = an important man | cibus gravis = heavy (to digest) food |
| periculum grave = serious problem | vulnus grave = a deep wound |
| tempus anni grave = oppressive time of year | vox gravis = a deep voice |

in medio oppido
in the centre of the city

## New adverb

> vehementer = violently, loudly

### Exercise 7.4    Translate into English

1. princeps iratus in medio proelio vehementer clamabat.
2. multae naves ventis gravibus ad insulam agebantur.
3. nonne illum iuvenem fidelem ad cenam invitare vis?
4. o comites, nonne cum Troianis pugnare vultis?
5. Romani rempublicam diu bene gesserunt.
6. nos laboribus omnium civium hostes superare potuimus.
7. 'tibi semper fideles erimus' clamaverunt milites.
8. nocte Romani castra in summo monte celeriter posuerunt.
9. militem stultum atque lentum leo ferox tandem in silva conspexit.
10. pueri ad summum montem quam celerrime cucurrerunt.

1 nauta miser discedere volebat.
2 femina et miles cantare voluerunt.
3 nauta laetus cum femina pulchra sedere vult.
4 magister perterritus domum ire vult.
5 nauta reginam de periculo monere voluit.

### Exercise 7.5E    Translate into English

1. victoriane ab imperatore mox nuntiabitur?
2. quo modo hic puer lentissimus ad mediam urbem duabus horis advenire potest?
3. eo tempore is imperator crudelior ceteris erat.
4. cur hic servus sic vehementer clamat?
5. tres custodes in horto imperatoris vinum bibebant.
6. 'qualis leo effugit?' 'et magnus et ferocissimus.'
7. milites fideles discedere nolebant.
8. milites stulti in animo signa relinquere habuerunt.
9. tempus est illos senatores ad cenam invitare.
10. miles fidelis vulnus gravissimum forte accepit.

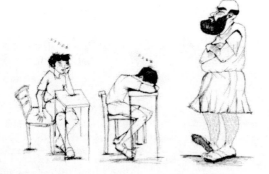

1 pueri libros legere volebant.
2 magister laetus dormire vult.
3 tres senes scribere nolebant.
4 magister pulcher discipulos punire volebat.
5 discipuli scribere nolebant.

### Exercise 7.6 Translate into Latin

1. Before the battle few soldiers were wanting to fight.
2. Because he had drunk a lot of wine, the general's companion was not wanting to leave.
3. O mistress, why do you want to sell that house?
4. The enemy does not want to hand over the young men.
5. The lazy boys will not want to perform (= do) these difficult tasks.

6. After they had eaten the heavy food, the merchants were unwilling to leave.
7. Where will you buy the gold, mother?
8. The new leader received a deep wound in the head.
9. Three wild lions remained in the forest for a long time.
10. The sailors were unwilling to sail in the heavy storm.

**Exercise 7.7E Translate into Latin**

1. At that oppressive time of the year, the consul wanted to stay on the island for a few days.
2. Will you drink this excellent wine?
3. How many letters did the faithful wife write?
4. What do you want to do now, young man?
5. How can we sail in this heavy storm?
6. Where are those dogs rushing to?
7. How big is the emperor's new villa?
8. Look! The old man is running to the pub!
9. Although the enemy was attacking the town, the citizens were unwilling to run away.
10. Where is the freedman going to?

1 miles felix puellam parvam terrere volebat.
2 nauta saevus puellam terrere vult.
3 senex malus feminam tristem ducere voluit.
4 dux fortis comitem laetam occidere volebat.
5 princeps de periculo uxorem monere volebat.

**Exercise 7.8E    Translate the following words into Latin and find them in the wordsearch**

```
A N N O S I M R L H H
Y R C O Y C Z E X I X
F R S W C S N S I X K
V M E D O T S U C D P
H U L C O U E B U E A
F R E S M L C I H B E
L W D A M T O V X K U
T W I R U U R A V T Q
A E F O S M E R K U Q
L K K H D G F G P I C
N R V R P B W D P F K
```

day *(acc.),* things *(nom.),* hours *(acc.),* night *(abl.),* years *(acc.),* guard *(acc.),* slow *(masc. acc. pl.),* stupid *(masc. acc.sing.),* top of *(neut. abl. sing.),* fierce *(fem. acc. pl.),* faithful *(fem. nom. pl.),* serious *(masc. dat. pl.)*

**Exercise 7.9E    Review  Complete the following and translate into English**

1. dux irat__   in medio proeli_   vehementer clamabat.
2. novem novae nav__   vent_   gravi age_____ .
3. o comites, nonne illos iuven__   fideles ad cenam invit____   vultis?
4. o milit__ , cur pugn___   non vultis?
5. Romani  bell__   diu gess_____ .
6. 'quales leon__   effugerunt?' 'et magni et ferocissimi.'
7. miles fidelis disced___   nolet.
8. dominus in anim_   signum nov__   emere habuit.
9. iam tempus est h__   oppidum oppugn___ .
10. milites fideles vulner_   gravissima in preli_   acceperunt.

# Chapter 8  Perfect passive tense

To correspond to the perfect tense active *I warned, I have warned, I did warn* **monui**, we have the perfect tense passive *I was warned, I have been warned.*

The perfect tense passive in Latin is made up of two parts:

The first part is the **perfect participle passive** and the second part is the **present tense** of the verb *sum* to be      *sum, es, est, sumus, estis, sunt*

The **perfect participle passive** is formed from the **supine** of the verb. Up to now we have had no need for the supine. However, when you look up a verb in a dictionary you will normally find four principal parts.

For example:

**amo**  1<sup>st</sup> pers. sing. pres.  **-are** infinitive  **-avi** 1<sup>st</sup> pers. sing. perfect **-atum** supine 1<sup>st</sup> conjug.

All verbs in the 1<sup>st</sup> conjugation follow this pattern. Thus,

| clamo | clamare | clamavi | clamatum |
| voco | vocare | vocavi | vocatum |

even

| do | dare | dedi | datum |
| sto | stare | steti | statum |

You may have noticed that taking off the **-um** and adding **-ion** will often give us an English word. (ex)clamation, vocation, station

However the supines of the 2<sup>nd</sup>, 3<sup>rd</sup> and mixed conjugation verbs need to be learnt. For ease of learning and reference, the principal parts of all the verbs met so far are listed below.

1 equa laeta ab aquila conspecta est.
2 aquila a phoca iam vulnerata est.
3 equa a phoca tandem conspecta est.
4 custos tamen a phoca occisus est.
5 phoca ab aquila iam conspecta est.

| accipio | ĕre | accepi | acceptum | 3½ | receive |
|---|---|---|---|---|---|
| ago | ĕre | egi | actum | 3 | do, act, drive |
| audio | ire | audivi | auditum | 4 | hear, listen to |
| bibo | ĕre | bibi | bibitum | 3 | drink |
| capio | ĕre | cepi | captum | 3½ | take, capture |
| colligo | ĕre | collegi | collectum | 3 | collect |
| conspicio | ĕre | conspexi | conspectum | 3½ | catch sight of |
| constituo | ĕre | constitui | constitutum | 3 | decide |
| consumo | ĕre | consumpsi | consumptum | 3 | eat |
| cupio | ĕre | cupivi | cupitum | 3½ | want |
| curro | ĕre | cucurri | cursum | 3 | run |
| defendo | ĕre | defendi | defensum | 3 | defend |
| deleo | ēre | delevi | deletum | 2 | destroy |
| dico | ĕre | dixi | dictum | 3 | say, tell |

| | | | | | |
|---|---|---|---|---|---|
| discedo | ĕre | discessi | discessum | 3 | depart |
| doceo | ēre | docui | doctum | 2 | teach |
| dormio | ire | dormivi | dormitum | 4 | sleep |
| duco | ĕre | duxi | ductum | 3 | lead |
| eo | ire | ii | itum | | go |
| effugio | ĕre | effugi | - | 3½ | escape |
| ĕmo | ĕre | ēmi | emptum | 3 | buy |
| exeo | ire | exii | exitum | | go out |
| facio | ĕre | feci | factum | 3½ | make, do |
| fugio | ĕre | fugi | fugitum | 3½ | flee |
| gero | ĕre | gessi | gestum | 3 | carry on, do, wage |
| iacio | ĕre | ieci | iactum | 3½ | throw |
| ineo | ire | inii | initum | | enter |
| invenio | ire | inveni | inventum | 4 | find, discover |
| iubeo | ēre | iussi | iussum | 2 | order |
| lego | ĕre | legi | lectum | 3 | read, choose |
| ludo | ĕre | lusi | lusum | 3 | play |
| maneo | ēre | mansi | mansum | 2 | remain |
| mitto | ĕre | misi | missum | 3 | send |
| moveo | ēre | movi | motum | 2 | move |
| occido | ĕre | occidi | occisum | 3 | kill |
| ostendo | ĕre | ostendi | ostentum | 3 | show |
| pereo | ĕre | perii | peritum | | perish, die |
| pono | ĕre | posui | positum | 3 | put |
| redeo | ire | redii | reditum | | return |
| reduco | ĕre | reduxi | reductum | 3 | led back |
| rego | ĕre | rexi | rectum | 3 | rule |
| respondeo | ēre | respondi | responsum | 2 | answer |
| rideo | ēre | risi | risum | 2 | laugh |
| ruo | ĕre | rui | rutum | 3 | rush, collapse, charge |
| scribo | ĕre | scripsi | scriptum | 3 | write |
| teneo | ēre | tenui | tentum | 2 | hold |
| terreo | ēre | terrui | territum | 2 | frighten |
| timeo | ēre | timui | - | 2 | fear |
| trado | ĕre | tradidi | traditum | 3 | hand over |
| traho | ĕre | traxi | tractum | 3 | drag |
| transeo | ire | transii | transitum | | cross |
| vendo | ēre | vendidi | venditum | 3 | sell |
| video | ēre | visi | visum | 2 | see |
| vinco | ĕre | vici | victum | 3 | conquer |
| vivo | ĕre | vixi | victum | 3 | live |

**Exercise 8.1**

Write down English words that come from the supines listed above by taking off **-um** and adding **-ion**. Some come with a prefix at the beginning of the English word.

It is useful to learn the principal parts of any new verb met.

To form the **past participle passive, PPP**, take off the **-um** from the supine and add **-us -a -um**

So from **monitum**, the supine of moneo, we get **monitus monita monitum**, the past participle passive.

The final stage is to put it with the verb **sum** to be

monitus sum    = I was warned, I have been warned

Of course, because the PPP functions as an adjective, if the speaker is female, this will be **monita sum**. Similarly, **moniti sumus** or **monitae sumus** = we were / have been warned.

So the full table will be:

|  | masculine | feminine | neuter |
|---|---|---|---|
| **singular** | -us | -a | -um |
| **plural** | -i | -ae | -a |

1 femina a comite audaci territa est.
2 nauta fortis a puella tristi territus est.
3 mater a filio saevo punita est.
4 puella misera a nauta crudeli territa est.
5 uxor sapiens a nauta de periculo monita est.

Examples:

servus captus est.        The slave was / has been captured.
puellae monitae sunt.     The girls were/ have been warned.
oppidum inventum est.     The town was / has been discovered.

**Exercise 8.2    Translate into English**

1.  epistula tertio die accepta est.
2.  vox pulchra mulieris ab iuvene audita est.
3.  hastae ducis a servo captae sunt.
4.  ceteri servi in medio oppido iam collecti sunt.
5.  puer a patre conspectus est.
6.  bellum a rege constitutum est.
7.  cibus gravis heri consumptus est.
8.  oppidum a civibus diu defensum est.
9.  muri ab iuvenibus deleti sunt.
10. haec verba a rege dicta sunt.
11. signa heri capta sunt.
12. quo modo aqua bibita est?
13. illae res celeriter gestae sunt.
14. paucae sagittae in oppidum iactae sunt.
15. hoc aurum Romae inventum est.
16. hic miles discedere iussus est.
17. dux pessimus a rege lectus est.
18. undeviginti milites ad urbem missi sunt.
19. equi quarta hora moti sunt.
20. servus miser secunda hora occisus est.
21. ianuae heri deletae sunt.
22. ceteri canes mortui e foro tracti sunt.
23. Romani diu a regibus recti sunt.
24. parva pars libri a tribus discipulis scripta est.
25. omnes libri a discipulo traditi sunt.
26. ille iuvenis Romae heri conspectus est.

**Exercise 8.3E    Translate into English**

1. castra hostium secunda hora capta sunt.
2. aqua ab equo celeriter bibita est.
3. omnes hastae ab iuvene captae sunt.
4. milites a duce iam collecti sunt.
5. interea hostes victi sunt.
6. bellum a principe tandem constitutum est.
7. cibus ab equo iam consumptus est.
8. urbs a civibus fortiter defensa est.
9. villa pulcherrima a custodibus deleta est.
10. haec verba a duce tristi dicta sunt.
11. illi milites Romam ducti sunt.
12. homo factus est.
13. hae res bene gestae sunt.
14. omnes hastae in hostes iam iactae sunt.
15. hoc aurum sub villa heri inventum est.
16. hic miles discedere iussus est.
17. dux optimus a militibus lectus est.
18. septem custodes ad mare missi sunt.
19. arma heri a puero audaci mota sunt.
20. princeps tertia hora occisus est.
21. aurum ibi heri positum est.
22. milites ad flumen reducti sunt.
23. haec taberna heri deleta est.
24. haec epistula a poeta claro scripta est.
25. servi miseri a domino traditi sunt.
26. bellum diu gestum est.

**Exercise 8.4    Translate into Latin**

1. All the pretty girls were invited to dinner.
2. The rest of the soldiers were collected at the top of the hill.
3. The deep voice of the general was heard by the soldiers.
4. Many large towns were destroyed by the enemy.
5. Those bad words were not said by our noble and wise leader.
6. The chieftain was killed in the battle yesterday.
7. A part of this book was written by the king.
8. All the soldiers were led back to Rome immediately.
9. Our books were handed over to the teacher yesterday.
10. Our town was defended for two years by the loyal citizens.

1 mater laeta a filio et filia laudata est.
2 puer et puella a matre dormire iussi sunt.
3 mater iratissima est.
4 puer et puella legere volebant.
5 uxor coniugem et filiam spectabat.

**Exercise 8.5E    Translate into Latin**

1. All these books were bought by our teacher.
2. A few slaves were sent to the field yesterday.
3. The deep voices of the merchants were heard in the forum.
4. All the country-houses were destroyed by the heavy winds.
5. These bad words were said by that young man.
6. The general was killed by a spear in the battle.
7. A large part of the book was written by a Greek slave.
8. These young men were led back to the city.
9. The book was handed over to the king.
10. The dead soldier's body was dragged down the street.

1 villa a servo deleta est.
2 murus ab uxore statim aedificatus est.
3 servus in muro vulneratus est.
4 murus a servo caro aedificatum est.
5 castra in agro aedificata sunt.

**Exercise 8.6E    Review  Complete the following and translate into English**

1. voces mulierum ab iuven_ audit__ sunt.
2. epistul__ domini a serv_ forte visae sunt.
3. proelium a duc_ tandem constitut__ est.
4. cib__ gravis a comit____ consumptus est.
5. haec verb_ clara a reg_ dicta sunt.
6. capita milit__ ab omnibus incolis vis_ sunt.
7. hast__ de muro ab iuvenibus iact__ sunt.
8. omn_ aurum in agr_ heri inventum est.
9. servi ad medi__ urbem heri miss_ sunt.
10. hic equus magn__ quinta hor_ ductus est.

29

# Chapter 9  Pluperfect passive tense

The **pluperfect passive** tense is formed by the **perfect passive participle** + the imperfect tense of sum:

servus captus erat.          The slave had been captured.
puellae monitae erant.       The girls had been warned.
oppidum inventum erat.       The town had been discovered.

### Exercise 9.1      Translate into English

1.  signum prima luce datum erat.
2.  vox mercatoris a puella audita erat.
3.  arma principis a servo capta erant.
4.  omnes servi in urbe iam collecti erant.
5.  puer a matre iam conspectus erat.
6.  bellum a principe constitutum erat.
7.  cibus ab equis heri consumptus erat.
8.  muri a civibus diu defensi erant.
9.  porta castrorum ab hostibus deleta erat.
10. haec verba mala a rege dicta erant.
11. canes a foro acti erant.
12. aurum a domina iam emptum erat.
13. hae res tandem gestae erant.
14. plurimae sagittae in oppidum iactae erant.
15. omne aurum in villa inventum erat.
16. hic iuvenis aurum tradere iussus erat.
17. dux sapiens a principe lectus erat.
18. undeviginti milites Romam missi erant.

### Exercise 9.2E     Translate into English

1. equus quinta hora motus erat.
2. princeps secunda hora occisus erat.
3. haec taberna heri deleta erat.
4. dux ab imperatore ad cenam invitatus erat.
5. Britanni diu a Romanis recti erant.
6. hic liber a poeta claro scriptus erat.
7. omnes servi a duce traditi erant.
8. comes meus in oppido heri visus erat.

### New Verbs

| convenio | ire | conveni | conventum | 4 | meet |
| credo | ĕre | credidi | creditum | 3 | believe, trust *(+dat.)* |
| custodio | ire | custodivi | custoditum | 4 | guard |
| interficio | ĕre | interfeci | interfectum | 3½ | kill |
| peto | ĕre | petivi | petitum | 3 | seek, ask for, make for, attack |
| relinquo | ĕre | reliqui | relictum | 3 | leave behind, to abandon |

Note    peto = to attack a person *v* oppugno = to attack or storm a city

### Exercise 9.3      Translate into English

1. pueri canes per viam petunt.
2. milites castra diu custodiunt.
3. ego amicos numquam relinquo.
4. miles fidelis principem non interficit.
5. domina pecuniam petit.
6. agricola miser iter petit.
7. pater filium domi relinquit.

**Exercise 9.4E    Translate into English**

1. agricola filium stultum petit.
2. custodes fessi muros custodiunt.
3. princeps uxorem in foro conspicit.
4. milites servum interficiunt.
5. venti saevi naves agunt.
6. servi miseri canes petunt.
7. duces milites in urbe relinquunt.

**Exercise 9.5    Put the sentences in Ex 9.4E into the passive without translating**

**Exercise 9.6E    Put the sentences in Ex 9.3 into the passive without translating**

**Exercise 9.7    Change the verbs in Ex. 9.3 from the present to the perfect tense**

**Exercise 9.8E    Change the verbs in Ex. 9.4E from the present to the perfect tense**

1 puella laeta a nauta crudeli iam territa erat.
2 nauta tristis ab uxore pulchra tandem territa erat.
3 coniunx misera a nuntio malo monita erat.
4 puella a nauta nono territa erat.
5 puella quarta a sene pessimo vulnerata erat.

**Exercise 9.9    Translate into English**

1. pueri a parentibus in foro relicti sunt.
2. omnes iuvenes in media urbe convenerunt.
3. uxor liberti a principe salutata erat.
4. servus a militibus interfectus est.
5. naves ventis saevis actae erant.
6. canis a servis miseris petitus erat.
7. milites in urbe a duce relicti sunt.
8. milites duci sapienti credit.
9. iuvenis in summo monte puellam reliquit.
10. muri a custodibus diu custoditi erant.

**Exercise 9.10E    Translate into English**

1. cives duci novo non credebant.
2. muri ab iuvenibus diu custodiebantur.
3. iuvenis ab uxore principis ad cenam invitatus est.
4. cur servus interfectus est?
5. quo modo navis deleta est?
6. canis ab servis petitus est.
7. mulieres in urbe a militibus relictae erant.
8. ego amicis semper credo.
9. senes in villa cras convenient.
10. quot milites ad flumen lente ierunt?

1 aqua a sene statim lata erat.
2 omne vinum a muliere bibitum erat.
3 vinum ad villam ab ancilla latum erat.
4 ancilla domum a coniuge reducta erat.
5 filia regis Romam cum fratre missa erat.

**Exercise 9.11 Translate into Latin**

1. The father hurried to the city with his wife.
2. The dogs were driven down the road by the old man.
3. We always trust our general.
4. The walls were being guarded by the loyal soldiers.
5. All the enemy soldiers were killed in the battle.
6. 'Believe me, father!' shouted the boy.
7. All the ships had been driven across the sea by the fierce winds.
8. The sad old man was looking for his companion.
9. We left the slaves at home and went to Rome.
10. With the help of our allies we drove the enemy from the town.

**Exercise 9.12E Translate into Latin**

1. The girl's mother will hurry to the river with her husband.
2. It's time to buy gold, for there will soon be war.
3. We never used to trust that evil man.
4. 'Don't sell your books, boys!' said the teacher.
5. By chance a soldier killed the old man with his sword.
6. The boy's father always believed his son.
7. All the ships had been driven across the sea by the fierce winds.
8. The son will look for his father in the centre of the town.
9. The leader had left the soldiers in the town.
10. With the help of these troops we'll drive the enemy from the city.

1 puella tristis a patre crudeli iam punita erat.
2 senex miser a filia irata punitus erat.
3 uxor fessa a coniuge sapienti non punita erat.
4 regina laeta in via a militibus non conspecta erat.
5 puella laeta a patre laudata erat.

**Exercise 9.13E   Review   Complete the following and translate into English**

1. puer a parentibus in for_  relict__  est.
2. omnes civ__ in medio oppid_  convenerunt.
3. uxor imperatoris a sen_  salutat_  erat.
4. servi miser_  a milit____  interfecti est.
5. centum nav__  vento grav_  actae erant.
6. can__ feroces a servis malis petit_  sunt.
7. puellae parv__  in media urb_  a liberto relictae erant.
8. nos amic__  semper credebamus.
9. mult_  incolae in foro  cras conveni___  .
10. quot puer_  ad flumen festinaverunt?

1 agricolae ventis territi erant.
2 senes mali ab aquilis ferocibus conspecti erant.
3 socii vento saevo ad insulam pulsi erant.
4 nautae miseri ab aquilis petiti erant.
5 nautae undis altis territi erant.

# Chapter 10        fero, totus, nullus, relative clauses

**fero**

The verb **fero** has a wide range of meanings: carry, bring, bring forth, produce, carry off, lead (road), endure (trouble), suffer, sustain. It has some irregular forms.

The principal parts of **fero**:        **fero        ferre        tuli        latum**

Note that the English words *translation* and *transfer* come from different parts of the same verb **fero**.

When we bring help to someone Latin uses the dative. Thus,

auxilium meis amicis semper fero.
I always bring help to my friends.

| active | present | imperfect | future | perfect | pluperfect |
|---|---|---|---|---|---|
| | fero | ferebam | feram | tuli | tuleram |
| | fers | ferebas | feres | tulisti | tuleras |
| | fert | ferebat | feret | tulit | tulerat |
| | ferimus | ferebamus | feremus | tulimus | tuleramus |
| | fertis | ferebatis | feretis | tulistis | tuleratis |
| | ferunt | ferebant | ferent | tulerunt | tulerant |

**infinitive** ferre  **imperative sing.** fer **pl.** ferte

| passive | present | imperfect | future | perfect | pluperfect |
|---|---|---|---|---|---|
| | feror | ferebar | ferar | latus sum | latus eram |
| | ferris | ferebaris | fereris | latus es | latus eras |
| | fertur | ferebatur | feretur | latus est | latus erat |
| | ferimur | ferebamur | feremur | lati sumus | lati eramus |
| | ferimini | ferebamini | feremini | lati estis | lati eratis |
| | feruntur | ferebantur | ferentur | lati sunt | lati erant |

**Uses of verb + complement  - note the use of the nominative after the verb**

ille senex nobilis esse videtur.
That old man seems to be noble.

Augustus per multos annos princeps mansit.
Augustus remained *princeps f*or many years.

ille miles dux mox legetur.
That soldier will soon be chosen as general.

dux mortuus fertur.

The general is reported dead.
ille poeta sapiens vocatur.
That poet is called wise.

### Exercise 10.1    Translate into English

1.  multos libros tuli.
2.  discipuli libros ad magistrum ferebant.
3.  quo modo pecuniam fers?
4.  coniunx dona ad uxorem tulit.
5.  dux omnia arma iam tulerat.
6.  servus cibum fert.
7.  servi epistulam ad regem ferent.
8.  hic mercator cibum bonum semper fert.
9.  cur pecuniam fers?
10. quale vinum amici tui tulerunt?

1 ancilla quae in illa villa laborat per viam currit.
2 reginam quae irata semper est specto.
3 femina cuius pater agricola est vinum fert.
4 ancilla quacum saepe in oppidum eo tristissima est.
5 mulier cui heri donum pulchrum dedi miserrima est.

### Exercise 10.2E   Translate into English

1.  mercator omnes libros ad forum tulit.
2.  discipulus tres libros admagistrum ferebat.
3.  epistulam domina heri tulit.
4.  pueri pater multa dona ad magistrum tulit.
5.  princeps omnes gladios iam tulerat.
6.  eo tempore venti naves ad Italiam ferebant.
7.  mater filiae donum tulit.
8.  o comes, quantam pecuniam mihi tulisti?
9.  miles multa et gravia vulnera ferebat.
10. illos gladios non feram.

### Exercise 10.3    Put the sentences in Ex 10.1 into
the passive without translating

### Exercise 10.4E   Put the sentences in Ex 10.2E into
the passive without translating

1 viri quorum dominus saevus est diu laborabant.
2. pueri quibuscum heri pugnavi in agro dormiunt.
3 hi sunt consules quos dominus saepe laudat.
4 hi sunt principes qui Romanos numquam laudant.
5 hi sunt senes quorum uxores saepe male se gerunt.

**totus, tota, totum** = whole, whole of is declined like **unus** and **solus**

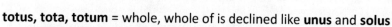

| singular | masculine | feminine | neuter |
| --- | --- | --- | --- |
| nom. | totus | tota | totum |
| acc. | totum | totam | totum |
| gen. | totius | totius | totius |
| dat. | toti | toti | toti |
| abl. | toto | tota | toto |
| | | | |
| **plural** | | | |
| nom. | toti | totae | tota |
| acc. | totos | totas | tota |
| gen. | totorum | totarum | totorum |
| dat. | totis | totis | totis |
| abl. | totis | totis | totis |

tota urbs deleta est.     The whole (of the) city was destroyed.

librum totum legi.     I have read the whole (of the) book.

**nullus, nulla, nullum** = none, **nullus, nulla** = nobody **nullum** = nothing
is also declined like **unus** and **solus**

|       | masculine | feminine | neuter  |
|-------|-----------|----------|---------|
| nom.  | nullus    | nulla    | nullum  |
| acc.  | nullum    | nullam   | nullum  |
| gen.  | nullius   | nullius  | nullius |
| dat.  | nulli     | nulli    | nulli   |
| abl.  | nullo     | nulla    | nullo   |

*nullius* gen. sing. and *nullo* abl. sing. of *nullus* are used as the gen. sing. and abl. sing. of *nemo* =
*nobody*

nullo modo
in no way

ego hoc consilium nulli dedi.
I have given this advice to no-one.

haec epistula a nullo visa erat.
This letter had been seen by nobody.

## Relative clauses and relative pronouns

Relative clauses in English are introduced by a relative pronoun (who, which, that) and refer back to
a person or thing just mentioned, the antecedent.

There are two kinds of relative clause in English:

1. non restrictive

The teacher punished the boys, who had been naughty.

with a comma - the meaning is that the teacher punished
all the boys mentioned.

2. restrictive

The teacher punished the boys who had been naughty.

without a comma - the meaning is the teacher punished
only the naughty boys, and not the others.

Latin does not make this distinction

magister pueros qui mali fuerant punivit.

Classical Latin did not have the level of punctuation that English has today. As is often the case, we rely on the context of the Latin.

The relative pronoun in Latin must agree with its antecedent in its gender and number, but not necessarily in its case.

Compare

miles qui bene laborat validus est.        The soldier, who works well, is strong.

where **qui** is masc. sing. subject of **laborat** and so is in the nominative, with

miles quem vides validus est.        The soldier (whom) you see is strong.

where **quem** is masc. sing. object of **vides**, and so is in the accusative.

Note:   quocum, quacum, quocum = with whom, with which
        quibuscum = with whom, with which

|  | masculine | feminine | neuter |
|---|---|---|---|
| **singular** | | | |
| nom. | qui | quae | quod |
| acc. | quem | quam | quod |
| gen. | cuius | cuius | cuius |
| dat. | cui | cui | cui |
| abl. | quo | qua | quo |
| **plural** | | | |
| nom. | qui | quae | quae |
| acc. | quos | quas | quae |
| gen. | quorum | quarum | quorum |
| dat. | quibus | quibus | quibus |
| abl. | quibus | quibus | quibus |

The following sentences will provide examples of the relative pronouns in their different cases.

**Exercise 10.5    Translate the following into English**

1. senex totam vitam Romae habitaverat.
2. paene tota urbs in qua habitabam in bello deleta est.
3. locus totus in quo pueri ludunt pulcherrimus est.
4. haec pars oppidi quam omnes cives amant pulcherrima est.
5. ego illi mulieri cuius filia pulcherrima est multa dona dedi.
6. illum puerum quem punivit magister in oppido cum amicis suis saepe videbam.

7.  fer, o serve, hos libros ad magistrum qui in oppido nunc est.
8.  vidistine iuvenem quocum heri pugnavi?
9.  hostes quibuscum pugnaverunt Romani celeriter effugerunt.
10. hae sunt puellae quibuscum saepe ludebam.

**Exercise 10.6E   Translate the following into English**

1.  copiae quae fessae erant pugnare nolebant.
2.  illi libri quos scripsit poeta notissimus pulcherrimi sunt.
3.  taberna in qua mercatores bibebant notissima est.
4.  Pompeius cui cives nomen Magnus dederant, ab omnibus salutatus est.
5.  ego viro cuius filiae pulcherrimae sunt multa dona dabam.
6.  pueros quos punivit magister in summo monte conspexi.
7.  ferte, o pueri, hos libros ad magistrum qui in villa dormit.
8.  vidistisne, o comites, iuvenes quibuscum heri pugnavi?
9.  Crassus, ubi duae legiones a servis victae sunt, per decem milites unum a comitibus occidi iussit.
10. mercatoribus qui in foro heri aderant libros vendidi.

**Exercise 10.7    Translate the following into Latin**

1.  The farmer was looking for the dogs which had been in the garden.
2.  The slaves whom the master never praised ran away.
3.  The walls that you can see were built by my slaves.
4.  The city in which we used to live has been destroyed by the enemy.
5.  The farmers who were working in this field had fought against the Romans.
6.  My friend, give me the food that you have brought from the town.
7.  I have brought all the gold that I found in the field.
8.  All the citizens praised the emperor whose courage was well-known.
9.  The man with whom I went to the town is my companion.
10. The farmer for whom I had brought the food was away.

**Exercise 10.8E   Translate the following into Latin**

1. The maid-servants were looking for the dogs that had escaped.
2. The boys whom the teacher often praised were happy.
3. That wall which I built yesterday has been destroyed by the naughty boy.
4. The villa in which the queen used to live was destroyed in the war.
5. The slaves who were sleeping in the field had drunk a lot of wine.
6. Companions, give me the swords that you brought from the king.
7. My son, have you seen the spears that I found in the field?
8. The general who had been sent to Africa destroyed the whole city.
9. The woman with whom I went to the town is my sister.
10. The sailors for whom I brought the wine had already left.

# is qui and ei qui

is qui = the one who, the man who, he who

Similarly

ea quae =  she who, the woman who ; id quod = that which

eos qui bene laborant laudare debemus.
We must praise those who work well.

**Exercise 10.9 Translate the following into English**

1. eos qui consulem laudant non amamus.
2. nolite credere eis qui haec dicunt!
3. id quod difficile est saepe praemia fert.
4. illi iuvenes eas quae pulcherrimae sunt semper spectant.
5. nos eos qui celeriter currebant capere non poteramus.

**Exercise 10.10E Review**          **Complete the following and translate into English**

1.  liberti qui fess_   erant discess___   nolebant.
2.  paene tot__   oppidum in qu_   habitabant delet__   est.
3.  totus locus in qu_   puer_   ludebant pulcherrim_   erat.
4.  haec pars urb__   quam spectas pulcherrim_   est.
5.  tune illi vir_   cuius filia pulcherrim_   est donum dedisti?
6.  conspexistine in media urb_   servos qu__   punivit dominus?
7.  ferte, o puer_  , hos libr__   ad magistr__   qui in villa dormit.
8.  conspexistine, o comes, iuven__   quibuscum heri pugnavimus?
9.  milit__   quibuscum ad oppid__   fugi non iam adsunt.
10. senibus qui in for_   heri aderant quattuor serv__   vendidi.

1 hae sunt puellae quarum matres male se gesserunt.
2 hae sunt feminae tristes quae a coniugibus numquam laudantur.
3 haene sunt puellae quas Romae heri conspexisti?
4 noli laudare eas puellas quae male se gerunt.
5 hae sunt dominae quarum coniuges semper absunt.

1 hic sunt feminae quibuscum saepe Romam eo.
2 uxores quas in oppido saepe video pulcherrimae sunt.
3 puellae quibus omnibus dona heri dedi pulchre cantant.
4 omnes ancillae quibuscum servi luserant clamabant.
5 tres puellae quae a magistro punitae sunt iam fugiunt.

# Chapter 11      Transitive v Intransitive verbs

Transitive verbs have a direct object:

mercator libros vendebat.
The merchant was selling some books.

Intransitive verbs do not have a direct object:

leones per silvam currebant.
The lions were running through the forest.

Note that only transitive verbs can have a passive voice and that verbs that take an indirect object
are not transitive.

**Further verbs**

| Transitive verbs | | | | | |
|---|---|---|---|---|---|
| ascendo | ĕre | ascendi | ascensum | 3 | climb |
| descendo | ĕre | descendi | descensum | 3 | go down, come down |
| quaero | ĕre | quaesivi | quaesitum | 3 | search for, look for, ask |

| Intransitive verbs | | | | | |
|---|---|---|---|---|---|
| lacrimo | are | lacrimavi | | 1 | weep, cry |
| sedeo | ēre | sedi | | 2 | sit |
| taceo | ēre | tacui | | 2 | be silent, quiet |
| accido | ĕre | accidi | | 3 | happen |
| procedo | ĕre | processi | | 3 | advance, proceed |
| resisto (+dat.) | ĕre | restiti | | 3 | resist |
| surgo | ĕre | surrexi | | 3 | get up, stand up, rise |
| vivo | ĕre | vixi | | 3 | live |

**Exercise 11.1      Translate the following into English**

1. copiae lente montem descendebant.
2. eo tempore omnes milites ad summum montem ascendebant.
3. mulier misera, quod pecuniam non iam habebat, ante tabernam lacrimabat.
4. pueri miseri in horto sedebant atque tacebant.
5. incolae, quod leones quaerebant, magna cum cura per silvam procedebant.
6. nullus huic iuveni feroci resistere poterit.
7. ego tertia hora semper surgo.
8. quid in foro heri accidit?
9. saepe facilius est montem ascendere quam descendere.
10. uxor semper tacebat ante imperatorem.

## Exercise 11.2E   Translate the following into English

1. canis ferox subito surrexit et puerum perterritum petivit.
2. libertus duo annos Romae vixit.
3. quo modo hostibus resistere possumus?
4. cives canes feroces in viis quaesiverunt.
5. vir miser lacrimabat ante tabernam in qua uxorem conspexerat.
6. milites, ad urbem quam celerrime procedite!
7. tempus est tacere et regem audire.
8. venti graves heri acciderunt.
9. cur ancillae in horto sedebant?
10. sagitta in corpus militis descendit neque dux eam extrahere potuit.

## Exercise 11.3   Translate the following into Latin

1. At first light we all went up the hill.
2. The dog who was sitting in front of the bar door suddenly got up.
3. It's time now to resist the wild inhabitants.
4. The enemy advanced with great care.
5. The woman was weeping because her sons had departed to Rome.
6. We lived for three years near the sea.
7. There were strong winds yesterday in Rome.
8. Why did you go up the hill, soldiers?
9. Why are you crying, my daughter?
10. The stupid man sat down in the middle of the road and was quiet.

1 domina laeta subito surgit.
2 puella in horto sedit.
3 mater agricolae in via lacrimat.
4 puella montem lente ascendit.
5 filia tristis matrem quaerit.

## Exercise 11.4E   Translate the following into Latin

1. The old man lived happily alone for many years.
2. The boy was crying because his mother had not bought him a present.
3. The senator suddenly got up and departed.
4. At that time all the Roman forces were going up the hill.
5. By day and night the enemy continued advancing towards Rome.
6. An arrow went into the head of the lion.
7. We shall advance to the town at first light.
8. You will live a happy life near the sea.
9. The inhabitants resisted the Romans for a long time but finally they were overcome.
10. The merchant was sitting in the forum with his dog.

## Exercise 11.5E   Review   Complete the following and translate into English

1. copiae Roman__    montem celeriter ascenderunt.
2. tempus est tac___ et magristr__ sapientem audire.
3. mulier laet_ , quod multum pecuniae habebat, ad oppid__   iit.
4. cur illi serv_  in hort_  sederunt?
5. venti saev_  prope Rom__  heri accid_____ .
6. hoc tempor_  omnes milit__  ad urbem descend_____.
7. pueri, ex urb_  quam celerrime proced___  !
8. pueri miseri in medi_  foro sed_____ atque tacebant.
9. milites Roman_ , quod hostes quaerebant, magn_  cum cura ad silvam processerunt.
10. hasta in caput duc__  descendit neque miles extrahere pot___ .

1 phoca mox surget.
2 phoca ad aquilam celeriter descendit.
3 phoca perterrita lacrimat.
4 phoca celeriter procedere non potest.
5 phoca misera aqulilae saevae resistere non poterit.

# Chapter 12     celer, alius, alter, ipse, note on the infinitive

## Third declension adjectives ending in celer = quick, swift

|  | masc. | fem. | neut. |
|---|---|---|---|
| **sing.** | | | |
| nom. | celer | celeris | celere |
| voc. | celer | celeris | celere |
| acc. | celerem | celerem | celere |
| gen. | celeris | celeris | celeris |
| dat. | celeri | celeri | celeri |
| abl. | celeri | celeri | celeri |
| | | | |
| **plural** | | | |
| nom. | celeres | celeres | celeria |
| voc. | celeres | celeres | celeria |
| acc. | celeres | celeres | celeria |
| gen. | celerum | celerum | celerum |
| dat. | celeribus | celeribus | celeribus |
| abl. | celeribus | celeribus | celeribus |

## alius alia aliud = other

Like unus = one, solus = alone and totus = whole, alius needs careful attention

|  | masc. | fem. | neut. |
|---|---|---|---|
| **singular** | | | |
| nom. | alius | alia | aliud |
| acc. | alium | aliam | aliud |
| gen. | alius | alius | alius |
| dat. | alii | alii | alii |
| abl. | alio | alia | alio |
| | | | |
| **plural** | | | |
| nom. | alii | aliae | alia |
| acc. | alios | alias | alia |
| gen. | aliorum | aliarum | aliorum |
| dat. | aliis | aliis | aliis |
| abl. | aliis | aliis | aliis |

Note:

In place of alius in the gen. sing. **alterius** is often used
*(see below)*

1 aquila celeris alium cibum quaerit.
2 phoca lenta flumen transit.
3 equus celer aliquam subito conspicit.
4 altera capra ab aquila occisa est.
5 aquila phocam celerem capere non poterit.

41

Examples:

hunc librum iam legi; fer mihi alium!
I have already read this book; bring me another (one).
alii milites fortiores his sunt.     The other soldiers
are braver than these.

Note:   alii ..... alii        some (men) ...others

alii in via ambulabant, alii in villa dormiebant.
Some men were walking in the road, others
were sleeping in the villa.

Note also

alii cum aliis pugnant.
Some men are fighting some men and others
are fighting others.

1 domina ipsa pecuniam seni misero dat.
2 vir cui femina pecuniam dat senator est.
3 mulier cui vir miser pecuniam dat regina est.
4 femina cuius pater senator est pecuniam non dat.
5 puella epistulam agricolae dat.

## alter altera alterum = one of two, the other

|  | masc. | fem. | neut. |
|---|---|---|---|
| **singular** | | | |
| nom. | alter | altera | alterum |
| acc. | alterum | alteram | alterum |
| gen. | alterius | alterius | alterius |
| dat. | alteri | alteri | alteri |
| abl. | altero | altero | altero |
| **plural** | | | |
| nom. | alteri | alterae | altera |
| acc. | alteros | alteras | altera |
| gen. | alterorum | alterarum | alterorum |
| dat. | alteris | alteris | alteris |
| abl. | alteris | alteris | alteris |

ille puer laetus est, alter lacrimat.
That boy is happy, the other (of two) is crying.

# ipse ipsa ipsum = (-self)

**ipse** is used to emphasise the noun or pronoun

|          | masc.   | fem.    | neut.   |
|----------|---------|---------|---------|
| singular |         |         |         |
| nom.     | ipse    | ipsa    | ipsum   |
| acc.     | ipsum   | ipsam   | ipsum   |
| gen.     | ipsius  | ipsius  | ipsius  |
| dat.     | ipsi    | ipsi    | ipsi    |
| abl.     | ipso    | ipsa    | ipso    |
|          |         |         |         |
| plural   |         |         |         |
| nom.     | ipsi    | ipsae   | ipsa    |
| acc.     | ipsos   | ipsas   | ipsa    |
| gen.     | ipsorum | ipsarum | ipsorum |
| dat.     | ipsis   | ipsis   | ipsis   |
| abl.     | ipsis   | ipsis   | ipsis   |

Examples

| | |
|---|---|
| ego ipse ducem vidi. | I myself saw the general. |
| regem ipsum in oppido conspexi. | I caught sight of the king himself in the town. |
| ipsae venient. | They themselves will come. |

**A note on the Infinitive**
The present infinitive can often be translated by '...ing'
laborare in illis agris difficile est.
It is difficult to work in those fields.
Working in those fields is difficult.

celeriter currere seni difficile erat.
Running quickly was difficult for the old man.

**Exercise 12.1    Translate into English**

1. in medio foro alterum consulem conspexi.
2. libertus, quod oppidum ante amicum advenire volebat, equum celerem cepit.
3. interea dux alias copias in summo monte reliquit.
4. num rex ipse cenam uxori tulit?
5. ancillaene aliam cenam paraverunt?
6. aliae ridebant, aliae dormiebant.
7. ego ipse hos canes ex horto heri agi.
8. quo modo hi iuvenes militibus restiterunt?
9. quot libros magister ipse tulit?
10. alii milites interfecti sunt, alii vulnera gravia acceperunt.

**Exercise 12.2E   Translate into English**

1. interea alii milites quam celerrime discesserunt.
2. dominus ipse dormiebat sed nullus servus fugit.
3. pater tamen alterum filium tandem legit.
4. rex ipse nec vinum bibit nec cibum consumpsit.
5. regina ipsa hos canes ex horto egit.
6. alii consumebant, alii bibebant.
7. regem ipsum in illo loco heri vidi.
8. hae res heri gestae sunt.
9. quid tibi heri advenit?
10. iuvenes celeres paene omnes canes capere potuerunt.

**Exercise 12.3   Translate into Latin**

1. I caught sight of the same young men in the centre of the city.
2. Some boys were fighting, others were playing.
3. My friend always arrives at the same time.
4. The emperor himself received a deep wound in his head.
5. How were you able to catch the swift boys?
6. We always see the same men in the bar.
7. The queen herself came to the town with her other daughter.
8. I left the other book near the garden gate.
9. Working in this bad light is very difficult.
10. Sailing to Italy will not be easy.

**Exercise 12.4E   Translate into Latin**

1. When did you see the other consul?
2. Sailing to Italy in that ship was difficult.
3. Some men were sitting, others were standing.
4. The other dogs were sleeping near the garden gate.
5. Reading the letters in this bad light is not easy.
6. The merchant was laughing and reading at the same time.
7. Why didn't you bring the other books?
8. How did the emperor himself receive this deep wound?
9. It will be very difficult to catch the swift messengers.
10. The other consul received the letters.

**Exercise 12.5   Review  Complete the following and translate into English**

1. conspexistine in medio for_  alterum consul__ ?
2. nonne serv__  ipse cen__  uxori tulit?
3. civ__  celeres paene omnes puer__  mal__  capere potuerunt.
4. alii  in taberna consumeb___ , alii in vi_  bibebant.
5. quid vobis heri adven__  ?
6. hae res cras ger_____  .
7. interea imperator copias ceter__  in medio oppid_  reliquit.
8. ancill___  aliam cenam paravit?
9. dux, quod Romam ante amicum adven___  volebat, equ__  celerem cepit.
10. num imperatorem ips__  in illo loc_  heri vidisti?

# Chapter 13 Conditional Sentences

A clause containing **si = if** is known as a conditional clause. In a sentence this clause is called the **protasis** and the main clause of the sentence is called the **apodosis**.

Fot GCSE we shall concentrate on what are called **simple** conditionals, as opposed to **hypothetical** conditionals

si tu laetus es, bene est.
If you are happy, all is well.

1 si phoca aqulilam videbit, laeta erit.
2 si aquila celeriter descendet, phoca eam non videbit.
3 si phoca ibi manebit, aquila eam videbit

si dux hoc fecit, stultus erat.
If the general did this, he was stupid.

4 si phoca aquilam occidet, partem parvam consumere poterit.
5 si aquila phocam occidet, sola partem magnam consumere poterit.

A negative conditional uses **nisi = if not, unless**

nisi tu hoc facies, ego donum tibi donum non emam.
If you do not do this / Unless you do this, I shall not buy you a present.

Note the use of the future here.

## Exercise 13.1 Translate into English

1. si tu huic liberto credes, stultissimus es.
2. iuvenis tristis erit, nisi amicam suam videbit.
3. si puer hunc leonem interfecit, fortissimus erat.
4. si dux hoc iussit, crudelis erat.
5. si viam duobus horis inveniemus, domum hodie advenire poterimus.
6. si libros magistri habes, eos statim mihi da!
7. si regem conspexistis, felices fuistis.
8. si dominus haec verba dixit, sapiens erat.
9. si leones occides, incolae non iam perterriti erunt.
10. si pacem mox habebimus, cives duci nostro credent.

## Exercise 13.2E Translate into English

1. si arma ducis habes, statim ea illi da!
2. si tu illis mercatoribus credetis, stultissimi estis.
3. si pacem mox habebimus, cives laeti erunt.
4. si illos canes feroces ex horto statim agetis, domina laeta erit.
5. si milites ducem ipsum conspexerunt, felices fuerunt.
6. si servus hoc fecit, eum statim puni!
7. si domi manebis, tibi donum non emam.
8. si canes feroces ex horto egisti, bene fecisti.
9. si pacem cupitis, patriam ad bellum parate!
10. si fessus es, mecum domi mane!

**Exercise 13.3    Translate into Latin**

1. If you are tired, stay here!
2. If you tell your mother this, I shall be angry.
3. If you don't prepare my dinner at once, I shall go to the bar.
4. If you warned your father about the danger, you did well.
5. Hurry if you want to see the beautiful girls!
6. If you receive this letter today, don't come!
7. If you want to see me, come in the middle of the night!
8. If you destroy my letters, I shall be very angry.
9. If you have no money, you cannot go to Rome.
10. If you want to see the other consul, come with me!

1 nisi effugies, te capiam.
2 nisi mihi pecuniam das, iratus ero.
3 si donum mihi emisti, benigne fuisti.
4 si fessa es, statim sede!
5 si pecuniam habes, noli mihi dare.

**Exercise 13.4    Review of conditional (si = if), concessive (quamquam = although), temporal (postquam = after) and causal (quod = because) clauses**

1. comes fratri 'quamquam' inquit 'ego Romae decem annos vixi, eum senatorem numquam vidi.'
2. Romani, quod nemo muros custodiebat, castra hostium facile inire potuerunt.
3. senex, postquam sex horas dormivit, surrexit et statim exiit.
4. milites, quamquam heri fugere cupiverant, nunc fortiter contra hostes se defendebant.
5. quid accidet si servi dominos sine poena necare possunt?
6. mater, quod filia Romam discesserat, tristissima erat.
7. nuntius, postquam ad castra hostium pervenit, ducem petivit.
8. puer, postquam donum pulchrum accepit, magnopere risit.
9. si leo illum incolam occidet, ceteri statim discedent.
10. dominus saevus, quamquam servus fidelis erat, eum saevissime punire constituit.
11. plurimi, quod senatorem clarum videre volebant, Romam iter heri fecerunt.
12. postquam nuntius haec imperatori nuntiavit, hic ipse signum dedit.
13. dei, quod homines eis dona non iam dabant, iratissimi erant.
14. libertus, quamquam multos annos Romae vixit, numquam imperatorem vidit.
15. si nobis pecuniam dabis, in hac taberna dona emere poterimus.
16. senex, quamquam multos annos in villa pulcherrima habitabat, semper miser erat.
17. postquam haec audivit, vir propter auxilium comitem laudavit.
18. quamquam iuvenis diu ancillas petebat, eas invenire non poterat.
19. 'si' inquit mercator 'hunc hortum emam, vinum facere potero.'
20. quamquam senes pecuniam non habebant, ad tabernam ierunt.

**Exercise 13.5E    Translate into Latin**

1. Although he had a lot of money, the old man was always unhappy.
2. The old man was very happy because he had a lot of money.
3. If he finds the money, the old man will be happy.
4. After he arrived in Rome the old man went to a well-known bar.
5. Although he had no money, the old man went into the bar.
6. If the old man has no money, he won't be able to buy any wine.
7. The old man can't buy any wine because he has no money.
8. Although he had drunk a lot of wine the old man was able to walk home on his own.
9. The old man wasn't able to walk home on his own because he had drunk a lot of wine.
10. If the old man has drunk a lot of wine he won't be able to walk home on his own.

# Chapter 14    Past participle passive

In Chapter 8 we met the perfect passive tense, formed of the past participle passive PPP plus the present tense of sum. We can use the **past participle passive** on its own – with the meaning of **having been ….**

Thus:    **amatus** = having been loved    **monitus** = having been warned

The PPP is an adjective and must agree with the subject.
Its endings are the same as those of **bonus**

Thus:

urbs **capta** deleta est. = Literally: The city
**having been captured** was destroyed.

This translation sounds a little unnatural. We can say

When the city had been captured, it was destroyed *or*
The city which had been captured was destroyed *or*
The city was captured and destroyed.

1 regina a coniuge ad oppidum ire iussa vinum iam ferebat.
2 ancilla a rege punita laborare nolebat.
3 ancilla ab domino vinum ferre iussa iam celeriter redibat.
4 ancilla a coniuge relicta miserrima erat.
5 puella ab aquila vulnerata domum celeriter currebat.

Depending upon the context, the PPP can have
the meaning of

when *the city had been destroyed ….*        temporal
because *the city had been destroyed….*      causal
although *the city had been destroyed ….*    concessive

Compare

pueri saevissime puniti magistrum amabant.
Although the boys had been very savagely punished,
they loved the teacher.

1 coniunx dominae in urbe conspectus iam domum redibat.
2 servus in urbe a domino conspectus quam celerrime fugit.
3 rex ab uxore in urbe conspectus iam ad villam currebat.
4 nauta ab aquila vulneratus iam miserrimus fuit.
5 agricola a domino punitus iam miser fuit.

with

pueri saevissime puniti magistrum non amabant.
Because the boys had been very savagely punished,
they did not love their teacher.

## Exercise 14.1    Translate into English

1. servi felices, a domino nobili liberati, laeti erant.
2. miles, dux a comitibus factus, bene se gessit.
3. senes a comitibus relicti quam celerrime effugerunt.
4. rex de periculo a comitibus monitus se bene gerere constituit.
5. pater petivit filium captum in omnibus partibus terrae.
6. milites ab hostibus vulnerati muros custodiebant.
7. corpus Augusti Romam latum in foro sine mora incensum est.
8. servi miseri, a domino laborare iussi, statim ad tabernam fugerunt.

9. paene omnes cives, ab hostibus vulnerati, ex urbe fugerunt.
10. oppidum diu oppugnatum tandem captum est.

## Exercise 14.1E   Translate into English

1. ventus navem deletam ad insulam egit.
2. agricola omnes canes in agro relictos diu petivit.
3. princeps omnia arma ad oppidum lata statim cepit.
4. regina sapiens a filia monita statim fugit.
5. haec templa duobus mensibus aedificata celeriter deleta sunt.
6. hostes muros fortiter a civibus custoditos deleverunt.
7. hostes milites in proelio victos tandem ceperunt.
8. equus ingens prope muros relictus in urbem tractus est.
9. naves conspectae tandem ad Britanniam advenerunt.
10. alios libros a magistro laudatos tribus diebus legi.

1 equus pro muro relictus iam dormiebat.
2 cur equum in agro relictum cepisti?
3 equus in via relictus ab aquila interfectus est.
4 equum in via relictum heri vidi.
5 equa in via relicta aquilam subito conspexit.

## Exercise 14.3   Translate into Latin

1. After the ship had been driven to the island it was destroyed by the inhabitants.
2. After the city had been attacked for two months it was finally destroyed by the enemy.
3. After the emperor had been warned about the danger, he departed immediately.
4. I shall give money to the boys who have been praised by the teacher.
5. The swift horses which had been captured yesterday were led to the town.
6. We saw the slaves who had been set free by their master.
7. We looked at a part of the city that had been destroyed by the enemy.
8. Within three days I shall read the books brought to me by my friend.
9. My son, bring me the dinner that has been prepared by the maid!
10. Where is the money that has been given by the queen?

## Exercise 14.4E   Review          Complete the following and translate into English

1. servi a domin_ relicti quam celerrim_ effugerunt.
2. dominus de pericul_ a comite monitus se bene ger___ constituit.
3. equus ingens prope murum relict__ ad mediam urb__ tractus est.
4. alterum libr__ a magistro laudat__ paucis diebus legi.
5. milit__ in proeli_ victos heri cepimus.
6. navis ventis paene delet_ tandem ad insulam adven__.
7. copiae Romanae mur__ fortiter a civ____ custoditum delere non potuerunt.
8. h___ tabernam a servis meis aedificat__ cras vendam.
9. servus felix, a domino nobili liberat__ , laetus erat.
10. mil__ alius, dux a comitibus su__ factus, bene se gessit.

1 senis a rege laborare iussus villam aedificabat.
2 ancilla a domino conspecta ad villam festinavit.
3 princeps a servo de muro monitus perterritus erat.
4 servus a domino laborare iussus murum parvum aedificabat.
5 servus a principe stare iussus murum custodiebat.

# Chapter 15      Present participle active

Latin has a **present participle active** (e.g. warning) and a **past participle passive** (e.g. having been warned). The present particle passive (e.g. being warned) and the past participle active (e.g. having warned) do not exist in Latin. Here we shall meet the present participle active.

Note that English verbal form ending in '-ing' has two completely different uses:

As a participle:          The girls were walking to the sea, *laughing*.

As a verbal noun          *Singing* is good for you.

Latin does not use a participle in this second case.

The present participle of amo **amans** is declined like **ingens**

|  | masc. | fem. | neut. |
|---|---|---|---|
| **Singular** | | | |
| nom. | amans | amans | amans |
| voc. | amans | amans | amans |
| acc. | amantem | amantem | amans |
| gen. | amantis | amantis | amantis |
| dat. | amanti | amanti | amanti |
| abl. | amanti | amanti | amanti |
| **Plural** | | | |
| nom. | amantes | amantes | amantia |
| voc. | amantes | amantes | amantia |
| acc. | amantes | amantes | amantia |
| gen. | amantium | amantium | amantium |
| dat. | amantibus | amantibus | amantibus |
| abl. | amantibus | amantibus | amantibus |

To form the present participle take off **-re** from the infinitive and add **-ns**. Hence:

amans, monens, regens, audiens, capiens

Note: **iens** participle from **eo** (I go) is declined:

iens euntem euntis eunti eunti
euntes euntes euntium euntibus euntibus

Note compounds: abiens (going away), exiens (going out), iniens (going in), rediens (returning), transiens (crossing)

1 mulieri per viam festinanti donum non dedi.
2 hodie puellam canem domum ferentem conspeximus.
3 subito filiam magistri vinum et aquam ferentem vidimus.
4 puellam pulchram in via dormientem conspeximus.
5 heri ancillam in via stantem conspexi.

Examples:

dux in proelio **pugnans** interfectus est.
The leader was killed    *fighting*         in the battle.
                    *whilst fighting / as he was fighting*

ducem ad urbem **redeuntem** conspeximus.
We caught sight of the general *(as he was)*
*returning* to the city.

turbam iuvenum ex oppido **fugientium** vidimus.
We saw a crowd of young men fleeing the town.

## Exercise 15.1    Translate into English

1. pueri in villa dormientes tuti erant.
2. iuvenis iam habens minus pecuniae miserior erat.
3. viri pessimi pecuniam nostram capientes ridebant.
4. cives principem bene se gerentem amabant.
5. paene omnes milites ab oppido discedentes princeps conspexit.
6. dux milites totam noctem templum custodientes laudavit.
7. nautae clamantes ad navem lati sunt.
8. milites fortiter pugnantes in proelio saevo interfecti sunt.
9. mater filios in via ludentes conspexit.
10. illum mercatorem libros domini vendentem conspexi.

1 mulier militi in via stanti pecuniam dedit.
2 mulier pecuniam viro in via stanti dare noluit.
3 vir miser in via stans pecuniam accepit.
4 puella senem in muro sedentem de periculo monuit.
5 regina senem pecuniam capientem non laudavit.

## Exercise 15.2E   Translate into English

1. libertos in oppidum ruentes custos conspexit.
2. pueri leonem saevum spectantes perterriti erant.
3. iuvenes mali omne aurum capientes ridebant.
4. cives regem male se gerentem ex urbe pepulerunt.
5. puellae in villa dormientes tutae non erant.
6. rex custodes totam noctem in muro manentes laudavit.
7. servi vehementer clamantes ad regem lati sunt.
8. centum milites fortiter pugnantes tandem interfecti sunt.
9. frater sororem in horto ludentem conspexit.
10. pater filium dormientem ante ianuam tabernae vidit.

1 puellae per viam ambulantes ridebant.
2 filios reginae in oppidum ineuntes vidimus.
3 ancillas in agros fugientes cepimus.
4 puellas miseras in via pereuntes vidimus.
5 hodie duas puellas per viam currentes conspeximus.

## Exercise 15.3    Match the following pairs

1. domina, ubi vidit iuvenes ad portam    a. in illa domo habitantes necaverunt.
2. incola crudelis leonem                 b. lacrimantem non audivit.
3. milites crudeles omnes servos          c. procedentes, iussit servos villam  contra eos defendere.
4. dux milites captivum                   d. 'omnes' inquit 'donum accipietis.'
5. mater tamen filiam                     e. muros novos aedificantes.
6. dominus ridens                         f. horto cum puellas ludentem.
7. nam miles in animo habebat             g. custodientes invenit.
8. milites invenerunt incolas             h. lacrimantem prope mare.
9. iuvenis credulis reliquit dominam      i. custodem ibi dormientem necare.
10. vir invenit uxorem in                 j. dormientem necare parabat.

**Exercise 15.4**          **Translate into Latin**

1. We caught sight of the slaves as they rushed along the street.
2. The young men heard the shouts of the soldiers as they stood in the street.
3. The slave killed the brave general as he slept.
4. The enemy attacked the sailors as they sailed to Italy.
5. The happy mother watched her sons playing in the field.
6. The dogs frightened the maids as they walked down the road.
7. The young men threw water at the guards who were sleeping near the wall.
8. The guards saw the soldiers as they crossed the river.
9. The general praised his soldiers as they captured the lions.
10. We saw the master teaching the slaves how to fight.

**Exercise 15.5E  Review**          **Complete the following and translate into English**

1. milites duce_    bene se gerentem amabant.
2. puellae in villa dormient__   tut__   erant.
3. mater fili__   dormientem ante ianuam tabern__   conspexit.
4. dux custodes prope ianuam diu manent__   laudavit.
5. mult__   mulieres e taberna exeuntes cum nautis laet__   conspexi.
6. pueri canes spectantes rideb___   .
7. viri mali omne aur__   nostrum capientes riserunt.
8. paene omnes milites fortiter pugnant__   occis_   sunt.
9. soror fratres in hort_   ludentes conspex__   .
10. servi fortiter clamantes ad imperator__   lat_   sunt.

**Exercise 15.6E  Translate the following verbs and find them in the wordsearch**

```
F Q L V Q A C C I D I T R
U U I T I V I T E P K A E
E A T N K L T S H P T B L
L E I N T A C U I T A A I
D S M U U E Q N I I B M Q
S I G W N R R X F D E I U
Y V T D Z K E F S E D R I
P I I K K R H N E R E C M
O T N U R E D N E C S A U
N H S U M I X I V V I L S
C U S T O D I E B A N T I
S U M I T I T S E R S O R
H D S P R O C E S S I T C
```

they gathered, she believes, they were guarding, he killed, she asked for, we left, they went up, he went down, he asked/ searched for, he was crying, she was sitting, he went silent, it happened, he advanced, we resisted, she got up, we lived

1 senex crudelis puellas dormientes saeve punire constituit.
2 pueri magistrum ridentem spectaverunt.
3 puer magistrum stantem spectavit.
4 magister iratus pueros dormientes spectavit.
5 dominus puerum et puellam dormientes conspexit.

# Chapter 16        Future participle active

The simplest way to translate the future participle active is e.g. *about to* prepare

|        | masculine | feminine | neuter |
|--------|-----------|----------|--------|
| nom.   | paraturus | paratura | paraturum |
| acc.   | paraturum | paraturam | paraturum |
|        | etc.      | etc.     | etc.   |

2$^{nd}$ conj.              3$^{rd}$ conj.              4$^{th}$ conj              3½ conj.

about to warn          about to rule          about to hear          about to take
moniturus -a -um     recturus -a -um      auditurus -a -um     capturus -a -um

The future participle active is formed by taking off **-um** from the supine and adding **-urus**.

Hence from *eo ire ivi itum* the future participle is *iturus*. The one exception is *futurus* from *sum*

The future participle active can be translated by *about to* … , *going to* … even, when there is a suggestion of purpose, *intending to* ….  Like the present particle active and the past participle passive, the future participle active is often better translated as a clause, using *when*, *since* or *as*. If the main verb is in a past tense, the participle needs to be rendered accordingly. Compare

milites oppidum oppugnaturi signum ducis exspectant.
About to attack the town, the soldiers are waiting for the general's signal.

milites oppidum oppugnaturi signum ducis exspectabant.
As they were about to attack the town, the soldiers were waiting for the general's signal.

Note the use of the imperfect eram with this participle = was going to happen:

miles hastam iacturus erat.
The soldier was about to throw the spear.

### Exercise 16.1    Translate into English

1.  domina librum lectura sedit.
2.  iuvenem se iacturum in flumen forte conspeximus.
3.  puerum pecuniam capturum conspexi.
4.  ego patrem de sene aurum capturo monui.
5.  dux signum proelii daturus erat.
6.  pueri canem ex horto acturi erant.
7.  ubi filia advenit, mater aurum emptura erat.
8.  quid tibi Romam discessuro accidit?
9.  imperator servos fessos puniturus filium parvum discedere iussit.
10. ubi Romani castra posituri erant, ventus gravis subito accidit.

1 mulier seni pecuniam datura erat.
2 senex sagittam parvam accepturus erat.
3 senator puellae parvae pecuniam daturus erat.
4 regina pecuniam senis captura erat.
5 imperator pecuniam reginae accepturus erat.

## Exercise 16.2E Translate into English

1. talem cibum dormiturus consumere non debes.
2. senator verba imperatoris narraturus omnes tacere iussit.
3. milites urbem oppugnaturi signum ducis exspectabant.
4. imperator victoriam claram nuntiaturus tandem surrexit.
5. salutavi comitem domum initurum.
6. senator surrecturus erat.
7. servum pecuniam in silva celaturum forte conspexi.
8. ancilla, ubi ego te conspexi, quid factura eras?
9. venti saevi deleverunt naves Romam discessuras.
10. servi, ubi dominus rediit quid acturi eratis?

## Exercise 16.3 Translate into Latin

1. We who are about to depart salute you.
2. What happened to you when you were about to get up?
3. The dog was about to get up.
4. What were you about to do when I arrived?
5. The poet was about to set fire to the letter.
6. When he was about to speak of the victory the general got up.
7. I warned my mother about the boy who was about to take the horse.
8. When the king was about to die, he handed his books over to his slave.
9. The citizens greeted the emperor as he was about to leave.
10. The general gave the signal to his soldiers as they were about to advance through the forest.

1 phoca lente discessura subito ridet.
2 aquila phocam petititura celeriter descendit.
3 aquila phocam consumptura ad montem ascendit.
4 phoca in flumen se iactura subito surgit.
5 aquila in terram discessura subito capram conspexit.

## Exercise 16.4E Review Complete the following and translate into English

1. o mater, talem cibum grav__ dormitura consum___ non debes.
2. senator verb_ ducis narraturus omnes comit__ stare iussit.
3. milites oppidum oppugnaturi signum duc__ exspectabant.
4. nuntius victoriam clar__ nuntiavit consulibus discessur__ .
5. comes me salutavit domum initurum.
6. pueri canem ex horto actur_ erant.
7. ubi vir forte adven__ , uxor omne aur__ venditura erat.
8. ubi hostes castr_ posituri erant, vent__ gravis subito accidit.
9. quid duci ad villam discessur_ accidit?
10. patremne de can_ cibum capturo monu_____ ?

# Chapter 17 Present infinitive passive

Corresponding to the present infinitive active e.g. *spectare = to watch*, there is a present infinitive passive e.g. *to be watched*

|   | Present infinitive active | | Present infinitive passive | |
|---|---|---|---|---|
| 1 | amare | *to love* | amari | *to be loved* |
| 2 | monere | *to warn* | moneri | *to be warned* |
| 3 | regere | *to rule* | regi | *to be ruled* |
| 4 | audire | *to hear* | audiri | *to be heard* |
| 3½ | capere | *to take* | capi | *to be taken* |

Note

There is no present infinitive passive of *facio*.
The 3rd conjugation passive infinitive has the same form as the dative singular of *rex = king*.
This unusual form for the 3rd conjugation passive infinitive may look like the 1st person singular of the perfect tense.

### Exercise 17.1    Translate into English

1.  dux a militibus audiri nolebat.
2.  clamores audiri non possunt.
3.  cives capi nolunt.
4.  canes agi in agrum non poterant.
5.  canis agi nolebat.
6.  mulier conspici nolebat.
7.  dux hunc cibum consumi iussit.
8.  dux muros fortiter custodiri iussit.
9.  rex urbem defendi iusserat.
10. princeps oppidum deleri non iubebit.
11. milites per viam duci noluerunt.
12. dux bellum geri cum hostibus statim iussit.
13. hae hastae in oppidum iaci non possunt.
14. aurum inveniri non poterit.
15. dux servos interfici iussit.
16. magister omnes libros legi iussit.
17. rex nuntium mitti Romam iussit.
18. dominus servum occidi iubebit.
19. dux aurum regi ostendi nolebat.
20. miles in hoc loco poni noluit.
21. equus duci a puero non vult.
22. rex aurum in illo loco peti iussit.
23. equi ad urbem reduci noluerunt.
24. Romani a regibus regi non iam volebant.
25. pueri Romae relinqui nolebant.
26. poeta hunc librum scribi non cupivit.

### Exercise 17.2    Translate into Latin

1.  The soldiers don't want to be captured by the enemy.
2.  The chief ordered the soldiers to be collected near the wall.
3.  The bad master ordered the slaves to be killed.
4.  The king ordered the walls of the town to be destroyed.
5.  These pupils do not want to be punished by the teacher.
6.  The girls did not want to be left in Rome.
7.  The king ordered the gold to be sent to the city.
8.  The teacher ordered the books to be read by all the pupils.
9.  The horses don't want to be driven by the boys.
10. The freedman wanted to be invited to dinner by the consul.

**Exercise 17.3   Review   Complete the following and translate into English**

1. clamores puellae miser___  a matre aud___   non poterant.
2. quis hunc cibum consum_   iussit?
3. imperator muros urbis defendi quam diutissime iuss___  .
4. rex bellum cum host____   tandem geri iussit.
5. num dux castr_   poni iussit?
6. aurum in hoc magno horto inven____   numquam poterit.
7. quo dux host___   agi iussit?
8. domina cenam par____   statim iussit.
9. dux benignus oppid___   hostium deleri noluit.
10. hae hastae grav___   in hostes iaci non poterunt.

1 libertus murum deleri voluit.
2 domina murum deleri iusserat.
3 senator murum aedificari nolebat.
4 dominus murum quam celerrime aedificari iusserat.
5 servus murum inveniri noluit.

# Chapter 18        Fourth declension nouns

## Fourth declension nouns

There is only a small group of nouns in the fourth declension. Here we concentrate on

| manus f. | = hand |
|----------|--------|
| domus f. | = house *(See Ch. 3 and box below)* |

|       | singular | plural  |
|-------|----------|---------|
| nom.  | manus    | manus   |
| voc.  | manus    | manus   |
| acc.  | manum    | manus   |
| gen.  | manus    | manuum  |
| dat.  | manui    | manibus |
| abl.  | manu     | manibus |

|       | singular        | plural           |
|-------|-----------------|------------------|
| nom.  | domus           | domus            |
| voc.  | domus           | domus            |
| acc.  | domum           | domus *or* domos |
| gen.  | domus *or* domi | domorum          |
| dat.  | domui *or* domo | domibus          |
| abl.  | domo            | domibus          |

## Exercise 18.1    Translate into English

1. senator ducem domum heri invitavit.
2. hi senatores domi tres dies manserunt.
3. prima luce dux domo discessit.
4. erat vulnus grave in manu militis.
5. oppidum in manibus hostium iam est.
6. sagitta in manum nuntii descendit.
7. senex librum in altera manu, in altera epistulam tenebat.
8. summa cum cura sagitta e manu militis a duce tracta est.
9. senator duas domus habet; altera Romae est, altera prope mare est.
10. tua vita in manibus meis est.

## Exercise 18.2    Translate into Latin

1. Where is your second home, senator?
2. The emperor's hands were very large.
3. This consul has two houses: one is near Rome; the other is on an island.
4. The soldier has a deep wound in one hand; in the other he is holding a spear.
5. The arrow went into the soldier's hand.
6. The city will soon be in the hands of the enemy.
7. At first light the maid left the house.
8. With great care the arrow was taken out of the soldier's hand.
9. The city remained in enemy hands for four days.
10. Why did you invite that senator to your house?

**Exercise 18.3E  Review  Complete the following and translate into English**

1.  dux domum inimici heri deleri iuss__ .
2.  num Roma in man____  hostium est?
3.  cur prima luce dom_  discessisti?
4.  erat vulnera gravia in man____  militis.
5.  num haec magna urb_  in manibus hostium diu mans__ ?
6.  sagitta in man__  nuntii forte descendit.
7.  senex duo libr__  in altera manu, in alter_ epistulam tenebat.
8.  summa cum cura sagitt_  e pede ducis a milit_  tracta est.
9.  senator du__  domus habet; una Romae est, altera prope mar_  est.
10. vita huius milit__  est in manibus imperatoris est.

1 puella manus amicae tenet.
2 puellae dormlentes ambulant.
3 duae puellae in horto domi dormiunt.
4 puellae perterritae e manibus dominae crudelis effugerunt.
5 duae puellae domum quam celerrime currunt.

# Chapter 19      Indirect Statement

## Indirect Statements: accusative and present infinitive

He says: 'Caesar is approaching.'

The actual words that are used by the speaker are in **direct speech**. Putting this into **indirect speech**:

He says that Caesar is approaching.

Latin puts the noun 'Caesar' into the **accusative** case and the verb 'is approaching' into the present **infinitive**; there is no verb for *that* here.

Thus:

Caesarem appropinquare dicit.

This construction is used not only after verbs of 'speaking' but also verbs like *writing, thinking* etc. followed by *that*. Such verbs as:

| | | | | |
|---|---|---|---|---|
| audio, clamo, credo, dico, invenio, lego, narro, nuntio, respondeo, scribo, video | | | | |
| plus new verbs | | | | |
| cognosco | cognoscĕre | cognovi | cognitum | = get to know, find out |
| intellego | intellegĕre | intellexi | intellectum | = understand |
| sentio | sentire | sensi | sensum | = feel, notice |
| scio | scire | scivi | scitum | = know |
| nescio | nescire | nescivi | nescitum | = do not know |

**Exercise 19.1      Translate into English**

1. scio domum magistri parvam esse.
2. poeta scribit principem bene regere.
3. credisne regem laudari?
4. audivistine imperatorem in urbe adesse?
5. hi cives dicunt hostes urbi appropinquare.
6. dux semper respondet milites has res nescire.
7. senex cognoscit equos in agro non iam adesse.
8. scisne mercatores in foro adesse?
9. rex intellegit aurum non iam in villa esse.
10. plurimi dicunt reginae manus pulchras esse.

All the main verbs in the sentences of Ex 19.1 are in the present tense. The present infinitive indicates that this action is going on at the same time as the main verb in the sentence. This also applies when the main verb is not in the present tense. For example, in the sentence

I **knew** that the leader **was** arriving.

the *knowing* and *was coming* are happening at the same time, hence

sciebam ducem advenire.
I **knew** that the army **was** coming.

puer clamavit iuvenes discedere.
The boy **shouted** that the young men **were** leaving.

Note that when translating into English we must adjust the tense of the verb in the *that* clause.

### Exercise 19.2    Translate into English

1. quis sciebat virum domi esse?
2. poeta narravit principem bene regere.
3. num credebas Romam insulam esse?
4. audivi multas copias urbi appropinquare.
5. illi cives dicebant hostes fugere.
6. dux semper respondebat milites suos has res nescire.
7. senex clamavit servos militibus tradi.
8. nonne sciebas illum virum senatorem esse ?
9. rex cognovit urbem iam in manibus hostium esse.
10. plurimi dixerunt regi manus minimas esse.

### Exercise 19.3    Translate into Latin

1. The messenger says that the enemy are approaching.
2. O slave, do you know that the master is at home?
3. The leader knows that the ships are near the island.
4. The general announces that the enemy army is in front of the city wall.
5. The young men said that the old men were in the centre of the city.
6. All the pupils knew that their teacher was in Rome.
7. I didn't know that the boy had all the books.
8. Very many men said that the storm was fierce.
9. The king said that the guards were very brave.
10. The old man says that he drinks a lot of wine.

### Exercise 19.3E    Match the following pairs

| | |
|---|---|
| 1. dux tamen omnibus | a. non senatoris inimicos esse. |
| 2. pater intellexit filium | b. crudelissimum esse. |
| 3. magna voce liberti nuntiaverunt se | c. manibus hostium esse. |
| 4. mercator audivit imperatorem | d. servos militibus tradi. |
| 5. rex cognovit urbem iam in | e. captum in insula iam vivere. |
| 6. scisne mercatores | f. insulam esse? |
| 7. mercator sensit | g. audientibus respondit nullum periculum esse. |
| 8. credebasne Romam | h. in foro adesse? |

**Exercise 19.5E   Review   Complete the following and translate into English**

1.  plurim_   milites diceb___   pedes maximos imperatori esse.
2.  dux mox cognov__   oppidum in man____   hostium iam esse.
3.  quis nesciebat illum virum gravem fuisse senator__   ?
4.  imperator semper respondebat viros su__   has res bene scire.
5.  nuntii dixerunt host__   iam urb_   appropinquare.
6.  quis aud____   imperatorem in urb_   iam adesse?
7.  nesciebam imperatori multos inimic__   esse.
8.  tum sensi omnes puell__   fugisse.
9.  quo modo tu cognov____   ducem Rom__   iam esse?
10. quis nesc__   nomen illius milit__   ?

**Exercise 19.6E   Translate the following verbs and find them in the wordsearch**

| | | | | | | | | | | |
|---|---|---|---|---|---|---|---|---|---|---|
| Q | T | A | B | E | I | C | S | S | W | A | J |
| E | N | V | O | P | E | O | Z | U | A | S | N |
| T | U | N | M | D | E | G | N | M | P | T | E |
| I | I | C | A | S | E | N | T | I | M | U | S |
| C | C | G | B | V | U | O | F | X | W | M | C |
| S | S | G | E | Q | J | V | V | E | X | V | I |
| O | N | D | I | L | S | I | M | L | S | N | M |
| N | E | O | C | F | L | T | Y | L | E | B | U |
| G | K | P | S | X | Z | E | O | E | N | D | S |
| O | N | N | E | I | V | K | T | T | F | I | T |
| C | V | T | N | U | R | E | S | N | E | S | N |
| Y | R | F | L | D | K | M | P | I | I | H | N |

she found out, she understands, we feel, they know, we don't know, he found out, we understood, they felt, she knew, I didn't know

1 libertus servum tristem esse vidit.
2 servus dominam in urbe esse nesciebat.
3 libertus senem laetum esse sensit.
4 princeps servum Graecum esse cognovit.
5 mater filium tristem esse sciebat.

1 aquila phocam dormire nesciebat.
2 phoca aquilam appropinquare sensit.
3 aquila phocam minimam vidit.
4 phoca aquilam fratrem habere sciebat.
5 aquila phocam appropinquare sensit.

# Chapter 20    Perfect infinitive, active and passive

## Perfect infinitive active

|   |       | perfect | perfect infinitive active | English |
|---|-------|---------|---------------------------|---------|
| 1 | amo   | amavi   | amavisse                  | to have loved |
| 2 | moneo | monui   | monuisse                  | to have warned |
| 3 | rego  | rexi    | rexisse                   | to have ruled |
| 4 | audio | audivi  | audivisse                 | to have heard |
| 3½ | capio | cepi   | cepisse                   | to have taken |
|   | sum   | fui     | fuisse                    | to have been |

## Perfect infinitive passive

|   |       | PPP     | Perfect Infinitive Passive | English |
|---|-------|---------|----------------------------|---------|
| 1 | amo   | amatus  | amatus esse                | to have been loved |
| 2 | moneo | monitus | monitus esse               | to have been warned |
| 3 | rego  | rectus  | rectus esse                | to have been ruled |
| 4 | audio | auditus | auditus esse               | to have been heard |
| 3½ | capio | captus | captus esse                | to have been taken |

Since the perfect passive participle is an adjectival form, it has to agree with the subject, which may be in the accusative in an indirect statement.

The **perfect infinitive** indicates that this action took place **before** that of the main verb. Thus,

scio puerum advenisse.
I **know** that the boy **has** arrived.

sciebat puerum advenisse.
I **knew** that the boy **had** arrived.

audivi hostes victos esse.
I **heard** that the enemy **had been** defeated.

pater mihi dixit reginam mortuam esse.
My father **told** me that the queen **had** died.

Note that since there is a perfect participle passive of facio **factus -a -um**, there is a perfect infinitive passive of facio: factus esse

scio haec a puero malo facta esse.
I know that these things have been done by the naughty boy.

We can say that the perfect infinitive goes one step further back that the main verb.

**Exercise 20.1    Translate into English**

1.  tum senex sensit duo ex canibus discessisse.
2.  frater nuntiavit oppidum ab hostibus captum esse.
3.  paene omnes cives iam sciunt principem mortuum esse.
4.  omnes discipuli sciebant magistrum librum clarissimum scripsisse.
5.  servus domino respondit equos ab hostibus captos esse.
6.  diu credebam regem ab his interfectum esse.
7.  frater mihi dixit ducem prima luce discessisse.
8.  rex nuntiavit omnes naves ante proelium deletas esse.
9.  dux nuntiavit tres milites e manibus hostium effugisse.
10. quis nesciebat principem sapientem esse?

## Future infinitive active

The future infinitive in the active voice (literally *to be going to*) is formed from the future active participle (see Chapter 16) with *esse*. The participle is naturally accusative in indirect statements, but can be any gender, singular or plural

dominus credit ancillas bene laboraturas esse.
The master believes that the slave-girls will work well.

## Personal pronouns in indirect speech

In direct speech the personal pronoun as subject is generally concealed in the verb itself. Thus discessi = I departed. Here the pronoun ego is not normally written; the ending **-i** tells us it is the 1$^{st}$ person singular.

However if we put **discessi** into indirect speech, we have to add the pronoun:

dicit me discessisse.
He says that I have left.

Similarly *discessisti = you left* becomes *dicit te discessisse = He says that you have left.*

The pronouns can be strengthened by the addition of **ipse** in the accusative.

pater dicebat me ipsum has res fecisse.
My father used to say that I myself had done these things.

If the speaker is the same as the person who has carried out the action, then **se** is used.

dominus dixit se ipsum illos servos liberavisse.
The master said that he himself had freed those slaves.

However, if the *he / she / they* is someone other than the *he /she / they* of the main verb, we should use *eum / eam / eos /eas.*

regina eam advenisse dixit.
The queen said that she (someone else) had arrived.

Some Latin verbs are followed by the future infinitive where English uses the present infinitive

| promitto | promittĕre | promisi | promissum 3 = promise |
| --- | --- | --- | --- |

pater promisit se filio canem empturum esse.
The father promised to buy a dog for his son.

## Negative indirect statements

In translating 'He says that the general has not arrived', Latin does not use dico followed by non, but instead **nego -are -avi -atum** = I say that … not'. Thus

negat ducem advenisse.  He says that the general has not arrived.

### Exercise 20.2    Translate into English

1.  negavi me hanc rem pessimam gessisse.
2.  quis te muros delevisse nuntiavit?
3.  militesne vobis se has res malas fecisse dixerunt?
4.  num iuvenes se a pueris parvis superatos esse nuntiaverunt?
5.  servus mihi saepe dicebat se aurum domini invenire non posse.
6.  vir uxori se aurum in foro empturum esse promisit.
7.  dux nuntiavit suas copias prima luce castra movere.
8.  custos negavit eum effugisse.
9.  parentes scripserunt se in urbe manere.
10. cur te ipsum hoc fecisse dicis?

### Exercise 20.3E  Translate into English

1.  princeps dicebat se rempublicam servare cupere.
2.  quis vos ad oppidum advenisse nuntiavit?
3.  num dux vobis se has res malas fecisse dixit?
4.  nonne iuvenes se pueros superavisse nuntiaverunt?
5.  pueri mali nobis saepe dicebant se canes vulneravisse.
6.  milites promiserunt se quam fortissime pugnaturos esse.
7.  socii magna voce clamaverunt se bellum novum cum hostibus gerere velle.
8.  custodes negaverunt hostes fugisse.
9.  pueri negaverunt se has res pessimas fecisse.
10. cur te ipsum hanc rem malam fecisse dicunt?

### Exercise 20.4E  Match the following pairs

| | |
| --- | --- |
| 1. multi credebant | a. audivi ducem novum esse ferocem. |
| 2. etiam ego | b. mortem crudelem non timere. |
| 3. quis | c. suam oppugnaturos esse. |
| 4. imperator credebat cives domum | d. regem sed fratrem eius interfecisse. |
| 5. num iuvenis senatoribus dixit | e. credebat hominem imperatorem esse? |
| 6. dux, ubi intellexit hostes | f. se consilium optimum habere? |
| 7. miles miser mox cognovit se non | g. victos esse, laetus ad castra rediit. |
| 8. dux vidit militem | h. Caesarem ducem optimum esse. |

**Exercise 20.5    Translate into Latin**

1. The boy said that he had not done this.
2. Who announced that the army had left?
3. The guards said that they had not seen the enemy.
4. I said that I had seen my friend in the city.
5. O brother, you did understand that our father was in Rome, didn't you?
6. I didn't believe that all the arrows and spears had been handed over.
7. The sailors were shouting that almost all the ships had been destroyed.
8. Who said that the woman had been saved?
9. The messenger promised to read the letter at once.
10. The general told the citizens that the city was no longer safe.

**Exercise 20.6E   Review  Complete the following and translate into English**

1. senex negat se illam rem passim__    gessisse.
2. cur nuntiavisti hostes muros urb__    delevisse?
3. imperator scrips__    se domi man___    velle.
4. custos negavit se prope mur__    dormiv____    .
5. omnes copiae promis_____    se quam fortissime pugnat____    esse.
6. ille miles mihi heri dix__    se aurum in agr_    invenisse.
7. omnes soci_    clamaverunt se bellum novum cum host____    gerere nolle.
8. nonne hi milit__    dixerunt se host__    vici?
9. vir uxor_    promisit se in illa tabern_    donum car__    empturum esse.
10. cur te ipsum hoc fec____    dixisti?

1 domina promisit se cibum ad villam laturam esse.
2 regina promiserat se aurum quam celerrime empturam esse.
3 domina negavit se vinum laturam esse.
4 ancilla promiserat se aquam et vinum ad villam laturam esse.
5 mea soror dicebat se aurum empturam esse.

1 phoca aquilam vulneratam esse credit.
2 aquila phocam bene consumpsisse nescit.
3 aquila phocam vulneratam esse nescit.
4 aquila phocam periculum cognoscere sensit.
5 phoca aquilam fratrem habere vidit.

# Chapter 21    Correlatives

| The words | qui = who, | qualis = of what kind, | quantus = of what size, | quot = how many, |
|---|---|---|---|---|
| answer to | is = he, | talis = of such a kind, | tantus = of such a size, | tot = so many |

**talis** est **qualis** semper fuit.
He is such as (of the same character as) he has ever been.

**tantam** habeo villam **quantam** tu.
I have as large a house as you.

**tot** erant milites **quot** incolae.
There were as many soldiers as inhabitants.

## Exercise 21.1    Translate into English

1. tot erant pueri quot puellae.
2. vir tantam pecuniam habebat quantam uxor.
3. pueri tales sunt quales semper fuerunt.
4. libertus tantam domum habebat quantam senator.
5. tot viros quot mulieres in taberna erant.
6. filius tantam pecuniam quantam pater habebat.
7. hostes tanta castra quanta Romani habebant.
8. habemus tot libros quot vos.
9. is qui hoc intellegere potest sapiens est.
10. vir talis est qualem tu eum esse scripsisti.

1 nauta puellam parvam timet.
2 puella audax nautam terret.
3 femina a nauta pulchro terretur.
4 ancilla laeta a sene crudeli terretur.
5 puella parva a nauta saevo terretur.

## Exercise 21.2    Translate into Latin

1. There were as many soldiers as farmers in the bar.
2. These soldiers are no longer such as they were before the battle
3. I have as large a garden as my friend.
4. The soldier had as large a shield as his leader.
5. Do you want as much money as your father?
6. This general will have as many victories as that one.
7. Do you have as much money as your friend?
8. There was as much danger during the day as the night.
9. The man is just like his father.
10. He who can understand the words of the poet is wise.

## Exercise 21.3E   Review   Complete the following and translate into English

1. hic agricola tantum agr__   habebat quantum domin__   meus.
2. mercator non tal__   est qualem me_   mater eum esse scripsit.
3. tot erant can__   in via quot in hort_   erant.
4. filia tantam pecuni__   quant__   mater habebat.
5. uxor tant__   pedes habebat quantos vir.
6. senator habebat tot puer__   quot consul.
7. volo habere talem hortum qual__   tu habes.
8. tu non iam tal__   es qualis ubi eras puer.
9. ego scripsi tot verb_   quot tu leg____  .
10. num pueri tal__   erunt quales puell__   ?

1 hastae ab uxoribus saevis iaciuntur.
2 sagittae magnae a nautis crudelibus tenentur.
3 sagittae magnae ab uxoribus saevis delentur.
4 sagittae parvae ab ancillis iaciuntur.
5 hastae a patre et filio tenentur.

# Chapter 22     Connecting relative

The connecting relative is the relative pronoun used to start a new sentence or clause. It is very common in Latin and it is very important not only to recognize it but also to be able to give a translation that flows naturally.

uxor tandem domum advenit. quam ubi vidit vir laetissimus erat.
The wife finally reached home. When her husband saw her, he was very happy.

milites tandem ad mare advenerunt. quod ubi conspexerunt laetissimi erant.
The soldiers finally reached the sea. When they saw it, they were very happy.

filia domini tandem domum advenit. quam ubi hic vidit laetissimus erat.
The master's daughter finally reached home. When he saw her, he was very happy.

Note that *quod* and *quam* can have several different meanings.

Note also the use of quod in the following, where it refers more loosely to the whole of the previous sentence.

filia domini tandem domum advenit. quod ubi hic vidit laetissimus erat.
The master's daughter finally arrived home. When he saw this, he was very happy.

## Exercise 22.1     Translate into English

1. nullum cibum habebat puer miser; cui volui cenam optimam parare.
2. milites fortiter pugnare dux vidit; qui post victoriam ad regem missi sunt.
3. canes in horto dormire conspexi; quos post cenam servos in viam agi iussi.
4. heri senatori donum pulchrum emi; quod ubi is accepit laetissimus erat.
5. soror tua in foro heri erat; quam ubi conspexi, ego statim salutavi.
6. consul habebat quattuor filios, e quibus unus miles erat.
7. nuntius verba imperatoris nuntiavit; quae ubi cives audiverunt irati erant.
8. fratri epistulam heri misi; quam is ubi accepit laetus erat.
9. magistro duos libros dedi; quos ubi vidit is risit.
10. mihi libros mercator vendidit; cui igitur pecuniam dedi.

## Exercise 22.2E     Translate into English

1. mater tua domi heri erat; cui ego ubi ad villam veni statim donum dedi.
2. senex verba ducis nuntiavit; quae ubi filius audivit iratus erat.
3. filios in via ludentes pater conspexit; quos domum statim redire iussit.
4. liberto aurum mercator heri vendidit; cui pecuniam cras dabit.
5. dux conspexit militem fortiter pugnantem; qui post proelium magnopere laudatus est.
6. dominae meae hanc epistulam heri ostendi; quam ubi vidit ea misera erat.
7. filius miserrimus erat; cui pater voluit dare donum optimum.
8. libertus habebat tres filias; e quibus duae pulcherrimae erant.
9. heri puella matri donum pulchrum emit; quod ubi ea accepit laetissima erat.
10. duci epistulam heri imperator misit; quam is ubi accepit iratissimus erat.

## Exercise 22.3E Review Complete the following and translate into English

1. filius laetissim__ erat; cui pater donum optim__ dederat.
2. heri puer matri dona pulchra em__ ; quod ubi ea accepit laetissim_ erat.
3. rex habebat quattuor fili__ ; e quibus una sola pulch__ erat.
4. canes in agr_ dormientes conspexi; quos ante cen__ servos expellere iussi.
5. pater tu__ in foro heri erat; qu__ ubi conspexi, ego statim salut___ .
6. dominae meae hunc libr__ heri ostendi; quem ubi vidit ea miser_ erat.
7. nullum cib__ habebat senex miser; cui volui cen__ optimam parare.
8. heri filiae don__ pulchrum emi; qu__ ubi ea accepit laetissima erat.
9. duci epistul__ heri imperator misit; quam is ubi accepit laetissim__ erat.
10. hos milit__ fortiter pugnantes dux vidit; qui post victoriam ad urbem miss_ sunt.

1 nauta saevus puellam parvam timebat.
2 puella crudelis nautam terrebat.
3 femina a comite pulchro terrebatur.
4 mulier laeta a sene crudeli terrebatur.
5 puella perterrita a nauta saevo terrebatur.

1 aqua ab ancilla portabatur.
2 vinum a matre bibebatur.
3 aqua a domino portabatur.
4 ancilla a servo malo spectabatur.
5 vinum optimum a custode tradebatur.

# Chapter 23    The imperfect subjunctive and purpose clauses

In Latin we have learned that there are two **voices** – **active** (he sees) and **passive** (he is seen). There are also three **moods**. We have already met two: the **indicative** and the **imperative**.

The **indicative mood** is used to express a fact:

princeps multos annos rexit.
The chieftain ruled for many years.

The **imperative mood** issues a command:

fer mihi vinum!
Bring me wine!

The third mood is called the **subjunctive** and is used to express a purpose, a fear, a wish, a request – something that might happen.

There is a corresponding subjunctive mood for most tenses of the indicative. For the moment we shall concentrate on the **imperfect subjunctive**.

---

**ACTIVE**

| | | | | | |
|---|---|---|---|---|---|
| amarem | monerem | regerem | audirem | caperem | essem |
| amares | moneres | regeres | audires | caperes | esses |
| amaret | moneret | regeret | audiret | caperet | esset |
| amaremus | moneremus | regeremus | audiremus | caperemus | essemus |
| amaretis | moneretis | regeretis | audiretis | caperetis | essetis |
| amarent | monerent | regerent | audirent | caperent | essent |

**PASSIVE**

| | | | | |
|---|---|---|---|---|
| amarer | monerer | regerer | audirer | caperer |
| amareris | monereris | regereris | audireris | capereris |
| amaretur | moneretur | regeretur | audiretur | caperetur |
| amaremur | moneremur | regeremur | audiremur | caperemur |
| amaremini | moneremini | regeremini | audiremini | caperemini |
| amarentur | monerentur | regerentur | audirentur | caperentur |

---

Note that the imperfect subjunctive active is formed by putting **-m -s -t -mus -tis -nt** on to the infinitive. Thus *amarem* etc.

| Note also: | **present infinitive** | **imperfect subjunctive** |
|---|---|---|
| sum | esse | essem |
| possum | posse | possem |

|       |       |        |
|-------|-------|--------|
| eo    | ire   | irem   |
| volo  | velle | vellem |
| nolo  | nolle | nollem |

In Latin **purpose clauses** which are in the past, the main clause is as normal in the indicative, but the verb in the purpose clause goes into the **imperfect subjunctive**.

Example

| Main clause | purpose clause |
|-------------|----------------|
| venimus | **ut** regem videremus. |
| We came | **in order to** see the king. |
| | |
| milites venerunt | **ut** pugnarent. |
| The soldiers came | **to** fight. |
| | |
| servus fugit | **ne** laboraret. |
| The slave fled | **in order not to** work. |

1 pater et filius hasta iaciebant ut phocam interficerent.
2 agricolae signa petebant ut equas occiderent.
3 pueri mali sagittas iecerunt ut aquilas necarent.
4 viri hastas iaciebant ut milites vulnerarent.
5 agricolae hastas iaciebant ne a phoca vincerentur.

Note the negative **ne** = **in order not**

In English we can translate **ut** by *to, in order to, so as to* and **ne** *in order not to, so as not to, to stop being, so that (they) would not be*

### Exercise 23.1         Translate into English

1. cives ad mediam urbem festinaverunt ut reginam viderent.
2. Romani fortiter pugnaverunt ut hostes vincerent.
3. servi celeriter effugerunt ne a domino punirentur.
4. iuvenes in agrum canes egerunt ut eos ibi necarent.
5. milites in oppido convenerunt ut alium ducem legerent.
6. milites statim fugerunt ne ab hostibus caperentur.
7. cives ex urbe quam celerrime exierunt ut hostes effugerent.
8. cives militesque murum ingentem ut urbem defenderent aedificaverunt.
9. puer ad oppidum cum patre iit ne in villa solus esset.
10. dominus iter ad forum facere constituit ut ipse servos novos videret.

### Exercise 23.2E         Translate into English

1. consul ad forum festinavit ut comitem videret.
2. cives celeriter convenerunt ut servos novos conspicerent.
3. hostes celeriter effugerunt ne a nobis vincerentur.
4. agricolae ceteros canes ex oppido egerunt ne cives perterriti essent.

1 uxor fugit ne coniunx eam peteret.
2 dux militum clamabat ut puella pecuniam traderet.
3 nauta saevus puellam terrebat ut pecuniam traderet.
4 puella perterrita fugit ne pecuniam traderet.
5 femina agricolae saevo pecuniam dedit ne ab eo puniretur.

5. milites in medium oppidum cucurrerunt ut ducem iterum viderent.
6. custodes statim fugerunt ne ab hostibus interficerentur.
7. paene omnes cives ex urbe discesserunt ut hostes effugerent.
8. milites ut valida corpora haberent multum cibi boni consumebant.
9. puella in villa mansit ut sola esset.
10. omnes hastae et sagittae ad villam latae sunt ut dux se defenderet.

**Exercise 23.3**          **Translate into Latin**

1. We went to forum to see the merchants.
2. Almost all the citizens ran away in order not to be captured by the enemy.
3. The soldiers brought the slaves back to the town in order to punish them.
4. The wretched slaves ran away so as not to be killed by their master.
5. We handed over the books in order not to be punished by the teacher.
6. The allies returned to the city so as to see the general.
7. The poet remained in his country-house to write a new book.
8. The general took all the weapons in order to defend himself well.
9. The general collected his troops in front of the walls in order to attack the city.
10. We worked for two hours in order to build a new wall as quickly as possible.

# A note on purpose clauses

In translating a sentence such as 'He sent slaves to work in the fields', instead of saying:

servos misit ut in agris laborarent

it is more common to say

servos misit **qui** in agris laborarent

dux ipse gladium ferebat **quo** se defenderet.
The general himself was carrying a sword with which to defend himself.

Note that in the above sentence *quo = with which* abl. sing. masc. of *qui*. This should not be confused with the following:

If there is a comparative in the purpose clause, **quo** must be used rather than *ut*:

dux his militibus, quo melius pugnarent, tela optima dedit.
The general gave the best weapons to these soldiers in order that they could fight better.

**Exercise 23.4**          **Translate into English**

1. pater misit Romam filium qui cum fratre ibi laboraret.
2. dux festinare iussit ad urbem milites optimos qui eam fortiter defenderent.
3. magister ostendit libros optimos discipulis quo melius scriberent.
4. dominus laudavit servum quo celerius curreret.
5. dux dixit haec verba militibus quo audacius pugnarent.
6. rex ipse advenit ad urbem quo milites fortius muros defenderent.
7. rex misit ad agros milites quo agricolae tutius laborarent.
8. dux misit ad oppidum milites qui muros delerent.

9. pater saevissime punivit filium quo melius laboraret.
10. dux tradidit optima arma militibus quo rem facilius gererent.

## Exercise 23.5       Translate into Latin

1. The general sent a messenger to tell the king about the danger.
2. The king himself praised his soldiers in order that they fight better.
3. The leader sent soldiers to overcome the enemy.
4. The guards were standing on the walls in order to see the enemy more easily.
5. I went into the garden to read the letter more easily.

## Exercise 23.6    Review       Complete the following and translate into English

1. mulier in villa mans__ ut sola esset.
2. paene omnes civ__ ex oppido discess_____ ut hostes saevos effugerent.
3. cives ad medi__ urbem contenderunt ut regem vid_____ .
4. viri crudeles in agr__ canes pepul_____ ut eos ibi necarent.
5. dominus servum quo melius labor____ saevissime punivit.
6. custos statim fugit ne ab host____ interficeretur.
7. imperator ipse ad urb__ quo milites fortius muros defenderent contendit.
8. dux tradidit optim_ arma militibus quo rem facilius ger_____ .
9. omnes hastae et sagitt__ ad urbem lat__ sunt ut cives se defenderent.
10. rex ad agros tres milit__ quo agricolae tutius laborarent mis__ .

1 puellae tristes domum redierunt ut fratrem viderent.
2 filiae miserae regis ad agrum fugerunt ne a patre punirentur.
3 feminae ad villam cucurrerunt ut a senibus malis effugerent.
4 pueri currebant ut ante noctemad villem advenirent.
5 puellae quam celerrime currebant ut equos viderent.

1 ancilla aquam ferebat ut equus biberet.
2 puella vinum portabat ut rex biberet.
3 poeta vinum ferebat ne rex iratus esset.
4 filia principis vinum ferebat ut aquila biberet.
5 frater regis aquam tulit ut phoca biberet.

# Chapter 24      Result clauses

A result clause gives the outcome of an action:

dominus **tam** saevus erat **ut** omnes ancillae timerent.
The master was so harsh that all the maids were afraid.

In the main clause there is a 'signpost' word (so etc) followed by ut (that) which introduces the result clause. the negative is **ut non**

Some other 'signpost' words that are used in result clauses

adeo = so much, so greatly
ita = to such an extent, so
talis -e = such
tam  = so
tantus -a -um = so great, such a great
tot = so many

quis erat **adeo** stultus **ut** hoc intellegere **non** posset?
Who was so stupd that he could not understand this?

ventus non erat **ita** gravis **ut** domum redire **non** possem.
The wind wasn't so strong that I couldn't return home.

cibus quem vendebat mercator erat **talis ut** emere **non** vellem.
The food that the merchant was selling was such that I didn't want to buy it.

libertus habebat **tantam** pecuniam **ut** omne aurum emere posset.
The freedman had so much money that he was able to buy all the gold.

consul habebat **tot** amicos **ut** omnes invitare non posset.
The consul had so many friends that he couldn't invite them all.

**Exercise 24.1**          **Translate into English**

1. aderant tot canes in foro ut mercatores discesserent.
2. vulnus tam grave erat ut dux mox domi diu manere deberet.
3. puer canes tam vehementer agebat ut pater iratus esset.
4. imperator tam sapiens erat ut consilium hostium facile intellegeret.
5. servus tanta cum cura laborabat ut dominus saepe laudaret.
6. leo adeo celer erat ut incolae necare non possent.
7. hostes multos Romanos tam graviter vulneraverunt ut hi eis resistere non possent.
8. erant tot canes in horto ut domina domo exire nollet.
9. libertus ita villam aedificavit ut uxor ibi habitare nollet.
10. venti adeo graves erant ut omnia castra delerentur.

**Exercise 24.2**                **Translate into Latin**

1. The man was so stupid that he understood nothing.
2. The senator invited so many colleagues that they ate all the food.
3. The wind was so fierce that all the ships were driven to the island.
4. The man had so much money that he could buy presents for all his friends.
5. The forces proceeded so slowly that they were unable to reach the town before night.

**Exercise 24.3E   Match the following pairs**

1. puer tam clare clamavit
2. adeo volebat imperatorem
3. tantum erat
4. dux tam clarus
5. pueri tantum clamorem
6. illo die venti tam saevi
7. dux tam fortiter pro urbe
8. ventus tam vehementer

a. periculum ut cives maxime timerent.
b. fecerunt ut pater eos iussit exire et in horto ludere.
c. videre ut Romam statim adiret.
d. erant ut nemo laborare vellet.
e. egit ut multae naves delerenter.
f. sua pugnabat ut cives eum laudarent.
g. ut pater vocem eius audiret.
h. erat ut multi ad villam venirent.

**Exercise 24.4E   Review  Complete the following and translate into English**

1.  aderant tot cives irati in for_   ut consules perterriti ess___  .
2.  vulnus tam grav_   erat ut dux in villa diu manere deb____  .
3.  vir canes tam vehementer ag____  ut uxor clamaret.
4.  imperator tam stult__   erat ut consilium hostium intelleg___   non posset.
5.  servi tanta cum cura labor_____   ut dominus eos laudaret.
6.  leo adeo ferox er__   ut omnes incolae perterrit_   essent.
7.  hostes mult__   Romanos vulneraverant tam graviter ut hi quam celerrime fug_____  .
8.  mercator tant__   aurum domi hab____   ut domo dicessere noll__  .
9.  libertus ita villam aedificavit ut uxor ibi vivere noll__  .
10. ventus adeo saev__   erat ut tres villae deler_____.

1 nauta adeo perterritus erat ut puella lacrimaret.
2 puella adeo lacrimavit ut nauta clamaret.
3 nauta adeo vehementer clamavit ut puella lacrimaret.
4 puella perterrita erat ut nauta lacrimaret.
5 puella adeo vehementer lacrimabat ut  nauta non clamaret.

1 puellae tam celeriter cucurrererunt ut mox advenirent.
2 mulieres tam lente cucurrerunt ut non fessae essent.
3 puellae adeo celeriter cucurrerunt ut mox fessae essent.
4 puellae tantam cenam consumpserant ut non iam currere possent.
5 ancillae tam celeriter ambulaverunt ut ad urbem mox advenirent.

# Chapter 25      Indirect commands

So far we have met only direct commands or imperatives:

serve, fer mihi illos libros!       Bring me those books!

We can make this an indirect command by

I asked the slave to bring me those books.

We could write:

servum illos libros mihi ferre iussi.
I ordered the slave to bring me those books.

1 nauta iratus reginam ut discederet rogavit.
2 agricola audax reginae ut maneret persuasit.
3 femina senem laetum ut sederet rogavit.
4 dux ancillae ut cantaret persuasit.
5 femina nautae ut ibi maneret persuasit.

> We can also use such verbs as **rogavi** (I asked), **monui** (I advised) and a new verb:
>
> persuadeo -ere persuasi persuasum *(+dat.)* = persuade
>
> with **ut** and the **subjunctive**; negative **ne**

dux militibus **ut** oppidum statim oppugnarent persuasit.
The general persuaded the soldiers to attack the town immediately.

magister pueros **ne** iterum clamarent monuit.
The teacher warned the boys not to shout again.

The construction of the indirect command is the same as for a purpose clause, because the underlying idea is similar.

epistulam ad uxorem scripsi **ut** aurum emeret.

This could be read as a purpose clause:
I wrote a letter to my wife so that she would buy some gold.

or as an indirect command
I wrote a letter to my wife telling her to buy some gold.

**Exercise 25.1**          **Translate into English**

1. magister sapiens discipulos ut libros optimos legerent monuit.
2. iuvenes ut a media urbe discesserent meus pater rogavit.
3. num cives persuaserunt vobis ut arma in flumen iacerent?
4. dux ipse persuasit omnibus militibus ut in urbe manerent.
5. nonne dux vos rogavit ut urbem defenderetis?
6. cur pater te monuit ut flumen transires?
7. quis te rogavit ut canes ex foro ageres?
8. dux milites audaces rogavit ut castra hostium tertia hora oppugnarent.
9. magister persuasit discipulis ut se bene gererent.
10. rex iratus servos rogavit ut cibum pararent.

**Exercise 25.2E**          **Translate into English**

1 agricola ancillae pulchrae ut discederet persuasit.
2 agricola feminae miserae ut ibi maneret persuasit.
3 nauta mulierem laetam ut maneret in oppido rogavit.
4 senex mulierem iratam ut statim abiret rogavit.
5 agricola puellam ne fugeret monuit.

1. pater filium ne libros pessimos legeret monuit.
2. magister pueris ut bene scriberent persuasit.
3. num dux vobis ut oppidum oppugnaretis rogavit?
4. regina ipsa filio ut maneret in urbe persuasit.
5. nonne rex vobis ut in urbe maneretis rogavit?
6. quo modo custos tibi ut in flumen te iaceres persuasit?
7. quis tibi ut canibus cibum ferres rogavit?
8. dominus servis ut cibum equis pararent rogavit.
9. custos milites eosdem ut a medio oppido discesserent rogavit.
10. dux, cum unum militem verbis monuisset, ceteris persuasit ut pugnarent.

**Exercise 25.3**          **Translate into Latin**

1. We advised the boys to read these books.
2. The king ordered the slaves to take all the gold.
3. Who ordered your troops to leave the city?
4. We persuaded the teacher not to punish the pupils.
5. The king asked the slaves to prepare the weapons.
6. Surely the general didn't order you to attack the city?
7. The parents persuaded their sons to behave themselves.
8. The mother told the girls not to play in the street.
9. I advised the king not to leave the city.
10. Surely you told the pupils to work well?

**Exercise 25.4E   Match the following pairs**

| | |
|---|---|
| 1. itaque mater misera deos | a. ut in villa sua manerent. |
| 2. ubi puer perterritus leonem ferocem | b. ut servum stultum puniret. |
| 3. liberti rogaverunt dominum | c. vidit, patrem rogavit ut se servaret. |
| 4. senex nobilis comites invitavit | d. monuit milites suos ne fugerent. |
| 5. quibus verbis gravibus filius patrem rogavit | e. auxilium sociis ferrent. |
| 6. dux rogavit nautis ut omnia | f. rogavit ut filiam servarent. |
| 7. dux militibus monuit ut | g. in mare statim inicerent. |
| 8. imperator saepe | h. meum ut se in villam acciperet. |

1 dominus viris ut dormirent persuaserat.
2 magister discipulos laborare iusserat.
3 dominus servos ut murum aedificarent rogavit.
4 magister pueros fessos ne dormirent monuerat.
5 princeps filiis ut murum aedificarent monuerat.

1 regina ancillam ut murum deleret monuerat.
2 dominus servo ut villam quam celerrime aedificaret persuaserat.
3 pater filium miserum ut villam aedificaret rogaverat.
4 dominus servum ut murum aedificaret rogavit.
5 servus regem ut oppidum novum aedificaret rogaverat.

## Exercise 25.5    Review  Complete the following and translate into English

1.  nonne dux te rogav___  ut discederes?
2.  imperator, cum unum milit___  verbis monuisset, ceter___  persuasit ut pugnarent.
3.  dux ipse omn_____  militibus ut in urbe man_____  tandem persuasit.
4.  dominus serv___  ut aqu___  equis ferret rogavit.
5.  quo modo custos vobis ut in flumen vos iaceretis persuasit?
7.  quis tibi ut can_____  cibum ferr___  rogavit?
8.  iuvenes ut ab medio oppid_  discesserent meus pater rogav___  .
9.  num cives vobis ut arma in castr___  relinqu_____  persuaserunt?
10. magister puer___  ut bene scriberent persuas___  .

# Chapter 26     cum + the imperfect subjunctive

**cum + the imperfect subjunctive** is a very common construction, where **cum** can mean 'when', 'while', 'because' 'since' or even 'although', depending upon the context.

milites nostri, cum hostes urbem oppugnarent, multas hastas iaciebant.

While the enemy were attacking the city, our soldiers were throwing many spears.

### Exercise 26.1     Translate into English

1. mercator, cum tandem senex esset, vitam laetam egit.
2. milites, cum hostes lente appropinquarent, fugere parabant.
3. cum rex hoc facere nollet, cives iratissimi erant.
4. hic puer, cum parvus esset, cum eis iuvenibus validis pugnare nolebat.
5. hic puer fortis, cum minimus esset, cum illis iuvenibus pugnare parabat.
6. illum principem, cum nec fortis nec validus esset, nemo amavit.
7. naves, cum venti saevi essent, ad insulam actae sunt.
8. cum servi celeriter currerent, nemo eos capere poterat.
9. cum custodes virum miserum ad mortem ducerent, subito imperator advenit.
10. pater pueri, cum magnopere iratus esset, ad magistrum statim iit.

### Exercise 26.2E  Translate into English

1. pueri, cum libros legerent, ridebant.
2. comites, cum amicus appropinquaret, in media via steterunt.
3. dux illam domum, cum periculum adesse credebat, intrare nolebat.
4. hoc templum, cum pulcherrimum et sacerrimum esset, hostes deleverunt.
5. dominus, cum servus semper bene laboraret, eum magnopere laudabat.
6. illae naves, cum ventis saevis agerentur, ad insulam advenire potuerunt.
7. cives perterriti, cum hostes adessent, ad mare festinaverunt.
8. agricola, cum in agris laboraret, equos non vidit.
9. milites audaces, cum fortiter in proelio pugnarent, multa et saeva vulnera acceperunt.
10. duae ex his navibus, cum ad Italiam lente navigarent, deletae sunt.

### Exercise 26.3     Translate into Latin

1. My father was very angry as we were shouting.
2. Since the enemy were advancing quickly, the citizens decided to flee.
3. Because the master used to punish his slaves severely, his sons were very sad.
4. Because the enemy had defeated our army, the citizens no longer had faith in the leader.
5. As the wind was very strong, the sailors prepared to defend themselves.
6. While the farmers were working in the fields, they saw an animal crossing the river.
7. While the sailors were preparing their ships, a strong wind suddenly arrived.
8. While we were sailing to that island, we caught sight of the king's ship.
9. While the dogs were being driven into the town centre, they were making loud cries.
10. Since the master was very cruel, the slaves made up their minds to flee.

**Exercise 26.4    Review  Complete the following and translate into English**

1.  hostes, cum Roman_ celeriter appropinquarent, fug___ parabant.
2.  hic puer fort__ , cum parvus esset, cum illis iuven____ pugnare parabat.
3.  servi, cum in agr__ laborarent, equos non vid_____ .
4.  miles audax, cum fortiter in proeli_ pugnaret, multa et saeva vulnera accep__ .
5.  mercator, cum tandem senex ess__ , Rom__ vivebat.
6.  hi pueri, cum parv_ essent, cum eis iuvenibus validos pugn___ nolebant.
7.  comites, cum amicus appropinqu____ , in medi_ via steterunt.
8.  naves, cum venti saev_ essent, ab insula act__ sunt.
9.  agricolae, cum in agris laborar___ , equos non viderunt.
10. h__ templum, cum pulcherrimum et sacerrimum ess__ , hostes deleverunt.

1 cum dominus adesset, servi lacrimabant.
2 cum dominus abesset, servi non laborabant.
3 cum dominus adesset, servi montem ascendebant.
4 cum dominus abesset, servi laborabant.
5 cum dominus adesset, servi sedebant.

1 cum magister iratus esset, discipuli non dormiebant.
2 cum magister dormiret, pueri ludebant.
3 cum magister non iratus esset, discipuli dormiebant.
4 cum magister laetus esst, discipuli dormiebant.
5 cum magister pueros historiam doceret, pueri dormiebant.

# Chapter 27    Pluperfect subjunctive, active and passive

The **pluperfect subjunctive active** is formed by taking the perfect stem and adding the following endings:

**-issem, -isses, -isset, -issemus, -issetis, -issent**

| | | | | | |
|---|---|---|---|---|---|
| amavissem | monuissem | rexissem | audivissem | cepissem | fuissem |
| amavisses | monuisses | rexisses | audivisses | cepisses | fuisses |
| amavisset | monuisset | rexisset | audivisset | cepisset | fuisset |
| amavissemus | monuissemus | rexissemus | audivissemus | cepissemus | fuissemus |
| amavissetis | monuissetis | rexissetis | audivissetis | cepissetis | fuissetis |
| amavissent | monuissent | rexissent | audivissent | cepissent | fuissent |

The **pluperfect subjunctive** of the **passive** voice is formed by taking the PPP **+ essem, esses, esset, essemus, essetis, essent**

| | | | | |
|---|---|---|---|---|
| amatus essem | monitus essem | rectus essem | auditus essem | captus essem |
| amatus esses | monitus esses | rectus esses | auditus esses | captus esses |
| amatus esset | monitus esset | rectus esset | auditus esset | captus esset |
| amati essemus | moniti essemus | recti essemus | auditi essemus | capti essemus |
| amati essetis | moniti essetis | recti essetis | auditi essetis | capti essetis |
| amati essent | moniti essent | recti essent | auditi essent | capti essent |

Instead of **ubi** or **postquam**, meaning **when** or **after**, we can use **cum + pluperfect subjunctive**

miles, cum ducem iratum esse vidisset, quam celerrime fugit.
When the soldier had seen that the general was angry, he fled as quickly as possible.

## Exercise 27.1        Translate into English

1. senes, cum iuvenes conspexissent, ad montes fugerunt.
2. milites, cum iter longissimum fecissetis, magnopere fessi eratis.
3. cum fortiter pugnavissetis, a rege atque a duce laudati estis.
4. dux, cum omnes milites sui fugissent, hostibus se tradidit.
5. discipulus, cum librum poetae clari legisset, alium legere voluit.
6. rex, cum verba nuntii audivisset, maxime timuit.
7. regem, cum sedisset, custos statim gladio occidit.
8. hi milites, cum fortiter in proelio pugnavissent, a duce laudati sunt.
9. dux milites miseros, cum periculum fugissent, saevissime punivit.
10. senes, cum vinum optimum bibissent, in silvam discesserunt.
11. dux, cum conspexisset milites occisos esse, consilium alium cepit.
12. cum pars oppidi ab hostibus capta esset, plurimi cives perterriti fugerunt.

1 cum pueri libros invenissent, magister iratus erat.
2 cum magister vinum bibisset, pueri fugerunt.
3 cum magister cibum consumpsisset, discipuli libros tradiderunt.
4 cum magister diu docuisset, discipuli dormiverunt.
5 cum pueri epistulas tradidissent, magister discessit.

**Exercise 27.2E**  **Translate into English**

1. domine, nonne iratus eras cum villam tuam deletam esse vento cognovisses?
2. milites, cum fortiter in proelio pugnavissent, a duce non laudati sunt.
3. dux custodes fortes, cum prope muros mansissent, magnopere laudavit.
4. senex, cum cibum gravem consumpsisset, exire non voluit.
5. cum omnes mulieres advenissent, a viris salutatae sunt.
6. cum vulnus saevum accepissem, montem ascendere non iam poteram.
7. cives laeti erant cum consilium novum imperatoris intellexissent.
8. milites, cum de periculo moniti essent, aliam viam per silvam legerunt.
9. interea milites, cum omnis cibus captus esset, discesserunt.
10. cives, cum ceterae copiae ab oppido discessissent, laetissimi erant.
11. dominus cum cognovisset unum e servis suis e villa tractum esse, iratissimus erat.
12. imperator, cum intellexisset virum non inimicum esse, eum liberare constituit.

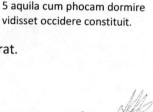

1 aquila cum phocam conspexisset statim ad terram descendit.
2 phoca cum aquilam conspexisset statim surrexit.
3 aquila cum phocam conspexisset statim ad montem ascendit.
4 phoca cum sensisset aquilam advenisse lacrimavit.
5 aquila cum phocam dormire vidisset occidere constituit.

**Exercise 27.3**  **Translate into Latin**

1. When the general had warned the citizens about the danger, the young men laughed.
2. After the soldiers had brought the weapons into the town, they quickly departed.
3. When they had caught sight of the beautiful girls, the young men were very happy.
4. When they had heard their daughters' voices, the parents laughed.
5. When he had freed the slaves, everyone praised the master.
6. After giving the book to the best boy, the teacher encouraged all the pupils to work.
7. When he had seen the fierce dogs, the old man was very scared.
8. When he had received very severe wounds, the soldier soon died.
9. After seeing the boys in the street, the father hurried home.
10. After reading this excellent book, I wanted to read another one.

**Exercise 27.4**  **Match the following pairs and translate**

1. cum cives imperatorem novum
2. cum dux in castra advenisset,
3. Caesar, cum hoc vidisset,
4. puer parvus cum canem
5. cum e nave discessissent, ventus
6. dux tamen, cum muri aedificati
7. iuvenis, cum ad suam villam
8. cum miles rogavisset quis

a. ipse in medios hostes processit.
b. saevus subito advenit.
c. esset, vir 'civis Romanus sum' respondit.
d. multi milites eum accipere nolebant.
e. conspexissent, clamor ad caelum ivit.
f. rediisset, forte sororem lacrimantem conspexit.
g. ingentem conspexisset perterritus erat.
h. essent, eis dona promissa tradere noluit.

**Exercise 27.5E  Review  Complete the following and translate into English**

1. cum pars urb__ ab hostibus capta esset, mult_ cives perterriti fugerunt.
2. cum miles fortiter pugnav_____ , atque a rege atque a duce laudat__ est.
3. imperator, cum conspexisset plurimos milites occis__ esse, consilium alium cep__ .
4. dux milites perterrit__ , cum periculum effugissent, saevissime puniv__ .
5. ceter__ militibus, cum omnes hastae ad urbem lat__ essent, non iam arma erant.
6. imperator, cum de pericul_ a sociis monitus esset, ali__ viam legere constituit.
7. dux, cum omn__ milites sui fugissent, host____ se tradidit.
8. consul, cum verba comitis audiv_____ , maxime timuit.
9. servus me__ , cum multum cib_ gravis consumpsisset, currere nolebat.
10. interea cives, cum omnis cibus in oppid__ latus esset, in forum festinaverunt.

# Chapter 28 Indirect questions

In the same way that a direct statement becomes an indirect statement after eg he said that ...., and a direct command becomes an indirect command after eg he ordered ...., a direct question becomes an indirect question after eg. he asked ....

As with final and result clauses, for GCSE we will restrict study to sentences where the main verb is in the past tenses.

Direct question:

o puella, cur rides?
Girl, why are you laughing?

Indirect question:

puellam rogavi cur rideret.
I asked the girl why she was laughing.

The verb in the indirect question here is imperfect subjunctive in Latin, where the two actions are going on at the same time.

Direct question

quis hunc librum scripsit?
Who wrote this book?

Indirect question

puer patrem rogavit quis hunc librum scripsisset.
The boy asked his father who had written this book.

The verb in the indiect question here is pluperfect subjunctive, as it took place before the main verb.

All the question words asking for information (cur = why? quam = how? quis = who?
quid = what? ubi = where? quo modo = how? quo = where to?
quantus -a -um = how big? quot = how many? qualis -e = what sort of?) are used in indirect questions just as in direct ones.

| Common verbs used in indirect questions | | | | | |
|---|---|---|---|---|---|
| rogo | rogare | rogavi | rogatum | 1 | = ask |
| scio | scire | scivi | scitum | 4 | = know |
| intellego | intellegere | intellegi | intellectum | 3 | = understand |
| nescio | nescire | nescivi | nescitum | 4 | = don't know |
| audio | audire | audivi | auditum | 4 | = hear |
| cognosco | cognoscere | cognovi | cognitum | 3 | = get to know, find out |
| quaero | quaerere | quaesivi | quaesitum | 3 | = search for, look for, ask |

Direct question

quo modo hostes oppidum oppugnaverunt?
How did the enemy attack the town?

Indirect question

dux cognoscere volebat quo modo hostes oppidum oppugnavissent.
The general wanted to find out how the enemy had attacked the town.

Direct questions which do not have a specific question word like *cur = why* use *-ne* (open question), *nonne* (expecting the answer yes) or *num* (expecting the answer no)

patremne meum vidisti?  nonne patrem meum vidisti?   num patrem meum vidisti?
Have you seen my father?  Surely you have seen my father?      Surely you haven't seen my father?

In indirect questions these three possibilities collapse down to

puer rogavit **num** patrem suum vidissem.
The boy asked **whether** (if) I had seen his father.

Notice also: direct question

quid accidit?     What happened?

Indirect question

facile non erat cognoscere quid accidisset.
It was not easy to find out what had happened.

Direct question

quid fecisti?
What have you done?

Indirect question

dominus servum rogavit quid fecisset.
The master asked his slave what he had done.

Note finally the difference between an indirect question and a relative clause:

Indirect question

matrem rogavi quem in foro vidisset.
I asked my mother whom she had seen in the forum.

Relative clause

matrem rogavi de viro quem in foro viderat.
I asked my mother about the man whom she had seen in the forum.

## Exercise 28.1          Translate into English

1. pueros rogavi num magistrum novum vidissent.
2. dominus servum quaesivit ubi esset equus.
3. pater cognoscere volebat cur filius discessisset.
4. dux nesciebat quo milites festinavissent.
5. audivistine quot naves appropinquavissent?
6. dux sciebat cur nuntius advenisset.
7. scisne quis omnes libros cepisset?
8. senator solus nesciebat quid accidisset.
9. agricola quaesivit qualis esset ventus.
10. eo tempore imperator cognovit quo modo hostes vicissent.
11. a duce imperator quaesivit cur hoc fecisset.
12. vir rogatus est quis esset.
13. dux militem rogavit quid sentiret.
14. ubi cognovit quid ancilla pararet, domina domum rediit.
15. cives perterriti erant cum non intellegerent quid accidisset.

## Exercise 28.2E          Translate into English

1. nonne intellegisti quo modo templum deletum esset?
2. non intellegi quid accidisset.
3. audivistisne quantam pecuniam ille vir haberet?
4. numquam intellegebam quid magister diceret.
5. nesciebam quo uxor ire vellet.
6. dux militem rogavit ubi equos reliquisset.
7. non audivi qualem villam libertus emisset.
8. dux cognoscere volebat cur prima luce milites discessissent.
9. senator rogavit quot nautae in taberna biberent.
10. puer tandem cognovit quid pater fecisset.
11. puella matrem rogavit quid facere deberet.
12. senex nescivit quid consumere deberet.
13. nulli dixi quid domi accidisset.
14. non iam constitueram quo irem.
15. puella perterrita rogata quis esset nihil dixit.

## Exercise 28.3    Match the following pairs

1. senex puer rogavit quis esset
2. mulier, ubi tandem cognovit
3. rex nesciebat cur nuntii
4. dominus fessus nolebat videre
5. pater sciebat quid filia
6. domina ancillam rogavit ut multum
7. civis perterritus erat, cum
8. mater irata filias rogavit quid
9. benene sciebas
10. nonne ceteri

a. sine epistulas venissent.
b. in villa pararet.
c. cibum in agrum ferret.
d. non intellegeret quid imperator dixisset.
e. quid patri accidisset, tristissima erat.
f. in foro facerent.
g. tu quid dux in animo haberet?
h. et cur canem parvum petivisset.
i. sciebant quid hic unus vellet facere?
j. quid servi stulti in horto facerent.

**Exercise 28.4    Translate into Latin**

1. The senator asked why the soldiers had fled.
2. The girl finally learned why her father had sold the house.
3. I didn't know who had taken the books.
4. The general asked how the enemy had escaped.
5. The man asked his wife how much money she had.
6. The master asked the slaves whether they had prepared dinner.
7. Do you know how large is the emperor's house?
8. I asked who had done this.
9. I asked the young man where he was running to.
10. The senator asked the woman how many dogs she had seen in the forum.

**Exercise 28.5E   Review  Complete the following and translate into English**

1. magister puer__ rogavit num libr__ novum legissent.
2. dominus servos quaes_____ ubi ess___ ancillae.
3. mater cognoscere vol_____ cur filia Romam discess_____ .
4. dux sol__ sciebat quo milit__ festinavissent.
8. dux cognosc___ volebat cur prima luc_ milites non discessissent.
9. senator rogavit quot naut__ in tabernam intraviss___ .
10. filius tandem cognovit quid pater feciss__ .
11. puella matrem rogavit quid facere deb_____.
13. ego nulli dix_ quid domi accidisset.
14. mercator non iam constituerat quo ir__ .
15. puella perterrita rogata quis ess__ nihil dix__ .

1 agricola rogavit nautam num in undas inire vellet.
2 nauta rogavit amicum num undas timeret.
3 pater filium rogavit num phocam conspexisset.
4 nauta matrem rogavit num undae saevae essent.
5 senator comitem rogavit quem in undas videret.

1 mulier rogavit nautam cur ad insulam venisset.
2 nauta nesciebat quis puella esset.
3 agricola rogavit mulierem num taberna prope villam esset.
4 mulier mox cognovit quo modo puer ad insulam advenisset.
5 nauta intellegere volebat cur filia domi maneret.

# Chapter 29     Some words easily confused

| | | |
|---|---|---|
| absum = I am away | adsum = I am present, here | |
| alter = the other (of two) | altus = high, deep | |
| carus = dear, expensive | clarus = clear, bright, famous | |
| dico = I say, tell | duco = I lead | |
| dominus = master | domus = house | |
| forte = by chance | fortis -e = brave, strong | fortiter = bravely, strongly |
| habeo = I have | habito = I live | |
| ita = in this way, so | itaque = and so, therefore | |
| iter = journey | iterum = again | |
| laetus = happy | latus = having been carried | |
| liber = book | liberi = children | libertus = freedman, ex-slave |
| novem = nine | nonus = ninth | novus = new |
| porta = gate | porto = I carry | |
| post = after *(prep.)* | postquam *(conj.)* = after | |
| redeo = I go back | rideo = I laugh | |
| res = thing | rex = king | |
| saepe = often | semper = always | |
| stat = he stands | statim = at once | subito = suddenly |
| summus = top (of) | sumus = we are | |
| tamen = however | tandem = at last | |
| terreo = I frighten | timeo = I fear | |
| trado = I hand over | traho = I drag | |
| vici = I conquered | vixi = I lived | |

**Exercise 29.1**     **Translate into English**

1. dominus hodie domi adest, sed uxor abest.
2. alterum flumen altum est.
3. miles fortis forte interfectus est.
4. habeo villam magnam quam cum liberis caris habito.
5. itaque hoc iter iterum heri feci.
6. fac ita laborem, stulte!
7. servus laetus ad villam domini latus est.
8. liberi liberti novem libros ad portam novam portabant.
9. dominus, postquam domum redit, vehementer clamavit.
10. res regis me terrent.

**Exercise 29.2E**     **Translate into English**

1. sumus in summo monte.
2. subito libertus surgit et statim cum liberis prope ianuam stat.
3. puer canem terret, sed leonem timet.
4. cives equum in medium oppidum tractum tandem consuli tradiderunt.
5. imperator, postquam hostes vicit, diu Romae vixit.
6. dux novus tres libros et novem liberos habet.
7. tandem librum nonum cepi.
8. 'duc me ad dominum!' dixit libertus.
9. Romani ita tandem vicerunt.
10. liberi cari domino sunt.

**Exercise 29.3**   **Translate into Latin**

1. Often I am away, but today I am present.
2. The other mountain is high.
3. I never give expensive gifts to the famous leader.
4. The master will return home tomorrow.
5. By chance the brave man was killed by a lion.
6. I live in a large country-house near which I have three fields.
7. In this way the lion escaped, and so all the inhabitants remained terrified.
8. I shall make this journey again tomorrow.
9. Having been carried along the road, the happy boy finally arrived home.
10. This feedman gave nine books to those children.
11. The ninth book is new.
12. After he (had) arrived home, the master drank some wine.
13. After dinner the master went into the garden.
14. When I go home I always laugh.
15. The king spoke about this matter again.
16. When I was standing near the door, my brother arrived.
17. We are now standing at the top of the mountain.
18. We finally arrived at the top of the mountain; however we were very tired.
20. They dragged the slave along the road and then handed him over to the king.

# Chapter 30    Revision of constructions with new vocabulary (i)

We begin the the Higher Tier by revising some constructions previously met but using new vocabulary.

New nouns, verbs and adjectives

| | | | |
|---|---|---|---|
| captivus -i 2 m | = captive, prisoner | | |
| praemium -i 2 n | = prize, reward, profit | | |
| princeps principis 3 m | = chief, emperor | | |
| | | | |
| oro    orare | oravi | 1 | = beg *(see below)* |
| impero imperare | imperavi *(+dat.)* | 1 | = order *(see below)* |
| | | | |
| iaceo   iacĕre | iacui 2 | | = lie |
| rapio   rapĕre | rapui | raptum 3½ | = seize, grab |
| reddo   reddĕre | reddidi | redditum 3 | = give back, restore |
| | | | |
| diligens diligentis | = careful | | |
| nonnulli | = some, several | | |

1. Conditional sentences

A negative conditional uses **nisi**, which can be translated either by **if not** or **unless**:

nisi mihi pecuniam statim reddes, tuos libros rapiam.
Unless you return the money to me, I shall seize your books.

2. Direct and indirect questions

**quando** mihi pecuniam reddes?
**When** will you return the money to me?

dux nesciebat **quando** milites ad castra advenissent.
The general didn't know when the soldiers had reached the camp.

**unde** milites veniunt?
**Where** are the soldiers coming **from**?

dominus sciebat unde servi cucurrissent.
The master knew from where the slaves had run.

3. Indirect commands

In addition to **iubeo**, which is followed by the accusative and infinitive, **impero** is often used, followed by **ut** and the subjunctive.

princeps servis suis imperavit ut cenam statim pararent.
The emperor ordered his slaves to prepare the dinner immediately.

Note *servis* is dative case.

**oro -are = I beg** takes the accusative of person and the subjunctive

libertus imperatorem oravit ut captivos redderet.
The frredman begged the emperor to give back the captives.

## Exercise 30.1    Translate into English

1. si captivi praemia in flumen iecerunt, stulti sunt.
2. princeps servis diligentibus imperavit ut domum omnia praemia ferrent.
3. patrem saepe orabam ut mihi aurum redderet.
4. nonnulli milites magna voce virtutem eius laudaverunt.
5. nesciebam unde illi captivi venissent.
6. princeps imperavit omnibus militibus ut arma statim redderent.
7. quando ad forum princeps advenit?
8. nemo sciebat quando princeps Romam advenisset.
9. princeps diligens ipse semper legebat omnes epistulas quas acceperat.
10. nonnulli servi miseri statim a militibus capti ad regem tracti sunt.

1 domum imperavit ancillae ne aquam ferret.
2 ancilla matri imperavit ut vinum ferret.
3 puella ancillae imperaverat ut libros ferret.
4 domina ancillae imperaverat ne vinum ferret.
5 domina imperavit ancillae ut vinum ferret.

## Exercise 30.2E   Translate into English

1. nisi praemia statim reddes, iratus ero.
2. puer miser matrem oravit ne mercatori praemia redderet.
3. quando emisti hos servos diligentes?
4. nonnulli captivi in summo monte cibum consumentes et vinum bibentes iaciebant.
5. sic princeps saepissime legiones vinci paratas vincere docuit.
6. eo tempore princeps imperavit duci ut milites oppidum oppugnarent.
7. vir rogatus quis esset et unde venisset 'civis Romanus sum' respondit.
8. dux nesciebat quando illi milites Roma discessissent.
9. servumne diligentiorem quam hunc umquam vidisti?
10. redde mihi statim eos libros, mi fili!

## Exercise 30.3E   Match the following pairs and translate into English

1. pater per omnes
2. tum domina domum
3. imperator revenit ut verba
4. multi liberti convenerunt
5. dei mali leones miserunt ut
6. tum ancillam oravit ut omnes
7. itaque libertus persuasit comiti
8. senex ad tabernam iit ut ibi

a. incolas terrerent.
b. terras ibat ut filium carum peteret.
c. suo ut Romam iret.
d. ducis civibus nuntiaret.
e. epistulas deleret.
f. vinum cum amicis biberet.
g. iit ut cenam pararet.
h. ut ducem salutarent.

## Exercise 30.4E   Match the following pairs and translate in English

1. senator virum rogavit quis esset
2. puella, ubi tandem intellexit
3. rex sciebat cur nuntii
4. dominus volebat videre
5. pater sciebat quid filius
6. domina ancillam rogavit ut multam
7. cives perterriti erant, cum
8. pater iratus filios rogavit quid
9. ceteri milites bene
10. nonne ceteri sciebant

a. venissent.
b. in horto pararet.
c. aquam in villam ferret.
d. non intellegerent quid imperator dixisset.
e. quid fratri accidisset, tristissima erat.
f. in via facerent.
g. sciebant quid dux in animo haberet.
h. et cur canem miserum petivisset.
i. quid hic unus vellet facere?
j. quid servi in horto facerent.

## Exercise 30.5E   Match the following pairs and translate into English

1. puella parva magna
2. mater maritum rogavit
3. vir uxorem rogavit ne ad
4. omnes senatores orabant ut miles
5. vir feminam salutatam invitavit ut in
6. tum Iuppiter deos convocatos rogavit
7. dux seni non potuit
8. iuvenis dominae

a. forum nocte iret.
b. villa sua paucas horas maneret.
c. ut ventum gravem in terram mitterent.
d. persuasit ut ad silvam secum iret.
e. voce matrem rogavit ut se servaret.
f. ut cum servo de auro invento diceret.
g. persuadere ut in navem ascenderet.
h. ipse nunc exiret.

## Exercise 30.6   Translate into Latin

1. The emperor ordered a slave to bring him the weapons.
2. Nobody knew where the merchants had come from.
3. 'Give me back my weapons!' begged the wretched soldier.
4. Some soldiers had taken the weapons from the town.
5. Did you know where the king had come from?
6. I begged the king to read the letter.
7. Nobody knew why the emperor had come to the town.
8. The general ordered the soldiers to show him the wall which they had destroyed.
9. If you don't do this, I won't be happy.
10. Slave, where do you come from?

1 femina rogavit nautam unde hoc aurum tulisset.
2 femina oravit nautam ut sibi pecuniam daret.
3 agricola miser feminam oravit ut sibi pecuniam daret.
4 femina nautam rogavit quando in insulam advenisset.
5 femina mercatorem rogavit ubi librum invenisset.

## Exercise 30.7E   Review  Complete the following and translate into English

1. si captivi praemia de mur__ iecerunt, stult_ sunt.
2. princeps milit____ diligentibus imperavit ut domum omnia arma ferr__ .
3. ducem saepe orabam ut mihi aurum red____ .
4. nonnulli magna voce virtut__ eius militis laudaverunt.
5. nesciebasne unde illi captivi venissent?
6. eo tempore princeps imperavit duci ut milites oppidum oppugnar___ .
7. senex miser rogat__ quis esset et unde venisset 'civis Roman__ sum' respondit.
8. dux nesciebat quando illi milit__ Roma discessiss___ .
9. ancillamne diligentior__ quam hanc umquam vidisti?
10. redde mihi statim praemi_ mea, mi fili!

# Chapter 31    Revision of constructions with new vocabulary (ii)

## New nouns, verbs, adjective and adverb

| | |
|---|---|
| inimicus -i 2 m | = (personal ) enemy |
| gens gentis 3 f | = family, tribe, race, people |
| scelus sceleris 3 n | = crime, evil deed |

| | | | |
|---|---|---|---|
| celo celare | celavi | celatum | 1 = hide |
| faveo favēre | favi | fautum *(+dat.)* | 2 = favour, support |
| incendo incendĕre | incendi | incensum | 3 = to burn, set on fire |

dirus -a -um = dreadful, horrible, fearful
plenus -a -um = full

libenter = willingly, gladly

Note that *celo* and *oro* takes two accusatives: one of the person, the other of the thing:

puer librum patrem celavit.
The boy hid the book from his father.

libertus auxilium amicum oravit.
The freedman begged his friend for help.

### New verbs that take the accusative and infinitive

| | | | |
|---|---|---|---|
| cogito | cogitare | cogitavi 1 | = think, consider |
| puto | putare | putavi 1 | = think |
| spero | sperare | speravi 1 | = hope |

homines ea sic accidere posse non cogitant.
Men don't think that these things can happen in this way.

hic senex se solum laetum esse putat.
This old man thinks he alone is happy.

senator sperabat se mox Romam adventurum esse.
The senator was hoping that he would soon arrive in Rome.

Note the use of the **future infinitive** here after **spero**.

| | |
|---|---|
| coepi    coepisse *irreg.* | = began |
| cogo    cogĕre coegi    coactum 3 | = force, compel |

coepi  = I began / have begun          coeperam = I had begun          coepisse = to have begun

hunc murum heri aedificare coepi.
I began to build this wall yesterday.

quis te emere hoc aurum coegit?
Who forced you to buy this gold?

omnes naves vento ad insulam coactae sunt.
All the ships were driven to the island by the wind.

## Exercise 31.1    Translate into English

1.  princeps sperabat se Romam duobus diebus adventurum esse.
2.  senator credebat servos suos murum iam aedificare coepisse.
3.  comes meus negavit se inimico meo fauturum esse.
4.  servi in agro diu laborare coacti sunt.
5.  nonnulli cogitant hos senatores diligentes esse.
6.  dux putabat se solum copias Romanas ducere posse.
7.  amicus meus illi senatori libenter favebat.
8.  imperator haec scelera dira uxorem diu celavit.
9.  nonnulli credebant imperatorem ipsum urbem incendisse.
10. mercator sperabat se omne aurum his mulieribus venditurum esse.
11. senex credebat se filiam numquam visurum esse.
12. libertus credidit se vitam laetiorem prope mare acturum esse.
13. promitto me leonem ferocissimum necaturum esse.
14. rex civibus promisit se urbem magnam facturum esse.
15. mulier tristissima erat quod credebat se filiam numquam visuram esse.

## Exercise 31.2E   Translate into English

1.  liberte, quando hanc villam aedificare coepisti?
2.  senex miser omne aurum vendere coactus est.
3.  pater de hac re paucas horas cogitabat, tum subito discessit.
4.  hic iuvenis est gentis notissimae et sperat se consulem paucis annis futurum esse.
5.  senator me oravit ut comiti suo faverem.
6.  libertus multa scelera dira Romae fecit
7.  quando in horto haec praemia celavisti?
8.  princeps nesciebat quando filius Romam advenisset.
9.  princeps sciebat neminem talia facturum esse.
10. libertus sperabat se Roman iturum esse et ibi laete victurum esse.
11. spero hos mercatores mox ab urbe discessuros esse.
12. iuvenis promisit se multas horas laboraturum esse.
13. pater dixit se omnes libros laturum esse.
14. inimico comitis mei numquam favebo.
15. hae gentes stultae silvam incendere constituerunt.

## Exercise 31.3    Translate into Latin

1.  The senator began to say bad things about his enemy.
2.  The freedman was forced to sell all his lands.
3.  The senator had hidden all his money from his wife.
4.  Will you support that diligent senator?
5.  If you give me some gold, I promise to support you.
6.  Why did the emperor begin to build the villa in that place?
7.  Very many citizens thought that Rome was a beautiful city.
8.  Did the emperor really set fire to the city?
9.  The old man thought that he would never see the emperor.
10. That senator begged me to support him.

## Exercise 31.4    Review  Complete the following and translate into English

1.  imperator haec scel___   saeva cives diu celavit.
2.  vosne credebatis imperator__   ipsum urbem incendisse?
3.  mercatores sperabant se omne aur__   mulieribus venditur__   esse.
4.  vir miser cred____   se filiam numquam visur__   esse.
5.  consul credebat se vitam laetior__   prope mare victur__   esse.
6.  promitto me leonem ferocissim__   necaturum esse.
7.  princeps civibus promisit se urb__   magnam paucis ann__   aedificaturum esse.
8.  senator credebat servos suos murum iam aedific___   coepisse.
9.  agricolae in agr_   diu laborare coact_   sunt.
10. liberte, quando hos muros aedificare coep____   ?

1 inimici nautae ridere coeperunt.
2 duo servi ferre ad villam cibum coacti sunt.
3 servi libenter laborabant.
4 duo servi murum aedificare iussi erant.
5 inimici sperabant se aurum inventuros esse.

1 nauta sperat feminam se ad cenam invitaturam esse.
2 nauta cogitat feminam saevam esse.
3 femina lacrimare coepit propter clamores diros nautae.
4 femina  sedere coacta est propter ventum saevum.
5 femina putavit nautam virum dirum esse.

# Chapter 32　　　Time expressions and time clauses

## New nouns, verbs and adjectives

imperium -i 2 n = empire, power, command
maritus -i 2 m = husband
tempestas -atis 3 f = storm

| | | | | |
|---|---|---|---|---|
| pello | pellĕre | pepuli | pulsum 3 | = drive |
| rumpo | rumpĕre | rupi | ruptum 3 | = break, burst |
| verto | vertĕre | verti | versus 3 | = turn |

brevis -e = short, brief
benignus -a -um = kind

## Expressions of time

A . Review

1 multis post horis aquila phocam tulit.
2 ante tempestatem phoca aquilam subito petivit.
3 post tempestatem aquila phocam conspexit.
4 paucis ante horis aquila hanc phocam iam necaverat.
5 prima luce phoca aquilam ferocem occidit.

| Preposition | Adverb | Conjunction | |
|---|---|---|---|
| ante | antea | antequam | before |
| post | postea | postquam | after |

ante cenam advenit.
He arrived before dinner.

antea servus miser erat, nunc libertus laetus est.
Before(hand) he was a wretched slave, now he is a happy freedman.

antequam respondi, de principe pauca dixi.
Before I answered, I said a few things about the emperor.

But note antequam is sometimes broken in two:

ante comitem ad cenam invitavi, quam ad forum ii.
I invited my companion to dinner, before I went to the forum.

post proelium milites fessi erant.
After the battle the soldiers were tired.

1 servus rumpere murum iussus erat.
2 maritus in agro murum parvum aedificabat.
3 maritus sperabat se in terra aurum inventurum esse.
4 senex incendere murum voluit.
5 puer stultus aurum celatum esse in muro putabat.

But note

multis post annis imperatorem iterum vidit.
Many years afterwards he saw the emperor again.

quid postea accidit?
What happened afterwards?

ad forum postquam adveni, multa dona emi.
After I (had) arrived at the forum, I bought many gifts.

Note that while English sometimes has the pluperfect here,
Latin uses the perfect tense.

1 magister dum pueri aderant dormiebat.
2 discipuli dum magister librum scribit discesserunt.
3 pueri dum magister librum legebat dormiverunt.
4 magister dum discipuli scribunt discessit.
5 pueri dum magister aderat dormiebant.

## New conjunctions and adverbs

dum = while *(see below)*
simulac, simulatque = as soon as

postridie = on the next day
primo = at first
simul = at the same time

1 vir dum in flumine stat pecuniam accepit.
2 senex cui femina pecuniam dederat valde iratus erat.
3 dum vir miser in via stat puella ei pecuniam dedit.
4 femina dum per viam ambulat pecuniam seni misero dedit.
5 regina dum per viam currit senem miserum vidit.

Note the two uses of **dum**

1. servi, dum dominus in villa dormiebat, in agro laborabant.
   While the master was sleeping in the villa, the slaves were working in the field.

Here while something was happening, something else was
happening throughout the same time.

2. dum in via ambulo, clamorem magnum subito audivi.
   While I was walking in the street, I suddenly heard a great shout.

Here, while something was happening, something new happened.
Here Latin uses the present tense in the *dum* clause.

After **simulac**, as with **postquam**, Latin uses the perfect tense.

mercator, simulac ad forum advenit, comitem conspexit.
As soon as the merchant (had) reached the forum, he caught sight of his companion.

### Exercise 32.1    Translate into English

1. dum senatores de hac re cogitant, magna turba civium in foro convenerunt.
2. postquam maritus discessit, uxor de sua vita misera cogitare coepit.
3. simulac dux intellexit hostes oppido appropinquare, epistulam ad imperatorem misit.
4. hoc modo benigne a senatore salutati, cives a foro reverterunt.
5. libertus miser erat. nam, cum senex esset, oppidum ab hostibus captum vidit.

6. multis post annis imperator tandem summum imperium accepit.
7. milites Romani castra intrabant; simul dux hostium fugere parabat.
8. postquam tempestas dira omnes naves e portu pepulit, dux non iam credebat se victurum esse.
9. dum milites ad portam villae adveniunt, dominus consilium audax cepit.
10. multi senatores, quod Caesar cum imperio erat, inimico eius favebant.

## Exercise 32.2E   Translate into English

1. simulac imperator de victoria audivit, ad senatores epistulam misit.
2. milites primo fortiter pugnaverunt; sed paucis horis ab hostibus victi sunt.
3. forte copiae Romanae viam per hostes viam ruperunt; ita eos vincere potuerunt.
4. tum senator ad comitem se vertit et benigne risit.
5. ille princeps propter multa scelera dira imperium breve accepit.
6. princeps in bello saevus et in pace benignus esse constituit.
7. uxor maritum in taberna cum muliere pulchra bibere forte conspexit; ei postea numquam credidit.
8. dum uxor incendit epistulam quam acceperat, maritus subito domum rediit.
9. simulac flammae corpus imperatoris consumpsunt, advenerunt venti graves.
10. eo tempore nonnulli Romani credebant multas gentes saevas in illa terra adesse.

## Exercise 32.3    Translate into Latin

1. After a crowd of citizens gathered in the forum, the general ordered his soldiers to take up arms.
2. While the soldiers were approaching the house, the master suddenly came out.
3. As soon as the storm arrived, we turned the ships towards the island.
4. The next day the whole town was destroyed by the heavy storm.
5. While the woman was driving the dogs out of the garden, her husband arrived home.
6. After holding power for ten years, the emperor was killed by one of his slaves.
7. Before the storm arrived, I built a huge wall.
8. At the same time the ships were driven to the island by the strong winds.
9. The storm was brief but very heavy.
10. At first the emperor ruled in a kindly way, but after the death of his son he was very cruel.

## Exercise 32.4    Review    Complete the following and translate into English

1. pauc__   post annis imperator tandem summum imperium accepit.
2. nunti__   castra intrabat; simul dux hostium fug___   parabat.
3. postquam tempestas dir_   omnes naves ab insul_   pepul__  , nautae non iam credeb___   se victur_   esse.
4. dum ego portae appropinqu_  , servos dormien___   conspexi.
5. nonnull_   senatores, quod Caesar cum imperio erat, inimic_   eius favebant.
6. copiae Romanae viam per hostes viam tandem rup_____  ; ita eos vinc___   potuerunt.
4. deinde pater ad filium se vert__   et benign_   risit.
5. cives hu__   senatori propter tam scelera saev_   non favebunt.
6. illo die nonnull__   naves ventis saevis ab urbe puls__   sunt.
7. uxor maritum in via cum mulier_   pulchra ridentem forte conspex__  ; ei postea numquam credidit.
8. dum filia leg__   epistulam quam acceperat, mater subito dom__   rediit.
9. hoc modo benign_   a filia salutata, mater ad villam revertit.
10. milites castra intr_____  ; simul dux hostium fug___   parabat.

# Chapter 33    idem quidam

## New nouns, verbs, adjectives, adverb, preposition and conjunction

```
gaudium -i 2 n    = joy
labor laboris 3 m = work, deed, difficulty
pes pedis 3 m     = foot
sanguis sanguinis 3 m = blood


cado          caděre       cecidi  casum  3      = fall
conficio      conficěre    confeci confectum 3½ = finish, wear out
tollo         tollěre      sustuli sublatum 3    = raise, lift up hold up
scelestus -a –um = wicked
verus -a -um     = true, real


magis = more (see below)
multo = much (see below)


apud (+acc.) = among, with, at the house of


enim = for (like autem, it never begins a sentence)
```

**magis** is often combined with **quam**

haec magis a feminis quam a viris intellegi possunt.
These things can be understood more by women than by men.

**idem = the same**

**is ea id** with **-dem** added, with a change in the accusative
singular and genitive plural

|  | masc. | fem. | neut. |
|---|---|---|---|
| **singular** | | | |
| nom. | idem | eadem | idem |
| acc. | eundem | eandem | idem |
| gen. | eiusdem | eiusdem | eiusdem |
| dat. | eidem | eidem | eidem |
| abl. | eodem | eadem | eodem |
| | | | |
| **plural** | | | |
| nom. | eidem | eaedem | eadem |
| acc. | eosdem | easdem | eadem |
| gen. | eorundem | earundem | eorundem |
| dat. | eisdem | eisdem | eisdem |
| abl. | eisdem | eisdem | eisdem |

1 duo servi laborabant cum magno gaudio.
2 servi quidam murum aedificabant.
3 multum sanguinis de pedibus servorum cadebat.
4 senatores cum magno labore canes agebant.
5 idem servus comitem tollebat.

Examples:

regina idem iter semper facit.   The queen always makes the same journey.
eosdem agricolas in oppido vidi. I saw the same farmers in the town.

**quidam, quaedam, quoddam = a certain person *or* thing**

|  | masculine | feminine | neuter |
|---|---|---|---|
| **singular** | | | |
| nom. | quidam | quaedam | quoddam |
| acc. | quendam | quandam | quoddam |
| gen. | cuiusdam | cuiusdam | cuiusdam |
| dat. | cuidam | cuidam | cuidam |
| abl. | quodam | quadam | quodam |
| **plural** | | | |
| nom. | quidam | quaedam | quaedam |
| acc. | quosdam | quasdam | quaedam |
| gen. | quorundam | quarundam | quorundam |
| dat. | quibusdam | quibusdam | quibusdam |
| abl. | quibusdam | quibusdam | quibusdam |

quidam ex inimicis suis est senator.
A certain one of his enemies is a senator.

quodam tempore Romae habitabat.
At a certain time he used to live in Rome.

1 libertus agricolam eundem scelus facere iussit.
2 senator nautae eidem imperavit ut scelus faceret.
3 libertus quidam hunc senem invitavit ut apud se duo dies maneret.
4 libertus agricolae dixit sanguinem ex pede cadere.
5 dux scelestus iussit agricolam tollere pedem vulneratum.

### Exercise 33.1    Translate into English

1. senator inimicum quendam prope ianuam tabernae stantem conspexit.
2. quattuor dies dux propter vulnus altum in pede apud se manere debuit.
3. pater Caesaris filium sustulit et dixit 'eum accipio.'
4. haec est res magni laboris; ego solus hanc conficere non potero.
5. hostes oppidum nocte intraverunt et omnia arma sustulerunt.
6. multum sanguinis de vulnere cadebat; miles autem nihil sentiebat.
7. huic senatori benigno multo magis quam illi scelesto faveo.
8. princeps ubi audivit Romanos hostes vicisse, plenus gaudii fuit.
9. comes quidam liberto appropinquavit lacrimans.
10. ante noctem has res difficiles conficere debeo.

### Exercise 33.2E   Translate into English

1. alii eundem laborem faciebant, alii in horto iaciebant.
2. apud se libertus tres horas mansit; cibum enim gravem consumpserat.
3. gaudium apud ducem breve fuit; postridie enim audivit filiam non redituram esse.

4. eaedem gentes haec scelesta semper faciunt.
5. iam senex, princeps vitam plenam gaudii petebat.
6. nonnulli cives putant principem novum scelestissimum esse.
7. tantus sanguis e pede ceciderat militis ut ambulare non iam posset.
8. ducem in pede grave vulneratum duo milites in equum maxima cum cura sustulerunt.
9. dum servus miser a custodibus abducitur, comes quidam ei appropinquavit.
10. alii alias feminas spectabant.

## Exercise 33.3E  Match the following pairs

1. cives tam clare
2. iuvenis tanto amore captus
3. rex ita terrebatur
4. hi tantum clamorem
5. tot tempestates descenderunt ut
6. ceteri tam gravibus vulneribus confecti
7. iuvenis tam vehementer clamavit
8. dux tam fortiter pro

a. est ut epistulam longam dominae scriberet.
b. faciebant ut etiam dux terreretur
c. patria pugnabat ut omnes ei faverent.
d. sunt ut armis hostium iam resistere non possent.
e. ut omnes canes fugerent.
f. clamabant ut imperator ipse perterritus esset.
g. plurimae villae delerentur.
h. ut nihil dicere posset.

## Exercise 33.4  Translate into Latin

1. The soldiers had to stay in the camp for two months because of their serious wounds.
2. The silly old man fell off his horse and injured himself in the head.
3. The leader lifted the soldier on to his horse because a lot of blood was falling from the wound.
4. Worn out by so much effort, the slave sat down in the garden.
5. The enemy were defeated because of the courage of a certain soldier.
6. When I went to town, I always used to see the same men drinking wine.
7. Some men were laughing, others were sleeping.
8. Full of joy, the father lifted up his little daughter.
9. I shall stay at my friend's house for five days.
10. This can be done by effort rather than by courage.

## Exercise 33.5E  Review  Complete the following and translate into English

1. nonnulli cives put___ hunc poetam sapient__ esse.
2. dum sanguis e vulnere puer_ cadebat, mater adven__ .
3. ducem in capite grave vulnerat__ duo milites in equum maxim_ cum cura sustulerunt.
4. dum servus miser a custodibus abduc____ , comites quidam ei appropinquaverunt.
5. alii iuvenes alias femin__ petebant.
6. dux inimic__ quendam prope ianu__ tabernae stant__ conspexit.
7. quinque dies dux propter vuln__ altum in capite apud se man___ debuit.
8. miles stultus de equ_ lente cecidit et se in ped_ grave vulneravit.
9. haec est res magni laboris; num tu sol__ hanc confic___ non poteris?
10. hostes urbem medi_ nocte intraverunt et nonnull__ cives occiderunt.

# Chapter 34     Verbs of Fearing

New nouns, verbs and adjectives

---

regnum -i 2 n = kingdom
legio legionis 3 f = legion
poenas poenarum 1 f pl. = punishment, *usually plural*

poenas dare = to be punished
opprimo     opprimĕre     oppressi     oppressum 3 = attack, crush
pervenio     pervenire     perveni     perventum 4 = reach, arrive at

infelix = unlucky, unhappy
proximus -a -um = nearest, next to

quam = as ... possible *(see below)*

---

**timeo**, called a verb of fearing, can take a direct object or an infinitive:

viri leones timebant.
The men were afraid of the lions.

puer hortum propter canes intrare timebat.
The boy was afraid to go into the garden because of the dogs.

**timeo** can also take a clause using **ne** and the imperfect subjunctive, expressing what someone feared might happen. In form this construction is like a negative purpose clause but it is not negative in English.

dux timebat ne urbs caperetur.
The general feared that the city would be captured.

A negative fear is expressed by **ne ... non** (or **ut**!)

senator timebat ne comes ad cenam non veniret.
senator timebat ut comes ad cenam veniret.
The senator was afraid that his colleague would not come to dinner.

Note the past participle passive of *perterreo = I frighten thoroughly* **perterritus** is used as an adjective meaning *terrified*.

**quam** is used with the superlative to express *as much as possible*:

ad villam quam celerrime festinavit.
He hurried to the house as quickly as possible.

Romam quam saepissime veniebat.
He came to Rome as often as possible.

quam maxima voce potuit clamavit.
He shouted as loudly as he could.

**quam** is also used to express to express surprise:

quam crudeliter a domino punitur!
How cruelly is he being punished by his master!

### Exercise 34.1    Translate into English

1.  puer parvus, quod erant nonnulli canes in via, discedere timuit.
2.  tantum erat periculum ut cives timerent ne hostes urbem caperent.
3.  quam libenter omnes ad domum invitat!
4.  timens ne filius in periculo esset, pater statim ad forum discessit.
5.  vir timebat ne illi scelesti venirent ut domum suam oppugnarent.
6.  timens ne filius infelix a leone occideretur, pater quam maxima voce potuit clamavit.
7.  pars legionis nonae duobus ante noctem horis tandem ad proxima castra pervenit.
8.  servi propter scelera scelesta poenas dederunt.
9.  post tot annos cives Romani saepe timebant ne unum virum regnum referre.
10. timens ne maritus ante noctem rediret, uxor epistulas quas acceperat incendit.

### Exercise 34.2E    Translate into English

1.  dux, timens ne imperator hoc cognosceret, librum celavit.
2.  illo tempore multi cives timebant ne hostes paucis diebus urbem oppugnarent.
3.  imperator timens ne gentes ibi convenirent duas legiones ad Germaniam misit.
4.  tantus erat clamor ut nonnulli cives timerent ad forum adire.
5.  libertus timebat ne illi milites venirent ut uxorem raperent.
6.  ancilla timebat ut dominus discesseret.
7.  dux, timens ne suae copiae ab hostibus opprimerentur, auxilium imperatorem oravit.
8.  post hoc scelus dirum nonnulli timebant ne omnes servi poenas darent.
9.  cives, timentes ne hostes ad portas urbis mox pervenirent, omne aurum celaverunt.
10. mane apud me quam diutissime, mi amice!

### Exercise 34.3E   Review  Complete the following and translate into English

1.  puer parvus, cum adess____ nonnulli canes in via, discedere timu__ .
2.  tot erant host__ pro muris ut cives tim_____ ne urbs caperetur.
3.  quam libenter h__ senator omnes comites ad dom__ suam invitat!
4.  timens ne filius in pericul_ esset, mater statim ad urb__ discessit.
5.  mercator timebat ne illi scelest_ venirent ut tabernam su__ incenderet.
6.  ancilla dominum adeo tim____ ut heri Romam fugeret.
7.  dux, timens ne suae copiae ab host____ vincerentur, auxilium imperatorem orav__ .
8.  post haec scelera dir_ nonnulli timebant ne illi servi poen__ darent.
9.  cives, timentes ne hostes ad portas urb__ mox pervenirent, omn__ arma celaverunt.
10. man___ apud me quam diutissime, m_ amici!

## Exercise 34.4    Translate into Latin

1.  All the citizens of the town were afraid of the storms.
2.  The Roman general never feared that his troops would be defeated.
3.  The father, fearing that his son would not work in the garden, hid all the books.
4.  The emperor went as often as possible to the island.
5.  Fearing that they would be punished by their master, the slaves ran away to the hills.
6.  How cruelly those slaves are being punished!
7.  After he had reached the next town, the general sent a letter to the emperor.
8.  The Romans crushed the people of that place as quickly as possible.
9.  The wretched emperor used to cry out 'Give me back my legions!'
10. Worn out after so many years of war, the citizens finally sought peace.

## Exercise 34.5E   Translate the following nouns into Latin and then find them in the wordsearch

```
T G I X R A M Z K H G U
R E L A B O R E S M A X
C N M U I M E A R P R O
A T N P R I N C I P E M
P E T M E G V W R G L R
T S O U U S A S E D E P
I H X I S C T U P T C P
V J N R P E I A D O S C
O I R E G N U M T I Z P
S Y K P A T U F I E U U
B D L M L E G I O N E M
M A R I T O K V N T I L
```

prize *(acc.)*, captives *(acc.)*, chief *(acc.)*, crimes *(nom.)*, tribes *(nom.)*, personal enemy *(acc.)*, husband *(dat.)*, storm *(abl.)*, command *(nom.)*, tasks *(acc.)*, feet *(nom.)*, blood *(gen.)*, joy *(acc.)*, rule *(acc.)*, legion *(acc.)*

1 nauta timebat ne puella eum tolleret.
2 nauta timebat ne puella scelus faceret.
3 puella timebat ne nauta eam peteret.
4 puella timebat ne alter pes nautae caderet.
5 puella timebat ne nauta poenas daret.

1 aquila timebat ut phoca effugeret.
2 aquila timens ne phoca effugeret auxilium comitem petivit.
3 phoca timens ne aquila eam peteret tandem dormivit.
4 phoca timebat ne aquila ad caelum effugeret.
5 phoca timebat ne aquila eam peteret.

# Chapter 35   4<sup>th</sup> and 5<sup>th</sup> declension nouns; malo; compounds of fero

## Some more 4<sup>th</sup> and 5<sup>th</sup> declension nouns

exercitus exercitus 4 m = army
vultus  vultus 4 m = expression, face
portus portus 4 m = port, harbour

**malo = I prefer** is normally introduced **with volo = I want**
and **nolo = I don't want**

| present | imperfect | imperfect subjunctive |
|---------|-----------|----------------------|
| malo    | malebam etc | mallem etc |
| mavis   |           |                      |
| mavult  |           |                      |
| malumus |           |                      |
| mavultis |          |                      |
| malunt  |           |                      |

| infinitive | perfect |
|------------|---------|
| malle      | malui etc |

1 in vultu pueri est spes victoriae.
2 iam vultu matris erat gaudium.
3 mater refert patri liberos bene se agere.
4 liberi dormire malebant quam matrem audire.
5 puer et puellae librum legere malebant.

1 in vultu ancillae omnes videbant eam tristem esse.
2 ancilla libros ad patrem referebat.
3 femina tristis auferre vinum maluit.
4 ancilla irata seni vinum offerebat.
5 ancilla vinum auferebat.

## The compounds of fero

| aufero | auferre | abstuli | ablatum = take away, carry off, steal |
| offero | offerre | obtuli  | oblatum = offer |
| refero | referre | rettuli | relatum = bring / carry back, report, tell |

**Exercise 35.1     Translate into English**

1. putans illum regem esse, libertus stultus ei donum pulchrum obtulit.
2. postquam hostes omnia arma abstulerunt, cives fugere coacti sunt.
3. duae ex his navibus, cum ad portum lente navigarent, tempestate saeva deletae
4. nonnulli clamaverunt principem portum hostibus tradidisse.
5. quo abstulisti meos libros et epistulas, serve?
6. plenus spei imperator duci imperavit ut in proelium exercitum duceret.
7. dux vulneribus gravibus confectus apud se sex menses mansit.
8. in vultu pueri parvi mater spem eum habere videbat.
9. postquam servi haec domino rettulerunt, filii eius miserrimi erant.
10. spes me tenet Romanos in proelio victuros esse.
11. dux hoc modo toti exercitui spem victoriae reddidit.
12. libertus prope mare vitam laetam agere quam in insula misera malebat.

**Exercise 35.2E    Translate into English**

1. filius tantae spei erat ut pater credebat eum paucis annis consulem esse.
2. pater libros abstulit ne filius parvus eos legeret.
3. senex domi multo magis manere quam ad tabernam ire malebat.
4. imperator omnem spem victoriae in virtute militum suorum posuit.
5. servus poenas dare quam fugere maluit.
6. prima luce imperator spei plenus exercitum e castris educit.
7. senex vultu canis sui intellexit eum tristem esse.
8. putans imperatorem paucis horis adventurum esse, dux legionem ad flumen duxit.
9. nuntii quidam referunt Romanos urbem iam cepisse.
10. poeta scribere quam legere multo magis malebat.
11. naves tempestate gravi in portum repulsae sunt.
12. Caesar, ubi caput Pompeii ei oblatum est, lacrimavit.

**Exercise 35.3    Translate into Latin**

1. There was no longer any hope on the face of the wretched general.
2. The brave soldiers preferred to die in battle rather to flee.
3. I much prefer to live near the sea than in Rome.
4. Thinking that she was the queen, the little boy gave the gift to that woman.
5. Many prisoners were carried off by the Roman army.
6. The messenger reported that a large part of the city had been destroyed.
7. Most men preferred to drink wine rather than water with their dinner.
8. The old man much preferred to stay in Rome than visit his friend who lived near the sea.
9. Full of hope the general led his troops into battle on the same day.
10. The little boy was hoping that his father would bring back some presents. for him.

**Exercise 35.4E  Review  Complete the following and translate into English**

1. plena spe_   regina duc_    imperavit ut in proelium exercitum duc____  .
2. miles vulneribus grav____   confectus apud se decem dies man___   debuit.
3. in vult_   puellae parv__   mater spem eam habere videbat.
4. postquam nuntius haec duci rettul__  , hic exercitum procedere iuss__  .
5. spes imperatorem tenet milit__   suos in proeli_   victuros esse.
6. prima luce dux spei plenus exercit__   e castris educi iuss__  .
7. senex vultu servi sui intellex__   eum tristem es__  .
8. putans imperatorem tribus hor__   adventurum esse, dux legionem ad mare dux__  .
9. nunti__   quidam heri rettulit Romanos urbem iam cep____  .
10. poeta legere quam scrib___   multo magis mal____  .

```
Z U C O O V O S U L X Q
I T O O R A P T L C V S
T N L E N U P C S E I N
R P C L Y F R R L L B F
R A A E S A E Z I A A A
T H P N N U S C T V T V
T I P U R D S B I I I E
R E D D I D I T L T U R
B X Z I A T T T U J C T
K B F Y C R M L P L A I
Z P X V P E R V E N I T
B A B G I A C D P E B T
```

**Exercise 35.5E          Translate the following verbs and then find them in the wordsearch**

she seized, he gave back, he lay down, she hid, he supported, she set on on fire, it drove,  it turned, he broke, she fell, he wore out, she raised, he overwhelmed, she arrived

103

# Chapter 36    Deponent Verbs

A deponent verb is a verb which is passive in form but active in meaning. In nearly all its parts it has the appearance of being passive.

**hortor -ari -atus sum = I encourage**

| present | imperfect | future | perfect | pluperfect |
|---------|-----------|--------|---------|------------|
| hortor | hortabar | hortabor | hortatus sum | hortatus eram |
| hortaris | hortabaris | hortaberis | hortatus es | hortatus eras |
| hortatur | hortabatur | hortabitur | hortatus est | hortatus erat |
| hortamur | hortabamur | hortabimur | hortati sumus | hortati eramus |
| hortamini | hortabamini | hortabimini | hortati estis | hortati eratis |
| hortantur | hortabantur | hortabuntur | hortati sunt | hortati erant |

**infinitive**: hortari

Other deponent verbs

| | | |
|---|---|---|
| conor, conari, conatus sum | 1 | try |
| egredior, egredi, egressus sum | 3½ | go out, leave |
| ingredior, ingredi, ingressus sum | 3½ | go in, enter |
| loquor, loqui, locutus sum | 3 | speak |
| miror, mirari, miratus sum | 1 | wonder at, admire |
| morior, mori, mortuus sum | 3½ | die |
| patior, pati, passus sum | 3½ | suffer, endure |
| precor, precari, precatus sum | 1 | pray to, beg |
| proficiscor, proficisci, profectus sum | 3 | set out |
| progredior, progredi, progressus sum | 3½ | go forward, advance |
| regredior, regredi, regressus sum | 3½ | go back, return |
| sequor, sequi, secutus sum | 3 | follow |

**Exercise 36.1    Translate into English**

1. pueri, quod hoc iter difficile esse sciebant, proficisci nolebant.
2. apud senatores consul diu locutus est; tum tandem sedit fessus.
3. nonnulli credent Romanos in bellum duobus annis ingressuros esse.
4. senes duas horas locuti sunt; tum egressi sunt.
5. novem milites profecti sunt; omnes autem in itinere mortui sunt.
6. miles multa et gravia vulnera passus est; tandem mortuus est.
7. legionem tres horas secuti sumus; tum ad oppidum regressi sumus.
8. dux dixit milites duabus horis profecturos esse et ante noctem regressuros esse.
9. quam crudeliter tot annos passus es!
10. dum milites ad portam villae progrediuntur, dominus consilium audax cepit.

**Exercise 36.2E  Translate into English**

1. plurimi cives, quamquam princeps crudelis mortuus erat, corpus eius timebant.
2. milites sperant se secunda hora egressuros esse et cras regressuros esse.
3. agricola quartus in villam duabus horis ingredietur.
4. mulieres iratae duas horas de sceleribus maritorum locutae erant.
5. regina tandem regressa est et in villa subito mortua est.
6. parentes clamores saevos puellarum parvarum patiebantur.
7. mirati sumus quod imperator bene cantabat.
8. imperator multa vulnera gravia passus est.
9. paene omnes copiae ad flumen progressae sunt et mox regressae sunt.
10. rex tribus diebus in itinere longo proficisci conabitur.

**Exercise 36.3  Translate into Latin**

1. The general always used to encourage his soldiers to fight bravely.
2. Many men tried to catch the animals but in vain.
3. We'll set out from the city at first light.
4. The enemy entered the town in the middle of the night.
5. We tried to sail to the island in these ships.
6. The father encouraged his sons to work well.
7. I shall try to build the wall tomorrow.
8. The general ordered the troops to advance as quickly as possible.
9. The old man had suffered many harsh things.
10. The teacher spoke about the battle to his pupils.

**Exercise 36.4E  Translate the following verbs and then find them in the wordsearch**

they encourage, she enters, she speaks, they endure, he begs, we admire, he advances, they return, I follow, they try, they go out

# Present, past and future participles of deponent verbs

## I    The present participle

The **present participle** has the **active form**, hence *conans = trying, loquens = speaking, sequens = following* etc.

Latin present participles are often best translated by a clause. So

feminas in via loquentes audivimus.
We heard the women as they spoke in the street.

### Exercise 36.5    Translate into English

1. ducem milites hortantem audivimus.
2. puer, vidistine servum opus suum facere conantem!
3. milites ex oppido egredientes conspeximus.
4. mulieres in villa loquentes nos effugimus.
5. copiis ad montem proficiscentibus paene omnes cives dormiebant.
6. hostibus effugere conantibus dux Romanus oppidum oppugnare constituit.
7. nolite credere viris haec loquentibus!
8. hostes copias proficiscentes subito petiverunt.
9. filius patrem ingredientem salutavit.
10. custodes viros ad oppidum progredientes pepulerunt.

### Exercise 36.6E    Translate the following present participles and then find them in the wordsearch

```
I S R O I O S M M L X S
S N E I D E R G O R P S
N A G K K O I Q H S E H
E N R R B H U G B F V O
I O E X E E I W X W I R
T C D L N D Q O N F L T
A D I T J L I U Y N O A
P R E C A N T E S Z J N
P S N S E Q U E N T E S
K L T M O R I E N T E M
A R E G X Y L O H E E N
D J S N A R I M S V T M
```

encouraging *(nom . sing.)*, entering *(fem. acc. sing.)* , speaking *(masc. pl.)*, enduring *(nom. sing.)*, begging *(fem. acc. pl.)*, admiring *(nom. sing.)*, advancing *(nom. sing.)*, returning *(fem. acc. pl.)*, following *(fem. acc. pl.)*, trying *(neut. acc. sing.)*, going out *(fem. acc. pl.)*

## 2    The past participle

As we have mentioned in chapter 15, Latin does not have a past participle active. So 'Having reached the city, the soldiers …..' would have to be translated as 'When they had reached the city, the soldiers …' . Deponent verbs however, passive in form but active in meaning, do allow us to translate such sentences as

The enemy, having advanced for two hours, suddenly fled.
hostes duas horas progressi subito fugerunt.

**Exercise 36.7    Translate into English**

1. postquam Sulla mortuus est, Caesar Romam statim rediit.
2. servus saepe effugere conatus sed frustra, in oppido manere constituit.
3. senes multas horas locuti tandem domum discesserunt.
4. milites in itinere longo profecti magnopere iam fessi erant.
5. copiae prima luce profectae tribus horis ad flumen advenerunt.
6. iuvenes viros trans montes secuti tandem eos prope flumen conspexerunt.
7. dominus puerum praemia capere conatum saeve punivit.
8. milites virum multa saeva passum reduxerunt.
9. milites nostri hostes oppidum oppugnare conantes petiverunt.
10. turba mulierum ab urbe prima luce profectarum quinque horas ambulavit.

**Exercise 36.8E    Translate the following past participles in the nominative masculine singular and then find them in the wordsearch**

```
J S E P P V C L S B S S
H E C K W O K C U U U T
I C X H N C N R S G T S
P U L A A H Z S S J A B
A T T N Z O E M E X C R
S U S S E R G O R P E N
S S V E G T I L G X R W
U U R N M A F P E R P J
S M I R A T U S R L N I
I S U T U U Q O L R L Y
O E Z U X S U U T R O M
R A I W I O L O L Z C X
```

having encouraged, having entered, having speaken,
having endured, having begged, having admired,
having advanced, having returned, having followed,
having tried, having gone out

**Exercise 36.9E    Translate into English**

1. exercitus, cum hostes adessent, ad mare progressus est.
2. turba iuvenum ab oppido prima luce profectorum tres horas ambulavit.
3. pueri, videtisne senem opus suum facere conantem?
4. viri paene omnes milites  oppidum oppugnare conantes interfecerunt.
5. gentes ex oppido egredientes dux conspexit.
6. magister pueros praemia delere conatos saevissime punivit.

7. pueri, quamquam hoc iter difficile esse sciebant, proficisci volebant.
8. nautae iuvenes trans mare secuti tandem eos in insula conspexerunt.
9. paene omnes cives ducem victum ad urbem regredientem viderunt.
10. mulieres prima luce profectae paucis horis ad flumen advenerunt.
11. dux Graecus hostes effugere conantes petere constituit.
12. milites tribus antea horis profecti celeriter ad locum advenerunt.
13. nolite loqui de hac re apud senatores!
14. coniuges multas horas locuti domum redierunt.
15. milites viros proficiscentes subito multis armis petiverunt.
16. ancilla canes pellere conata sed frustra, ad villam rediit.
17. filia matrem in templum ingredientem salutavit.
18. milites multa et saeva vulnera passi tandem mortui sunt.
19. custos virum ad oppidum progredientem petivit.
20. illae naves, cum ventis saevis pellerentur, in portum ingredi potuerunt.

### Exercise 36.10E Match the following pairs

| | | |
|---|---|---|
| 1. | noli credere puero de | a. crudelem occidere conabuntur. |
| 2. | dux solus nocte ex urbe egressus ad | b. virtutem mirabantur. |
| 3. | plurimi alii imperatorem | c. mirabantur ut eum libenter sequerentur. |
| 4. | dux adeo virtutem captivi mirabatur | d. iussisset, diu de virtute locutus est. |
| 5. | etiam hostes ducem Romanum propter | e. castra prima luce profectus est. |
| 6. | Romani virtutem imperatoris adeo | f. parentibus sic loquenti! |
| 7. | milites vocatos vehementer | g. ut portum custodirent. |
| 8. | quibus verbis pater filio persuadere | h. hortatus est ut hostes repellerent. |
| 9. | dux cives hortati sunt | i. conabatur ut in horto laboraret. |
| 10. | imperator, cum milites tacere | j. ut eum liberare constitueret. |

### Exercise 36.11  Translate into Latin

1. The guard was killed as he was setting out on his journey.
2. The husband greeted his wife as she entered the country-house.
3. Having set out at first light, the soldiers finally arrived at the sea.
4. Having advanced for two hours, the soldiers finally reached the city.
5. Having tried in vain to enter the city, the enemy went away in the middle of the night.
6. O king, don't believe the words of that evil general!
7. The teacher caught sight of the pupils as they were trying to run away,.
8. After following the animal for an hour, the boy finally threw a spear.
9. The enemy killed the soldiers as they were entering the harbour.
10. The enemy threw many arrows at the soldiers as they were advancing.

## 2  The future participle

The future participle of deponent verbs is formed in the same way by taking -us from the perfect and adding -urus. Thus from  *egredior egredi egressus sum*  we get *egressurus = about to depart*

### Exercise 36.12  Translate into Latin

1. ave, imperator, nos morituri te salutamus.
2. dux profecturus Roma apud senatores locutus est.
3. imperator apud senatores locuturus surrexit.

4. captivi poenam mortis passuri se iecerunt ad pedes imperatoris.
5. mater filium ad summum montem secutura multum aquae bibere constituit.
6. maritus domum regressurus uxori donum pulchrum emit.
7. vir tabernam ingressurus forte comitem conspexit.
8. imperator in bellum ingressurus centum naves aedificari iussit.
9. maritus domo profecturus 'vale, mea vita' uxori inquit.
10. imperator apud cives locuturus primo risit.

**Exercise 36.13E Review**　　　　**Complete the following and translate into English**

1. decem milit__ profecti sunt; quattuor autem in itiner_ mortui sunt.
2. miles multa vulner_ gravia passus est et duobus post diebus mort___ est.
3. paene omnes copi__ ad oppidum profect__ sunt et heri regress__ sunt.
4. rex paucis diebus in itin___ longo proficisc_ conabitur.
5. nolite cred___ mulieribis haec loquentibus!
6. hostes copi__ ab oppido proficiscentes subito petiverunt.
7. filii patrem ingredient__ salutaverunt.
8. dominus puerum praemia capere conatum saeve pun____ .
9. milites virum multa saeva pass__ reduxerunt.
10. turba mulier__ ab urbe prima luce profect____ quinque horas in silva mansit.

1 magister discipulos laborare hortabatur sed frustra.
2 magister loquebatur dum discipuli legunt.
3 magister tacebat dum discipuli loquuntur.
4 magister regressus est dum discipuli ludunt.
5 dum magister librum legit discipuli egressi sunt.

1 aquila phocam effugere hortabatur.
2 phoca celeriter in flumen progreditur dum aquila ad caelum ascendit.
3 aquila phocam effugere conabatur.
4 phoca progrediebatur et aquila celeriter descendebat.
 5 diu aquila clamores diros phocae morientis passa est.

# Chapter 37      Semi-deponent Verbs

Some verbs have a present of active form but a perfect of passive form: they are called semi-deponents

| | | | |
|---|---|---|---|
| audeo | audēre | ausus sum 2 | = dare |
| gaudeo | gaudēre | gavisus sum 2 | = be pleased, rejoice |
| soleo | solēre | solitus sum 2 | = be accustomed |

nocte puer per viam currere ausus est.
The boy dared to run along the road at night.

## Exercise 37.1 Translate into English

1. vir apud senatores dicere ausus est imperatorem crudelem esse.
2. quis tantum scelus facere ausus est?
3. dux sperabat milites oppidum oppugnare ausuros esse.
4. ipse solus per silvam procedere ausus est.
5. illo tempore nemo apud senatores loqui ausus est.
6. tanta ira civium erat ut senator apud eos loqui non auderet.
7. dux, quod milites hostes vicerant, magnopere gaudebat.
8. maxime gaudentes quod dona acceperant, pueri domum laeti redierunt.
9. nolite auferre haec dona quae deis offerri solent.
10. si unus servus dominum suum interfecerat, Romani illius omnes servos necare solebant.

## Exercise 37.2E Translate into English

1. quis apud senatores ita loqui audebit?
2. pater sperabat filium flumen altum transire ausurum esse.
3. tanta virtus illius militis erat ut solus ipse montem ascendere auderet.
4. mater, quod filius tot praemia acceperat, magnopere gavisa est.
5. senator apud comites dicere ausus est ducem exercitum male ducere.
6. eosdem mercatores in foro videre solebam.
7. quis solus nocte in castra hostium intrare audebit?
8. illo tempore nemo Romam proficisci audebat.
9. maxime gaudens quod filius tot dona acceperat, pater domum rediit.
10. ipsa sola per viam procedere ausa est.

## Exercise 37.3    Translate into Latin

1. The old man rejoiced when he saw his son after so many years.
2. The freedman was accustomed to sleep in his garden after a heavy dinner.
3. This soldier alone dared to ask the general why he had attacked the town.
4. Who dared to laugh while the emperor was talking?
5. When the messenger related the victory to him, the chief greatly rejoiced.
6. Nobody dared to go into the forest because of the danger of lions.
7. Who will dare to cross this small river and follow me to Rome?
8. The cruel master was accustomed to punish all his slaves.
9. If my friend arrives today, I shall greatly rejoice.
10. Everyone rejoiced when they saw the excellent dinner.

**Exercise 37.4E  Translate the following adjectives and then find them in the wordsearch**

```
N T X S J L M K Q D O E
I Q S U T U X P I V D H
N M C A N A K L I V F E
F B E E N L I S T W A P
E B L V U G O S O P T A
L P E G E M O C Z G D F
I O S N I R B J V C S A
C V T X I G B W J K F F
E E O D A G N A I I A P
M R S W F Y N E I J E S
P O I Y X C G O V M E F
V S E I C G T A S A Y V
```

careful *(masc. acc. sing.)*, dreadful *(masc. acc. pl.)*,
brief *(fem. acc. sing.)*, kind *(masc. acc. pl.)*,
wicked *(masc. acc. pl.)*, real *(masc. acc. pl.)*,
nearest *(masc. acc. pl.)*, unlucky *(fem. acc. sing.)*

**Exercise 37.5E  Review        Complete the following and translate into English**

1. tanta ira patr__  erat ut filius loqui non aud____ .
2. dux, cum milites hostes viciss___  , non gavisus est.
3. maxime gaudent__  quod dona acceperant, pueri dom__  redierunt.
4. servi, nolite auferre h___  cibum qu_  equis nostris offerri solent!
5. quis apud senator__  ita loqu_  audebit?
6. ego eosdem agricol__  in agris videre sol____.
7. qu__  solus nocte in castra host___  intrare ausus est?
8. ill_  tempore pauci Romam proficisci audebant.
9. tanta virt__  militum erat ut ducem in proeli__  ducere auderent.
10. regin_  ipsa sola per viam procedere aus_  est.

1 femina pecuniam servo reddere solebat.
2 femina servo pecuniam dare ausa est.
3 agricola miser feminam pecuniam petere ausus est
4 femina ubi agricola ei pecuniam dedit gavisa est.
5 dux ubi femina benigna ei pecuniam dedit gavisus est.

1 magister, quamquam discipuli dormirent, discedere solebat.
2 magister ubi discipuli dormiebant librum legere solebat.
3 magister cum discipuli dormirent magnopere gaudebat.
4 magister, cum pueri libros legerent, dormire ausus est.
5 pueri apud magistrum dormire audebant.

# Chapter 38    Copulative Verbs

Verbs which link a subject and complement are called copulative verbs. Others besides **sum** are

| | | | |
|---|---|---|---|
| appareo | apparēre | apparui 2 | = appear |
| maneo | manĕre | mansi 2 | = remain |
| videor | videri | visus sum 2 | = seem |

The noun or adjective in the complement remains in the nominative case.

Note:    The passive of video = I see **videor = I seem** or **I appear**

magister iratus esse videtur.
The teacher seems to be angry.

The passives of verbs of making, saying, thinking and choosing (known as factitive verbs) are also used as copulative verbs. Similarly, the noun in the complement remains in the nominative case.

| | | | | |
|---|---|---|---|---|
| feror | ferri | latus sum | *irreg.* | = am reported |
| legor | legi | lectus sum | 3 | = am chosen |
| putor | putari | putatus sum | 1 | = am thought |
| vocor | vocari | vocatus sum | 1 | = am called |

## ut followed by the indicative = as

ut solebant, nonnulli senatores eodem tempore loquebantur.
As was their wont, several senators were speaking at the same time.

ut bene scis, dominus iam discessit.
As you well know, the master has already departed.

ut sperabas, ita res est.
The situation is as you were hoping.

**Exercise 38.1    Translate into English**

1. ille vir senator paucis ante diebus lectus erat.
2. hic Augustus ab omnibus civibus iam vocatur.
3. dux miser in insula captivus tres annos manere debebat.
4. dux heri mortuus a nuntio quodam latus est.
5. ille consul, ut a nonnullis fertur, mox discedet.
6. post mortem canis carissimi senex semper tristis videbatur.
7. illa femina ancilla apud imperatorem multos annos mansit.

8. hic miles fortior omnibus comitibus esse putabatur.
9. rex diligens omnibus esse videbatur.
10. hic canis, ut me saepe monuisti, ferocissimus est.

## Exercise 38.2E  Translate into English

1. cur haec ancilla diligens esse ferebatur?
2. hic apud senatores sapiens semper videbatur.
3. num hic miles infelix dux a comitibus legetur?
4. illae feminae ancilla apud me novem annos mansit.
5. imperator heri mortuus a civibus quibusdam latus est.
6. ille senator paucis ante diebus consul lectus erat.
7. post victoriam exercitus princeps tristis non iam videbatur.
8. haec femina benignius quam maritus servos se gerere putabatur.
9. neque Crassus neque Pompeius maior videri alteri voluit.
10. post victoriam Crassus et Pompeius consules facti sunt.

## Exercise 38.3  Translate into Latin

1. After the death of his little son, the emperor often appeared sad.
2. The wretched man remained a slave all his life.
3. The brave soldier was chosen to be their leader by all his colleagues.
4. After many years the emperor Octavian was called Augustus by the citizens of Rome.
5. That poet was considered to be very wise by all his friends.
6. After the battle the very seriously wounded general was reported dead.
7. The maidservant seemed to be working without any care.
8. That old man has remained on his own for ten years.
9. Who is thought wiser than the emperor?
10. Nobody is considered more diligent than that slave.

## Exercise 38.4E  Review  Complete the following and translate into English

1. ante mort__  canis carissim_  senex semper laetus videbatur.
2. illa puella ancilla apud patr__  meum tres annos mans__ .
3. hic dux fortior omn____  militibus esse putabatur.
4. cur hic magist__  diligens esse ferebatur?
5. hic agricol_  diligens maxima cum cura semper labor___  videbatur.
6. ille vir paucis ante annis consul lect__  est.
7. ante victoriam exercit__  princeps trist__  videbatur.
8. haec mulier benignius quam marit__  servos aud___  putabatur.
9. hic servus stult__  sine cur_  cenam parare videbatur.
10. num ille imperator mortu__  latus est?

1 ut videmus, nauta et domina tristes sunt.
2 ut saepe accidebat, ubi dominus aberat, uxor bene non se gerebat.
3 uxor domini omnibus irata apparebat.
4 nauta rex a femina lectus est.
5 ut solebant, servus et ancilla bene laborabant.

# Chapter 39      The Gerundive

The gerundive is a participle or verbal adjective, passive in meaning:

amandus -a -um = fit to be loved      monendus -a -um = fit to be warned
regendus -a -um = fit to be ruled      audiendus -a -um= fit to be heard
capiendus -a -um = fit to be taken

It has a number of uses. We shall focus here on just one. Rather than **ut** plus the subjunctive, occasionally **ad** with the gerundive is used to express purpose. Note how the gerundive agrees with the following noun.

Romam ad petendam pacem venerunt.
They came to Rome to seek peace.

Note that *petendam* agrees with the noun following, here acc. fem. sing.

## Exercise 39.1 Translate into English

1. imperator consilium audacissimum fecit ad patriam e periculo servandam.
2. servi perterriti omnia parabant ad iuvenes feroces repellendos.
3. milites missi sunt ad omnes servos occidendos.
4. cives ad forum festinaverunt ad ducem clarum conspiciendum.
5. ubi Caesar Circum Maximum intravit omnes senatores surrexerunt ad salutandum eum.
6. imperator milites misit ad urbem servandam.
7. multi cives ad mediam urbem adierunt ad reginam audiendam.
8. multae naves ad Graeciam missae sunt ad servos capiendos.
9. nuntius heri missus est ad cives de periculo monendos.
10. Sabini Romam venerunt ad feminas rapiendas.

## Exercise 39.2E Translate into English

1. imperator ducem misit ad urbem delendam.
2. nonnulli milites fortes missi sunt ad omnes leones occidendos.
3. multi cives ad mediam urbem convenerunt ad reginam audiendam.
4. iuvenes ad forum festinaverunt ad feminas pulchras conspiciendas.
5. vir domum regressus est ad pecuniam quaerendam.
6. senex in tabernam intravit ad vinum bibendum.
7. quando consilium facies ad omnes canes ex oppido pellendos?
8. cives perterriti arma parabant ad hostes repellendos.
9. pater ad servos emendos Romam venit.
10. cum satis pecuniae haberet, libertus Romam venit ad aurum emendum.

## Exercise 39.3    Translate into Latin

1. Many soldiers were sent to the town to take prisoners.
2. The emperor devised a bold plan to save the city.
3. The freedman came to Rome to buy four slaves.
4. The woman returned home to take more money.
5. We have come to the city centre to listen to the emperor.
6. The sixth army was sent to destroy the town.

7. We all hurried to the city centre to catch sight of the emperor.
8. Some brave soldiers have gone into the wood to search for the lion.
9. The old man went into the garden to hide his money in the ground.
10. I'm off to the pub to see my friends.

### Exercise 39.4E  Review  Complete the following and translate into English

1. imperator milites mis__  ad oppidum delend__  .
2. nonnulli milites fortes miss_  sunt ad leones feroces occidend__  .
3. mult_  cives ad mediam urb__  festinaverunt ad regin__  conspiciendam.
4. iuvenes ad forum festinav_____  ad femin__  pulchras conspiciendas.
5. vir domum regressus est ad libros quaerend__  .
6. quis ad for__  heri iit ad imperatorem audiendum?
7. Hannibal montes transiit ad Roman__  petendos.
8. nonnullae nav__  ad Graeciam missae sunt ad servos capiend__  .
9. dux cum militibus suis flumen parv__  transiit ad urb__  oppugnandam.
10. Sabini ad urbem venisse feruntur ad feminas rapiend__  .

1 pueri per viam currebant ad canes petendos.
2 puellae per viam currebant ad amicas videndas.
3 feminae agrum transibant ad perveniendum ad oppidum.
4 puellae ad oppidum ambulabant ad cibum petendum.
5 tres puellae domo discesserunt ad cibum emendum.

1 aquila e caelo descendebat ut phocam petendam.
2 phoca ad petendam aquilam surrexit.
3 aquila ad caelum ascendit ad phocam quaerendam.
4 phoca ad flumen progrediebatur ad aquilam occidendam.
5 aquila ad silvam profecta erat ad phocam servandam.

# Chapter 40     Ablative absolute

The **ablative absolute** construction consists of a **past participle passive (PPP)** or a **present participle active** agreeing with a **noun** in the ablative. It is important to note that these words must not be related to any other words in the sentence.

urbe deleta Romani discesserunt.
The city having been destroyed, the Romans departed.

Of course, a more natural translation would be:

With the city destroyed …. or When the city had been destroyed ….. or Once the city had been destroyed …..

filio ludente mater librum legit.
The mother read a book while her son was playing.

Note that in the ablative absolute construction, the present participle ends in **-e** rather than **-i**

Note that there is no present participle of *sum*. It can be simply *understood*. In the sentence

Caesare duce, milites laetissimi erant.

When Caesar was leader, the soldiers were very happy.
We can translate it as:  Caesar (being) leader …..

**Exercise 40.1     Translate these phrases using 'when … had been …'**

1. praemiis acceptis …
2. clamoribus auditis ….
3. armis captis ….
4. copiis collectis ….
5. hostibus conspectis  ….
6. die constituto ….
7. cibo consumpto ….
8. urbe defensa ….
9. oppido deleto ….
10. verbis dictis ….
11. equis ductis ….
12. itinere facto ….
13. bello gesto  ….
14. hastis iactis ….
15. auro invento ….
16. milite iusso ….
17. libro lecto ….
18. nuntio misso ….
19. gladiis motis ….
20. militibus occisis ….
21. auro ostento ….
22. libris positis ….
23. militibus reductis  ….
24. urbe recta ….
25. libro scripto ….
26. servis traditis ….
27. monte viso ….
28. canibus fugere coactis ….
29. iuvene custodito ….
30. principe interfecto ….
31. navibus pulsis ….
32. puella petita ….
33. auro relicto ….
34. urbe oppugnata ….

**Exercise 40.2    Translate these phrases  using 'While ….. was / were …..'**

1. pueris praemia accipientibus ….
2. duce domum adveniente ….
3. principe appropinquante ….
4. leonibus clamores audientientibus ….
5. milite arma capiente ….
6. duce milites colligente ….
7. nautis insulam conspicientibus ….
8. duce hoc constituente ….
9. custode ad urbem festinante ….
10. civibus in oppido convenientibus ….
11. equo celeriter currente ….
12. militibus muros custodientibus ….
13. civibus urbem defendentibus ….
14. hostibus oppidum delentibus ….
15. patre hoc dicente ….
16. gente ex oppido discedente ….
17. Tarqinio rege ….
18. captivis castra effugientibus ….
19. matre exeunte ….
20. amico me exspectante ….
21. nauta hanc rem faciente ….
22. iuvenibus ad oppidum festinantibus ….
23. hostibus fugientibus ….
24. duce has res male gerente ….
25. custode ducem interficiente ….
26. agricola aurum inveniente ….
27. dis spectantibus ….
28. patre in oppido laborante ….
29. magistro hoc iubente ….
30. poeta hunc librum legente ….
31. domino servum liberante     ….
32. pueris in via ludentibus ….
33. matre in villa manente ….
34. rege nuntium mittente ….
35. servo regem monente ….
36. nautis navigantibus ….
37. magistro hoc narrante ….
38. agricola canem necante ….
39. custode haec nuntiante ….
40. hostibus cives occidentibus ….
41. hostibus oppidum oppugnantibus ….
42. fratre librum ostendente ….
43. ancilla cibum parante ….
44. tempestate navem pellente ….
45. cane in agro pereunte ….
46. servo dominum petente ….
47. militibus in oppido pugnantibus ….
48. magistro discipulos puniente ….
49. principe Romam redeunte ….
50. agricola servos reducente ….
51. principe Romae regente ….
52. puero praemium relinquente ….
53. puella respondente ….
54. discipulis ridentibus ….
55. cane ad servum ruente ….
56. magistro me salutante ….
57. puero scribente ….
58. patre filiam servante ….
59. nauta mare spectante ….
60. hostibus Romanos superantibus ….
61. leonibus pueros terrentibus ….
62. domino servos tradente ….
63. milite flumen transeunte ….
64. amico Romam veniente ….
65. sociis periculum videntibus ….
66. militibus hostes vincentibus ….
67. matre filium vocante ….
68. milite senem vulnerante ….

**Exercise 40.3    Translate into English**

1. multo cibo gravi consumpto, dominus iit ad hortum ut dormiret.
2. morte imperatoris crudelis cognita plurimi cives laeti erant.
3. hoc consilio a senatoribus laudato, senex tandem sedit.
4. vir malus gladio celato ad forum iit.
5. cena domini parata ancilla in hortum discessit.
6. vulnere in pede militis conspecto dux de equo descendit.
7. cane caro in via interfecto senex miser solus vivebat.
8. qua epistula accepta iuvenis diu lacrimabat.
9. nomine imperatoris audito, plurimi cives clamorem fecerunt.
10. armis depositis, ianuae lente appropinquaverunt.

**Exercise 40.4    Translate into English**

1. quo facto omnes abierunt.
2. hoc viso, milites antea perterriti nunc fortius pugnare coeperunt.
3. puella e periculo servata omnes laeti domum redierunt.
4. domino sic mortuo, omnes servi miseri erant.
5. paucis oppidis resistentibus Caesar cum legionibus mox ad oppidum pervenit.
6. ianua pulsa miles in villam intravit.
7. quibus rebus factis, senatores discesserunt.
8. naves omnibus civibus spectantibus Troiam profectae sunt.
9. his verbis auditis puellae tristissimae erant.
10. urbe tandem capta dux discessit.

**Exercise 40.5    Translate into Latin**

1. When all the troops had been gathered, the Greeks quickly departed.
2. Once they had seen the mountain, the soldiers rejoiced.
3. As the enemy fled, the emperor ordered his men to attack the town.
4. As the people left the city, I caught sight of my friend.
5. As the leader was reaching home, a messenger suddenly arrived.
6. Once the leader had been killed, the remainder of the troops fled.
7. Once the book had been read, the boy went to town.
8. The angry teacher went out as the pupils laughed.
9. When the children had been taken away by the soldiers, the mothers cried for a long time.
10. As the dogs rushed down the street, the sailors went into the bar.

# Translating complex sentences into English

A **complex sentence** has a main clause and one or more subordinate clauses, as opposed to a **compound sentence**, which has more than one main clause joined by a conjunction.

To help make the translation into English read more smoothly, it is often better to break long complex Latin sentences into shorter sentences, where the emphasis is put on brevity and clarity. So, the sentence

milites, postquam in castra venerunt, cibum petiverunt

is best rendered by putting *the soldiers* inside the subordinate clause:

After the soldiers arrived in the camp, they asked for food.

This is especially important when translating participles

libertus comitem conspectum salutavit.
*literally* The freedman greeted the having been caught sight of colleague.
i.e. The freedman greeted the colleague he had caught sight of.
*or* The freedman caught sight of the colleague and greeted him.

Notice that as the ablative absolute contains a participle, in a passage where there is sufficient context, the particular force of the phrase, whether temporal (when), causal (because, since as), or concessive (although) should be rendered in the English translation.

**Exercise 40.6E   Review   Complete the following and translate into English**

1. quibus verb___   dictis imperator discess___  .
2. host_____   subito conspectis milites nostri fugerunt.
3. consule de victori_   locuto plurim_   cives gavisi sunt.
4. ancillis surgere iuss___   domina in hort___   exiit.
5. imperatore mortu_   novum ducem Romani leg___   debuerunt.
6. servis malis vendit___   dominus bonos em____   constituit.
7. senex hort_   tempestate deleto diu trist___   mansit.
8. Caesare consul_   plurimi cives laeti erant.
9. cen_   iam parata ancillae discedere iuss___   sunt.
10. omnibus epistulis ab imperatore lectis senatores egressi sunt.

1 his verbis dictis duae puellae cantare coeperunt
2 matre ingressa puellae clamare coeperant.
3 patre viso ancillae laborare coeperunt.
4 matre egressa puellae cantare coeperant.
5. auro invento tres puellae loqui coeperunt.

1 pueris loquebentibus magister gaudebant.
2 magistro dormiente pueri librum legebant.
3 magistro librum legente pueri dormiebant.
4 discipulis dormientibus magister ridebat.
5 pueris dormientibus magister tacebat.

# Chapter 41　　　Compound verbs

Be on the lookout for **compound verbs**, which are formed by using a **prefix** plus a **verb**. The most common prefixes are:

## ad-, e(x)-, in-, re-, trans-

The meaning of the compound verb should be clear from the prefix plus the root verb. In a few cases the meaning of the compound is slightly different. Some of the more common compound verbs from the verbs we have met are:

## ad-

**adduco** = to draw to oneself, to bring; **adeo** = to come to; **admiror** = to admire; **admitto** = to send to, to let go (a horse at full speed), to admit a person; **admoneo** = to remind, advise; **admoveo** = to move, bring to; **advenio** = to come to; **adverto** = to turn towards, steer; **advoco** = to summon, call

### Exercise 41.1 Translate into English

1. adductus spe victoriae facilis, imperator prima luce proficisci constituit.
2. dum naves ad portum adeunt, dux milites egredi in mare iussit.
3. Caesar res a militibus fortissimis suis gestas saepe admirabatur.
4. equo admisso nuntius mox ad urbem advenit.
5. imperator nuntium hostium tandem admisit.
6. ante proelium dux milites de periculo admonuit.
7. senator comitem admonuit ne illam insulam emeret.
8. dux, quod illa nocte oppidum capere volebat, milites suos muris celeriter admovit.
9. dux quo facilius muros oppidi oppugnaret suas copias admovere constituit.
10. princeps sensit periculum ad urbem advenire.
11. post multos annos pacis, princeps animum ad bellum advertit.
12. nesciens quid facere deberet, senator comitem in consilium tandem advocavit.

## e(x)-

**educo** = to lead, draw out, bring up, rear; **emitto** = to send forth, servum manu emitto = to free; **emoveo** = to move out; **enavigo** = to sail away; **erumpo** = *with se* to break out; **evenio** = to come out, turn out, happen; **everto** = to overturn, destroy; **evoco** = to call out, summon; **evinco** = to conquer utterly, subdue; **excurro** = to run out; **exeo** = to go out; **exoro** = to entreat earnestly; **expello** = to drive out, banish; **expono** = to set out; **expugno** = to take by storm, capture; **extraho** = to extract

### Exercise 41.2 Translate into English

1. imperator naves e portu quam celerrime educi iussit.
2. pater filios prope mare educere constituit.
3. hostibus fortiter resistentibus, imperator copias suas ex urbe eduxit.
4. multi et boni domini servos manu emittebant.
5. adductus spe victoriae, Caesar milites suos in hostes statim emisit.
6. princeps omnes canes e foro removeri iussit,
7. sociis Graecis Aulide collectis nautae Troiam sine mora enavigaverunt.

8. Caesar copias suas e castris se erumpere ex oppido iussit.
9. senex, ut saepe eveniebat, domi pecuniam reliquerat.
10. forte evenit ut omnes milites ad oppidum ante noctem pervenirent.
11. post proelia saeva Carthago a Romanis tandem eversa est.
12 tres naves tempestate saeva eversae sunt.
13. barbaris Romam procedentibus, Romani ad bellum socios evocaverunt.
14. timens ne a leone feroci occideretur, incola miser deos evocavit.
15. signo dato cives ex omnibus portis oppidi excurrerunt.
16. heri conspexi comitem e villa exeuntem.
17. Romani regem saevum Roma tandem expulerunt.
18. magister benignus praemia pulchra tribus ex discipulis exposuit.
19. dux hastam e capite militis vulnerati magna cum cura extraxit.
20. poeta promisit se scelera imperatoris crudelis in lucem extracturam ese.

## in-

**incurro** = to attack, happen; **indico** = to make publicly known, declare (war); **induco** = to lead; **ineo** = to enter; **infero** = to carry in, charge; **ingero** = to heap on; **inscribo** = to inscribe; **invoco** = to call upon

### Exercise 41.3 Translate into English

1. cum intellegebant milites Romanos fessos esse, hostes in eis incurrere constituerunt.
2. vultus imperatoris iram saevam clarissime indicabat.
3. Caesar Romam iniit ad pecuniam capiendam militibus suis qui diu pugnaverant.
4. nocte hostibus dormientibus imperator milites in pugnam induxit.
5. postridie Caesar in hostes signa inferre constituit.
6. barbaris Romam celeriter procedentibus consul cives ad urbem defendendam invocavit.
7. milites hastas in hostes fugientes ingerebant.
8. hostibus fortiter oppidum defendentibus imperator Romanus consilium novum iniit.

## re-

**recurro** = to run back; **reduco** = to bring back, lead back; **refugio** = to flee away, take flight; **remaneo** = to remain; **remitto** = to send back, relieve; **removeo** = to remove; **renuntio** = to bring back word; **reparo** = to prepare anew; **repello** = to drive back; **repono** = to place back, lay aside; **reporto** = to bring back; **reputo** = to think over; **rescribo** = to write again; **resurgo** = to rise again; **retraho** = to draw back; **reverto** = to return, come back; **revoco** = to summon again

### Exercise 41.4 Translate into English

1. hostibus victis imperator legiones Romam reduxit.
2. plurimi senes e castris in montem refugerunt.
3. Romani hostes tandem ad mare repulerunt.
4. multi milites Romani in exercitu viginti annos remanserunt.
5. iuvenis epistulam quam dominae missuram esse rescripsit.
6. quando pater ex itinere revertit?
7. Caesar viros suos hortatus est. 'in virtutem' inquit 'omnem spem ponite.'
8. Cicero dixit Caesarem victoriam non pacem domum reportavisse.
9. urbe ab hostibus deleta princeps dixit urbem novam mox surrecturam esse.
10. post victoriam imperator exercitum a Germania reportavit.

# trans-

**transeo** = to go over, pass (time): **transfero** = to carry out, translate: **transgredior** = to go across, pass over; **transmitto** = to send across

## Exercise 41.4 Translate into English

1. senex duos annos prope mare transit.
2. tres legiones per montes altissimos transgressae sunt.
3. imperator duas legiones celeriter ad Britanniam transmisit.
4. princeps epistulam transferri iussit.

# Chapter 42      Conversational Latin

salve! mihi nomen est _____; sedecim annos natus sum. habito in domo quae est sita in septentrionibus Londinii cum parentibus et cum fratre. huic nomen est _____ et decem annos natus est. habemus canem et duos feles.

in domo mea sunt tria dormitoria, duo sessoria, unum triclinium et culina magna sed hortus parvus est.

obeo ad scholam secundariam cui nomen est _____ . ea sita est in _____ . hoc anno sum in octavo gradu. amo omnes disciplinas praeter historiam. postmeridie saepe athleticis ludimus. pedifolle et tenisia ludo. per agros saepe curro. est in schola piscina parva in qua natare possumus.

domum advenio sexta hora post meridiem et cum familia septima hora ceno. post cenam praescripta domestica in cubiculo meo facio. deinde, si tempus mihi est, librum lego aut lusum computatralem ludo aut televisionem specto. decima hora dormitum eo.

fine hebdomadis saepe certamen pedifollis specto aut amicos meos visito aut ad concentum eo aut ad tabernas eo.

| | |
|---|---|
| 1. quid est nomen tibi? | mihi nomen est _____. |
| 2. ut vales? | bene mihi est. |
| 3. ut valet familia tua? | omnes domi bene se habent. |
| 4. habesne fratres vel sorores? | ita vero, unum fratrem habeo. |
| 5. quis domi tuae habitat? | ego et pater et mater. |
| 6. quot annos natus es tu? | _____ annos natus sum. |
| 7. quot sorores habes? | sororem non habeo. |
| 8. quot fratres habes? | duos fratres habeo. |
| 9. quid facis fine hebdomadis? | in cinemateum eo; televisionem specto; amicos meos visito; ad concentum eo; librum lego; pedifolle ludo; tenisia ludo; ad tabernas eo; lusum computatralem ludo. |
| 10. quibus athleticis ludis? | pedifolle et tenisia ludo. in piscina saepe nato. |
| 11. quo mense natus es? | ego mense Ianuario natus sum. |
| 12. quota hora est? | est fere*(almost)* decima hora et semihora. |
| 13. quota hora mane surgis? | septima hora mane surgo. |

14. quota hora prandium sumis?  plerumque prima hora prandium sumo.

15. quis in medio oppido facis?  in tabernas eo; amicos meos visito.

16. quot cubicula in tua domo sunt?  sunt quattuor cubicula.

17. habetne domus tua hortum magnum?  minime, habet hortum parvum.

18. habesne delicias domi?  duos canes habeo.

19. quae urbs est caput Britanniae?  Londinium est caput Britanniae.

20. quid flumen per Londinium fluit?  flumen Tamesis nomine per Londinium fluit.

**domi**

| | | | |
|---|---|---|---|
| cubiculum -i | bedroom | sessorium -i | sitting-room |
| triclinium -i | dining-room | culina -ae | kitchen |

**quota hora est?**

hora prima secunda tertia quarta quinta sexta septima octava nona decima undecima

ante post meridiem  est prima fere *(about)* hora

hora septima et semihora  mane *(in the morning)*

**menses anni**

| | | | |
|---|---|---|---|
| Ianuarius -i | Februarius -i | Martius -i | Aprilis -is |
| Maius -i | Iunius -i | Iulius -i | Augustus -i |
| September -bris | October -bris | November -bris | December -bris |

**ludi**

ludo pedifolle *(football)*, harpasto ludere *(play rugby)*, hocceio ludere *(play hockey)*, tenisia ludere *(play tennis)*, ludus baluci et pilae *(cricket)*,

**ubi est ...?**

| | | | |
|---|---|---|---|
| a septentrionibus | on the north | a meridie | on the south |
| ab oriente | on the east | ab occidente | on the west |

**deliciae** *(pets)*

canis -is *(dog)*  feles -is *(cat)*  cuniculus -i *(rabbit)*

# Chapter 43      Passages and sentences for vocabulary building and to help reading fluency

The following passages provide practice to improve reading fluency. They are adapted from Ritchie's *Fabulae Latinae*. Words not on the prescribed GCSE list are underlined and are to be found in the word list on page 135. There is scope for laying the basis for wider reading in the sentences on page 131. They cover the remaining words prescribed for the GCE AS syllabus; new underlined words are listed in the same word list.

> **ULYSSES** *Ulysses, a famous Greek hero, took a prominent part in the long siege of Troy. After the fall of the city, he set out with his followers on his homeward voyage to Ithaca, an island of which he was king; but being driven out of his course by northerly winds, he was compelled to touch at the country of the Lotus-eaters, who are supposed to have lived on the north coast of Africa. Some of his comrades were so delighted with the lotus fruit that they wished to remain in the country, but Ulysses compelled them to embark again and continued his voyage. He next came to the island of Sicily, and fell into the hands of the giant Polyphemus, one of the Cyclopes. After several of his comrades had been killed by this monster, Ulysses made his escape by stratagem and reached the country of the winds. Here he received the help of Aeolus, king of the winds, and having set sail again, arrived within sight of Ithaca; but owing to the folly of his companions, the winds became suddenly adverse and he was again driven back. He then touched at an island which was the home of Circe, a powerful enchantress, who exercised her charms on his companions and turned them into swine. By the help of the god Mercury, Ulysses not only escaped this fate himself, but also forced Circe to restore her victims to human shape. After staying a year with Circe, he again set out and eventually reached his home.*

## 1      HOMEWARD BOUND

urbs Troia a Graecis decem annos <u>obsidebatur</u>; qua tandem per <u>insidias</u> capta, Graeci longo bello confecti domum quam celerrime redire festinaverunt. cum <u>spolium</u> ac <u>praedam</u> cepissent, et omnibus rebus ad discedendum paratis, naves in aquam deduxerunt, et tempestate bona et magno cum gaudio domum enavigaverunt. erat inter primos Graecorum Ulixes quidam, vir <u>nobilis</u> et <u>peritus</u>, quem dicunt nonnulli <u>dolum</u> clarum <u>excogitavisse</u> quo Troianis deceptis urbem captam esse fertur. hic regnum insulae Ithacae <u>obtinuerat</u>, et <u>paulo priusquam</u> cum <u>reliquis</u> Graecis ad bellum profectus est, puellam pulcherrimam, nomine Penelopen, in <u>matrimonium</u> <u>duxerat</u>. nunc igitur cum iam decem annos afuisset, Ithacam redire maxime volebat ad uxorem et filium carum videndos.

## 2      THE LOTUS-EATERS

paulo tamen postquam a <u>litore</u> Troiae progressi sunt, tam gravis <u>hiems</u> subito accidit ut naves cursum tenere non possent sed <u>passim</u> <u>disicerentur</u>. navis autem, qua ipse Ulixes <u>vehebatur</u>, tempestate gravi coacta decimo die ad <u>litus</u> Libyae <u>denique</u> <u>appulsa</u> est. ancoris iactis, Ulixes, quod iam <u>inopia</u> cibi erat, tres e sociis in terram misit, qui aquam et <u>frumentum</u> ad navem referrent et qualis esset <u>natura</u> eius terrae cognoscerent. hi igitur e nave egressi quod iussisset Ulixes <u>efficere</u> parabant. dum tamen aquam quaerunt, forte <u>obviam</u> <u>ierunt</u> quibusdam incolis qui eos benigne acceperunt. <u>plerique</u> autem incolarum consumebant <u>mirabilem</u> quemdam <u>fructum</u> cui nomen 'lotum' dabant. quem cum tres Graeci semel consumpsissent, patriae et sociorum statim obliti dixerunt se semper in ea terra mansuros esse ut illum fructum mirabilem cotidie consumerent.

3    THE RESCUE

Ulixes cum ab hora septima ad vesperum viros exspectavisset, veritus ne hi in periculo fortasse essent, duos e reliquis misit, ut quae causa esset morae discerent. hi igitur ad mediam insulam festinaverunt; quo cum venissent, comites suos quasi vino ebrios invenerunt. tum ubi cur venissent docuerunt, comitibus persuadere conabantur ut secum ad navem redirent. illi tamen resistere ac manu se defendere coeperunt, iterum atque iterum clamantes se illic manere velle. quae cum ita essent, duo viri ad Ulixem redierunt. his rebus cognitis ipse cum omnibus qui in nave relicti erant ad oppidum venit; et viros suos frustra hortatus ut libenter redirent, manibus post terga vinctis eos invitos ad navem reduxit. tum Graeci ancoris sublatis quam celerrime e portu enavigaverunt.

4    THE ONE-EYED GIANT

postquam eam totam noctem navigaverunt, postridie mane ad terram advenerunt. tum, quod nesciebat qualis esset haec terra, ipse Ulixes cum duodecim e comitibus in terram egressus loca explorare statuit. paulo a litore progressi ad speluncam altam et latam pervenerunt, quam habitari senserunt; eius enim aditum manu factum esse viderunt. mox, quamquam intellegebant se non sine periculo id facturos, speluncam paulatim intraverunt; quod cum fecissent, magnam copiam lactis in vasis ingentibus conditam invenerunt. dum tamen mirantur quis in hac spelunca habitaret, oves currentes repente audiverunt, et ecce! viderunt appropinquare monstrum ingens, corpore et vultu humano; et ubi viderunt unum oculum modo habere in ore positum, intellexerunt hunc esse unum e Cyclopibus. hi erant gens gigantium de quibus famam iam acceperant.

5    THE GIANT'S SUPPER

Graeci igitur simulac monstrum viderunt, terrore capti in interiorem partem speluncae refugerunt et se ibi celare conabantur. Polyphemus autem (sic enim erat nomen huius Cyclopis ) oves suas in speluncam egit; deinde, cum saxum ingens ad aditum posuisset, ignem in medio antro fecit. hoc facto, oculo omnia inspexit, et cum vidisset homines haud procul stantes, magna voce exclamavit: "qui homines estis? mercatores an viri mali?" tum Ulixes respondit se neque mercatores esse neque ad auferendas oves venisse; sed a Troia redeuntes vi tempestatum gravium a recto cursu depulsos esse. tum Polyphemus quaesivit ubi esset navis qua vecti essent; sed Ulixes, cum se magno in periculo esse bene intellegeret, respondit navem suam in rupes coniectam omnino fractam esse. Polyphemus autem nullo responso dato duo e sociis manu dextra repente corripuit, et eos vivos statim consumere coepit.

6    A DESPERATE SITUATION

dum haec geruntur, Graecorum animos tantus terror occupavit ut ne vocem quidem emittere possent, sed omni spe salutis deposita mortem exspectabant. Polyphemus iam laboribus suis defessus humi iacuit et somno se dedit. quod cum vidisset Ulixes, credens se tantam occasionem salutis capere debere,  monstrum gladio interficere voluit. sed intellexit se prius videre debere quo modo se et viri sui ex antro effugere possent. at cum saxum ingens ad aditum positum animadvertisset, nihil usui esse intellexit si Polyphemum interficerent. tantum enim erat saxum ut ne a viginti quidem hominibus amoveri posset. quae cum ita essent, Ulixes  rediit ad suos viros qui cum intellexissent quo in loco res essent, nulla spe salutis oblata de fortunis suis desperare coeperunt. ille tamen, vir summi ingenii, etsi adhuc consilium non invenerat, viros suos ne desperarent vehementer hortatus est.

## 7    A PLAN FOR VENGEANCE

prima luce postridie mane Polyphemus iam e somno excitatus rursus correptos duos e reliquis viris sine mora consumit. tum, cum saxum amovisset, ipse cum ovibus suis ex antro ad campos exiit; quod cum Graeci vidissent, magnam in spem venerunt se post paulum effugituros esse. mox tamen ab hac spe repulsi sunt; nam Polyphemus, postquam omnes oves exierunt, saxum in locum reposuit. viri omni spe salutis deposita miserrimi erant; Ulixes, vir summi ingenii, etsi intellegebat rem in angusto esse, nondum desperabat. tandem, postquam diu haec toto animo cogitavit, consilium cepit: sumpsit palum magnum et durum qui forte prope iacebat. hunc palum viris suis adiuvantibus diligenter gladio acri paratum bene tetegit. deinde omnes paulisper exspectaverunt dum Polyphemus rediret.

## 8    A GLASS TOO MUCH

sub vesperum Polyphemus rediit, et ovibus in speluncam actis eodem modo quo antea cenavit. tum Ulixes unum ex utribus vini aperuit, quos viri secum attulerant,  et monstro ad bibendum obtulit. Polyphemus, qui numquam antea vinum biberat, adeo amavit ut utrem secundum deinde tertium posceret. tum, cum quaesivisset quid esset nomen Ulixis, ille respondit nomen suum neminem esse; quod cum audivisset, Polyphemus ita locutus est: 'hanc tibi gratiam pro tanto beneficio referam; te postremum omnium consumam.' hoc cum dixisset, cibo vinoque gravis iacuit humi et brevi tempore somno oppressus est. tum Ulixes sociis convocatis, 'nunc denique occasionem habemus,' inquit,' hanc  tanta bona fortuna uti debemus."

## 9    THE BLINDING OF POLYPHEMUS

hac oratione habita, Ulixes imperavit viris suis ut partem pali paratam in igni paulisper ponerent et auxilio comitum palum in oculum Polyphemi dormientis vehementer egit. hic dolore acerrimo oculi e somno repente excitatus est. tantus clamor ex ore monstri ortus est ut Graeci terrore correpti fugere non possent.  Polyphemus per speluncam errat, clamans et Graecos capere conans; cum tamen viri oculo eius nocuisset, nullo modo hoc efficere potuit. interea duo alii Cyclopes, clamore audito, ad speluncam cucurrerunt, et pro aditu adstantes quid Polyphemus ageret quaesiverunt, et quam ob causam tantum clamorem sustulisset. ille respondit se graviter vulneratum esse et oculum vehementer dolere. cum tamen postea quaesivissent quis ei nocuisset, respondit ille Neminem id fecisse; quibus rebus auditis unus e Cyclopibus: "at si nemo," inquit, "te vulneravit, nonne dei, quibus parere necesse est, morbum ad te misit." hoc cum dixisset, abierunt Cyclopes credentes eum mentem amisisse.

## 10    THE ESCAPE

Polyphemus, ubi socios suos abiisse sensit, furore impulsus Ulixem iterum quaerere coepit; tandem cum aditum invenisset, saxum ingens abstulit ut oves in agros exirent. tum ipse in ianua sedit, et ut quaeque ovis ad hunc locum veniebat, eius in tergum manus ponebat, ne viri inter oves exire possent. quod cum animadvertisset Ulixes, intellexit omnem spem salutis in dolo magis quam in virtute poni necesse esse. itaque hoc consilium iniit. primum tres oves delegit, quas cum inter se viminibus coniunxisset, tum iussit unum ex sociis suis ventribus earum ita subiacere ut omnino se celaret; deinde oves hominem secum ferentes ad aditum egit. id accidit quod futurum esse sperabat. Polyphemus enim postquam manum in terga ovium ponit, eas exire passus est. Ulixes ubi rem tam feliciter evenisse vidit, omnes socios suos ex ordine eodem modo emisit; quo facto ipse postremus exiit et cuncti se fugae mandaverunt.

## 11    OUT OF DANGER

sic reliqui Graeci mortem vitaverunt. Ulixes timens ne Polyphemus se a Nemine deceptum esse sentiret, cum sociis quam celerrime ad oram contendit; quo cum venissent, ab eis qui in nave manserant magno cum gaudio accepti sunt. hi enim nesciebant quid comitibus accidisset, sed suspicati (id quidem quod erat) eos in aliquod periculum magnum incidisse, ipsi ad auxilium ferendum egredi parabant. tum Ulixes credens non satis esse tutum in eo loco manere, quam celerrime proficisci constituit. iussit igitur omnes se imponere in navem, et ancoris sublatis paulum a litore in altum navigaverunt. tum magna voce exclamavit: "tu, Polypheme, qui nec moribus nec legibus hominum pares, iustam et debitam poenam sceleris tui dedisti." hac voce audita Polyphemus ira vehementer commotus ad mare se contulit, et ubi navem paulum a litore remotam esse intellexit, saxum ingens manu dextra correptum in eam partem iecit unde vocem venire sensit. Graeci autem, etsi saxum haud procul ab nave advenit, cursum rectum tenere potuerunt.

## 12    THE COUNTRY OF THE WINDS

inde pauca milia passuum ab eo loco progressus Ulixes ad insulam Aeoliam navem appulit. haec patria erat ventorum,

"hic vasto rex Aeolus antro
luctantes ventos tempestatesque sonoras
imperio premit ac vinclis et carcere frenat."        (Virgil  Aeneid Book I  Lines 51-3)

ibi rex ipse hospites Graecos accepit, atque eis persuasit ut ad quietem capiendam paucos dies in ea insula manerent. septimo die, cum socii e laboribus se recepissent, Ulixes, ut tempestate idonea uteretur, sine mora proficisci constituit. tum Aeolus, qui sciebat Ulixem cupidissimum esse patriae videndae, ei iam profecturo magnum saccum dedit, in quo ventos omnes praeter unum posuerat. Zephyrum tantum solverat, quoniam ille ventus ab insula Aeolia ad Ithacam naviganti idoneus est. Ulixes hoc donum libenter accepit, et gratiis pro tanto beneficio actis hic sociis iuvantibus saccum cum reliquis bonis in navem attulit. tum omnibus rebus ad iter paratis navem a terra solvit.

## 13    THE WIND-BAG

hinc novem dies secundissimo vento cursum tenuerunt, iamque ad patriam perveneniebant, cum Ulixes ad quietem capiendam iacuit. at socii, qui mirabantur quid in illo sacco esset, cum ducem somno oppressum viderent, se tantam occasionem non perdere debere crediderunt; eis enim persuasum erat aurum et argentum et alia munera ibi esse. itaque spe capiendae praedae adducti saccum sine mora aperuerunt. quo facto venti "velut agmine facto,  qua data porta, ruunt et terras turbine perflant."        (Virgil Aeneid Book I  Lines 82-83)

hic tanta tempestas subito orta est ut illi cursum tenere non possent et in eandem insulam unde erant profecti referrentur. Ulixes e somno excitatus quo in loco res esset statim intellexit; saccum apertum et Ithacam post tergum relictam vidit. tum vero iratissimus fuit quod socii stulti spe pecuniae adducti occasionem patriae videndae perdiderat.

## 14    DRAWING OF LOTS

brevi spatio intermisso, Graeci insulae cuidam appropinquaverunt in qua Circe, filia Solis, habitabat. quo cum navem appulisset, Ulixes, in terram ad petendum frumentum egredi constituit; nam cognoverat viros in nave cibo egere. sociis igitur ad se convocatis quo in loco res esset et quid fieri vellet ostendit. cum tamen omnes in mente haberent quam crudeli morte necati essent ei qui antea nave egressi essent, nemo erat qui hoc negotium suscipere vellet. quae cum ita essent. tandem Ulixes socios in duas partes divisit, quarum alteri Eurylochus, vir summae virtutis, alteri ipse praeesset. tum hi inter se sortiti sunt uter in terram egrederetur. hoc facto, Eurylocho sorte evenit ut ille cum duobus et viginti sociis rem susciperet.

## 15    THE HOUSE OF THE ENCHANTRESS

his rebus ita constitutis ei qui sortiti erant ad mediam insulam profecti sunt. tantus tamen timor animos eorum occupaverat ut certi erant se morti obviam ituros. vix quidem poterant ei qui in nave relicti erant lacrimas tenere; credebant enim se socios suos numquam post hoc tempus visuros. illi per silvam paulatim progressi ad villam quandam pulcherrimam pervenerunt. quam dum appropinquant, vocem pulchram, sicut adulescentis, audiebant. repente leones sedentes inter arbores ubique viderunt, sed attoniti erant ubi viderunt hos leones placidos esse. mox ipsa Circe canens e villa exiit, et benigne omnes in suam domum invitavit. solus Eurylochus non satis confisus verbis huius mulieris mirabilis et suspicatus insidias sibi comparari, cavebat et in horto exspectare constituit. reliqui spe cenae adducti in villam intraverunt cenam et optimam omnibus rebus instructam invenerunt. at Circe in vinum quod servi fundebant quoddam potens ac mirabile prius clam addiderat; quod simulac Graeci biberunt, gravi somno subito oppressi sunt.

## 16    THE CHARM

tum Circe, quae artium magicarum peritissima erat, baculo  quod gerebat capita hospitum suorum leviter tetigit; quo facto omnes in porcos subito mutati sunt. interea Eurylochus attonitus quod socii in porcos factos esse quam celerrime ad oram cucurrit. huc cum venisset, adeo metu captus erat ut quae vidisset vix clare narrare posset. Ulixes autem satis intellexit socios suos in periculo esse, et gladio infra vestem celato Eurylocho imperavit ut sine mora viam quae duceret  ad villam monstraret. ille tamen multis cum lacrimis Ulixem orare coepit ne in tantum periculum se committeret; si quid gravius ei accideret, omnium salutem in summo periculo futuram. Ulixes autem respondit se neminem invitum secum adducturum; socios posse, si mallent, in nave manere; se sine ullo praesidio iturum esse; nam opus esse se ipsum rem suscepturum. hoc cum magna voce dixisset, e nave egressus et nullo sequente solus in viam se dedit.

## 17    THE COUNTERCHARM

ubi paulisper progressus ad quamdam villam pulchram pervenit et statim intrare statuit; intellexit enim hanc esse eandem domum de qua Eurylochus dixisset. at dum villae appropinquat, subito ei obviam stetit adulescens pulcher baculum gerens. hic Ulixem iam domum intrantem manu corripuit et, "quo ruis?" inquit. "nonne scis hanc esse Circes domum? hic adsunt amici tui quos Circe in porcos mutavit. num ipse porcus fieri vis?" Ulixes simulac vocem audivit, adulescentem esse deum Mercurium sciit; cum Mercurius sensisset Ulixem consilio suo desinere nolle, herbam quandam ei dedit, quam contra carmina multum valere dicebat. "hanc cape," inquit, "et si Circe te baculo tanges, tu aggrediens illi gladio minare." Mercurius postquam haec dixit,

"mortalis visus medio sermone reliquit, et procul in tenuem ex oculis evanuit auram."

(Virgil  Aeneid Book IV Lines 277-8)

## 18    THE ENCHANTRESS IS FOILED

brevi intermisso spatio Ulixes ad ianuam villae procedens ab ipsa Circe benigne acceptus est. omnia eodem modo atque antea facta sunt. cenam optime instructam vidit et cenare iussus est. sed, antequam cibum consumere coepit, Circe vinum in poculum fudit Ulixi et hospiti obtulit. ille etsi suspicatus est dolum, vinum bibit; quo facto Circe postquam caput eius baculo tetigit, ea verba locuta est quibus socios eius antea in porcos mutaverat. res tamen non accidit quo modo illa speraverat. tanta enim vis erat eius herbae quam Ulixi Mercurius dederat ut Ulixes somno non opprimeretur. at hic, ut eum monuerat Mercurius, gladio aggressus mortem illi minatus est. Circe cum artem suam nihil valere sensisset, multis cum lacrimis eum orare coepit ne sibi vitam adimeret.

## 19    MEN ONCE MORE

Ulixes autem ubi sensit eam timore captam esse, postulavit ut socios suos sine mora iam porcos in homines rursus mutaret; nisi id faceretur, se debitas poenas sumpturum promisit. Circe his rebus graviter commota ei ad pedes se proiecit, et multis cum lacrimis promisit se quae ille imperavisset omnia facturam. tum porcos in villam agi iussit. illi dato signo intraverunt, et cum ducem suum vidissent, magnopere dolebant quod nullo modo eum de rebus suis certiorem facere poterant. Circe tamen capita porcorum  baculo tetigit; quo facto omnes statim in genus humanum rursus mutati sunt. Ulixes, gavisus cum viri sui non iam porci essent, nuntium ad litus misit, qui reliquos Graecos illic manentes arcesseret. at illi his rebus cognitis hinc statim domum Circes se contulerunt; quo cum venissent, comites suos magno cum gaudio salutaverunt.

## 20    AFLOAT AGAIN

postridie mane Ulixes ex hac insula quam celerrime discedere in animo habebat. Circe tamen cum haec cognovisset, ex odio ad amorem conversa eum orare coepit ut paucos dies apud se moraretur; per eos proximos dies tanta beneficia in eum contulit ut facile ei persuadere posset ut diutius maneret. postquam tamen unum annum apud Circen consumpserat, Ulixes viris ad se convocatis haec verba dixit:

'comites mei, nec aequum  nec iustum est patriam ita neglegere. multos menses iam hic in otio vivimus; ita vero, est culpa mea. nunc navem parare opus est.'

ubi tamen ad litus descendit, navem suam tempestatibus paene deletam invenit. hac re cognita omnia quae ad naves reficiendas usui essent comparari iussit. tribus diebus omnia parata sunt. quod tamen ubi Circe vidit, miserrima erat et Ulixem vehementer orabat ut eo consilo desineret. ille tamen, ut ventis secundis uteretur, navem statim solvit. antequam in patriam suam perveniret, multas quidem clades duras Ulixes passurus erat; quas tamen hoc loco longum est perscribere.

These sentences complete the words prescribed for the GCE AS syllabus. Familiarity with this vocabulary will be useful for the unseen AS papers and help with vocabulary building, so necessary for students embarking on passages from the major authors.

1. dux militibus imperavit ut fossam latam extra moenia oppidi foderent.
2. postridie mane multae arae pulcherrimae deorum incendio deletae sunt.
3. cum equites ad castra pervenissent, Caesar impetum in hostes a latere statim iussit.
4. paucis annis hic mercator per facinora pessima ex pauperrimo dives factus est.
5. Graeci poetas suos in summo honore semper habebant.
6. mercator dubius sententiae  tandem fregit foedus quod cum socio suo tribus ante annis fecerat.
7. haec certe est causa omnium horum scelerum atque criminum.
8. post hiemem longam Romani in finibus hostium bellum gerere inceperunt.
9. servus Graecus omnes res summa cum dignitate semper gerebat.
10. plurima aedificia pulcherrima in incendio recenti deleta sunt.
11. dux ex aliis militibus soli huic fidem habebat.
12. imperator potestatem legati fratri uxoris dedit.
13. hac re audita consuli permissum est ut in provinciam duas legiones mitteret.
14. imperator se in fidem et potestatem populi permisit.
15. consul laetus erat quod in hac re nemo adversus ibat.
16. poeta miserrimus in exilio aut legebat aut scribebat.
17. quo audito Verres tam incensus est ut Diodorum ad se vocaret ac argentum posceret.
18. Caesar oppidum in proelio captum retinere non potuit.
19. Romani omni ope atque operā oppidum obsidere conati sunt.
20. amica misera deos superos in caelo ridentes oravit et rogavit.
21. puer cognoscere volebat quae essent rationes belli gerendi.
22. postquam ultimus rex Roma expulsus est, praetor iussit inscribi in omnia aedificia publica litteras SPQR - senatores populusque Romanus.
23. quibus rebus auditis Caesar cohortes in hiberna mittere constituit.
24. Crassus pontem ad alteram ripam fluminis ante hiemem facere constituit.
25. Caesar ad occupandum oppidum praesidium misit.
26. praetor sperabat iudicem veterem optime se gesturum esse.
27. Caesar legionem in fines gentium inimicarum misit.
28. imperator magnam laudem ob virtutem quam in proelio ostenderat tandem adeptus est.
29. Iulius Caesar cibum plebi Romanae saepe praebebat ut gloriam adipisceretur.
30. dux telis hostium sine ullo metu semper se praebuit.
31. eo tempore Romae nemo Crassum divitiis superavit.
32. uterque parens filio opem attulit.
33. Pompeius cives qui eo tempore Romae aderant ad bellum contra Caesarem incitavit.
34. postquam sacerdos caedem fecit multum sanguinis in aram fusum est.
35. dux curavit ut omnes pedites pila optima haberent.
36. dux quod militum virtuti non satis confisus est oppidum eo tempore oppugnare non ausus est.
37. imperator familiae servorum parvam fidem habebat.
38. Caesar virtuti militum suorum semper fidebat.
39. meā sententiā hoc aedificium pulcherrimum est.
40. senex vitā quam Romae agebat defessus,  ruri vivere constituit.
41. Agrippina, filia Germanici, maxime idonea videbatur.
42. praetor in senatu remansit quoad senatus dimissus est.
43. Caesar castra fossā latā quam celerrime munire constituit.
44. senex silentium ruris quam tumultum urbis malebat.
45. sententiā omnium dissimilis est militum causa et tua.
46. cives Romani, de morbo imperatoris certiores facti, undique ad templa concurrerunt.

47. dux milites qui in prima <u>acie</u> positi erant optimis armis <u>ornari</u> iussit.
48. hoc fieri et <u>oportet</u> et <u>opus est</u>.
49. hi milites <u>spreverunt</u> senatores qui in tali otio vitam totam agebant.
50. quo responso accepto dux magnopere motus est.
51. imperator agricolis <u>restituere</u> constituit hortos quos milites ceperant.
52. dux <u>exemplum</u> litterarum ad <u>legatum</u> misit ut eum certiorem de impetu hostium faceret.
53. bellum gerimus etiam in Italia, <u>sede</u> nostra.
54. facto non consulto in tali periculo opus est.
55. Caesar et pedites et equites post proelium ob virtutem <u>palam</u> laudavit.
56. praetor in Sicilia frumentum emendum et ad urbem mittendum <u>curavit</u>.
57. Romani post proelium saevum tandem urbe <u>potiti sunt</u>.
58. mercator multum temporis dormiendo in horto perdidit.
59. poeta <u>multitudinem</u> litterarum quas acceperat in incendio perdidit.
60. dux arma similia dedit duobus militibus ut in <u>certamine</u> <u>pares</u> essent.
61. optimi milites in <u>latere</u> <u>sinistro</u> positi sunt quo facilius hostes repellerentur.
62. hi milites fortissimi pugnare quam fugere maluerunt.
63. hic vir qui Romae <u>natus est paulo</u> sapientior quam ille qui ruri vitam egit..
64. dux fortis gladio <u>cinctus</u> in proelium aciem ducit.
65. nonnulli cives apud consulem <u>iniurias</u> gravissimas quas acceperant <u>querebantur</u>.
66. hic senator maria montesque palam civibus <u>pollicebatur</u> sed paucissimi ei credebant.
67. nonnulli dicunt <u>initium</u> sapientiae timorem domini esse.
68. dux milites suos multis vulneribus in proelio <u>exceptis</u> se recipere <u>vetavit</u>.
69. incolae qui erant socii Romanorum Poenos montes transire non <u>siverunt</u>.
70. signo dato milites in hostes <u>adhuc</u> dormientes plurima pila iecerunt.
71. soror imperatoris <u>sono</u> simili qui sub <u>tecto</u> villae <u>ortus</u> erat e somno <u>bis</u> excitata est.
72. uxor servos perterritos ab ira imperatoris <u>tegere</u> conata est.
73. talia <u>ne</u> tibi <u>quidem</u> agere licet.
74. haec gens <u>civitatem</u> Romanam tandem adepta est.
75. hunc virum non esse <u>liberum</u> puto.
76. poeta post mortem uxoris carae multum laborem et operam in his litteris consumpsit.
77. non operae est legere hunc librum.
78. equus miser onere gravi adeo opprimebatur ut non iam montem ascendere posset .
79. quamquam res <u>angustae</u> essent, senatores <u>officia</u> <u>rei publicae</u> <u>perficere</u> conabantur.
80. <u>condemnatus</u> iniuriarum gravissimarum senator in <u>exilium</u> abire coactus est.
81. mulier laeta hoc aurum parvi <u>pretii</u> emit.
82. sacerdos <u>tacitus</u> dum prope aram stat sonum magnum audivit.
83. dux multos <u>obsides</u> in proelio captos accepit.
84. eques vulneratus ex equo <u>lapsus est</u> et paulo post mortuus est.
85. nuntio de clade accepto dux litteras per omnes <u>provincias</u> dimisit.
86. inimicus quidam famam praetoris apud cives palam <u>laesit</u>.
87. hostes fugā salutem petere <u>contenderunt</u>.
88. post <u>exitium</u> urbis plurimi cives effugerunt ad mare.
89. <u>opus</u> poetae notissimi in manibus meis iam habeo.
90. mercator se socio opem allaturum esse promisit.
91. eo tempore multi cives notissimi in exilium missi sunt et pauci redierunt.
92. iudex saevus servum miserum capitis condemnavit.
93. hostes haec omnia flammā ac <u>ferro</u> deleverunt.
94. opera huius poetae bene adhuc non <u>novi</u>.
95. eo postquam Caesar pervenit, obsides armaque poposcit.
96. miles pilum magnum <u>dextrā</u> et scutum leve <u>sinistrā</u> tenebat.
97. Caesar virum fortissimum in exercitu <u>praefecit</u>

98. mercator domo incendio <u>omnino</u> deleta opem ab socio petivit.

99. consul apud senatores <u>recitavit</u> nomina eorum qui naves hostibus <u>prodiderant</u>.

100. duabus <u>aquilis</u> in proelio cum Germanis amissis, dux Romanus manus sibi <u>intulit</u>.

101. dux <u>negavit</u> se obsidibus in proelio recenti captis <u>parsurum</u> esse.

102. milites perterriti mortem fugā <u>vitaverunt</u>.

103. cum mihi diutius abesse non <u>placeret</u>, redire Romam quam primum constitui.

104. <u>ergo</u> pater monuit filium ut sapientiam <u>coleret</u>.

105. post cladem recentem Caesar <u>numerum</u> legatorum <u>augere</u> constituit.

106. hae gentes foedere diu <u>iungebantur</u>.

107. <u>quotiens</u> Romam is?

108. ne hic vir malus quidem tale facinus perficere potuit.

109. natura <u>pudorque</u> me <u>impedivit</u> talia verba dicere.

110. hoc tempus <u>opportunum</u> ad pugnam non est.

111. hic dux qui tantas victorias adeptus est summa laude <u>dignus</u> est.

112. quotiens Romam advenerat, ingens turba ad eum spectandum contendebat.

113. princeps, clamoribus <u>precantium</u> e somno excitatus, erat iratisssimus.

114. etiam hostes, qui cum Romanis eo tempore bellum gerebant, pugnare <u>desierunt</u>.

115. eo equites defessi tandem pervenerunt.

116. pater et filius ad templum <u>una</u> pervenerunt.

117. ubi arma esse sciam, <u>huc</u> veniam.

118. sic inde huc omnes cucurrerunt.

119. dux milites suos extra moenia oppidi instruxit.

120. hic vir magnum odium <u>erga</u> inimicum multos per annos habebat.

121. filius meus Romam, <u>seu</u> vult <u>seu</u> non vult, cras ibit.

122. <u>sive</u> amicus litteras scribit <u>sive</u> non scribit, puella misera erit.

123. ille eques sex dierum spatio provinciam transcurrit.

124. equitibus extra moenia oppidi manentibus dux in aciem pedites instruxit.

125. inimici in <u>certamine</u> saevo pugnaverunt.

126. ante proelium timor mentes peditum occupavit.

127. agricola defessus tanto labore prope arborem magnam se iecit.

128. post proelium minima pars exercitus <u>superfuit</u>.

129. dux aciem hostium lente procedere <u>cernebat</u>.

130. consul <u>prioris</u> anni in provinciam iam discessit

131. rex paulo ante advenerat.

132. acies hostium <u>adversus</u> castra nostra instructa est.

133. rebus undique arcessitis dux milites castra ponere iussit.

134. dux duobus tribus<u>ve</u> horis redibit.

135. servus bene non laborat, <u>praeterea</u> stultus est.

136. imperator, victor trium simul bellorum, ab omnibus laudabatur.

137. in omni sede ac loco ferrum <u>flammamque</u> timemus.

138. necesse erat in loco angusto ac <u>iniquo</u> <u>usque</u> ad noctem pugnare.

139. hic senatus apud nonnullos cives auro <u>insignis</u> erat.

140. <u>interim</u> iuvenis dum stat ante templum repente <u>amicam</u> conspexit.

141. Cicero <u>operam</u> maximam <u>dabat</u> ut rem publicam servaret.

142. poeta suis laboribus dignitatem salutemque <u>peperit</u>.

143. <u>centurio</u> duobus diebus omne opus <u>effecit</u>.

144. ante primam lucem pedites iter iam effecerunt.

145. acie instructa dux milites impetum in hostes facere iussit.

146. servi Romani in <u>potestate</u> tota dominorum erant.

147. dux haud dubius erat quin victor futurus esset.

148. hoc tacitus praeterire non possum.

149. suo quisque studio maxime ducitur.

150. neque mens neque vox iuvenis perterriti apud senes diu constitit.

151. vir vel studiorum vel officorum vel vero etiam negotiorum iam peritus factus est.

152. cives mox intellegebant quis tot scelera committeret.

153. nonnulli credebant se sub nomine Neronis scelera similia committere posse.

154. hunc librum legisti? ita vero.

155. centurio se paratum ad proelium esse negavit.

156. 'odi' inquit Hannibal 'odioque sum Romanis'.

157. pedites paulo minus quinque milia passuum processerunt.

158. Cicero praetorum auxilio semel usus est.

159. imperator Romanus Hannibalem in proelio vix vicit.

160. Hannibal duci Romano non iam odio erat.

161. imperator et domi et in provinciis aequus erat.

162. quisquis es, quicquid tibi nomen est, Graecus esse videris.

163. quoquo modo res se habent, postridie mane Romam discedam.

164. brevi tempore Agrippina cum imperatore habitabat sicut uxor.

165. multi credebant cladem diram civitati incasuram esse.

166. nemo aut nobilioris generis aut melioris ingenii erat quam Agrippina.

167. deinde Nero turbam militum sibi iunxit.

168. Nero hortatus est milites ut gladiis contra cives uterentur.

169. tandem urbs tanta vi oppressa est ut nemo esset qui non de vita desperaret.

170. Cicero senatum consuluit quid fieri vellet de re publica.

171. brevi tempore iniuriae adversus nonnullos viros insignes augebantur.

172. acerrimae et fortissimae sententiae a quibusdam senatoribus dictae sunt.

173. res publica maximis periculis mox liberabitur.

174. agricola ita defessus erat ut agros colere omnino neglegeret.

175. Nero dum nocte per vias Romae errabat servi vestem gerebat ne cognosceretur.

176. imperator hic comitibus imperavit ut aggrederentur omnes qui resisterent.

177. Cicero dicebat se pro bono publico semper agere.

178. Cicero socio pro suo summo beneficio gratias egit.

179. milites in hibernis ob frigus grave diu manere nolebant.

180. Cicero causa salutis publicae semper se agebat.

181. milites usque ad vesperum celeriter processerunt.

182. ad urbem intra tres dies perveniemus.

183. tibi licet omnes libros legere.

184. dux culpam cladis in legatum posuit.

185. miles gladium in dextra strictum tenebat.

186. eo tempore nonnulli cives libertatem perdere dixerunt.

187. plurimi cives fidem erga imperatorem conservaverunt.

188. his equitibus data est potestas augendae dignitatis.

190. regibus expulsis populus consulibus rempublicam permisit.

191. milites dicebant ducem omnes virtutes corporis animique habere.

192. bello confecto hic mercator de negotiis consuli solebat.

193. erat acies tredecim aquilis constituta.

194. poeta miser dixit se patriam et libertatem perdidisse.

195. legatus id querebatur caput esse exitiorum omnium.

196. tempestate gravi subito orta hostes se recepere constituerunt.

197. Hannibal tot milia militum Romanorum occiderat ut Romani timerent ne urbs ipsa caperetur.

198. illo die quo mortuus est arae deorum deletae sunt.

199. quo audito ingens turba civium ad imperatorem spectandum contendit.

200. consul in senatum ingressus senatores hortatus est bellum statim gerendum esse

## A

| | |
|---|---|
| acer acris acre | keen, sharp, fierce |
| acies aciei 5 f | line, battle line, army |
| addo -ere addidi additum 3 | add, join |
| adhuc | till now, still |
| adimo -ere ademi ademptum 3 | take away, remove |
| adipiscor -i adeptus sum 3 | obtain |
| *aditus aditus m 4 | entrance |
| adiuvo adiuvare adiuvi adiutum 1 | help |
| adulescens adulescentis 3 c | youth |
| adversus +acc. | against, up(hill) |
| adversus | against, opposite |
| aedificium -i 2 n | building |
| aequus -a -um | equal, fair, favourable, calm |
| *affero afferre attuli allatum | carry, bring to |
| aggredior -i aggressus 4 | attack, approach |
| agmen agminis 3 n | column of men, army |
| aliquis aliquid | someone / thing, anyone / thing |
| *altum -i 2 n | the deep (sea) |
| amica -ae 1 | girl-friend |
| amitto -ere amisi amissum 3 | lose |
| an | or |
| *ancora -ae 1 f | anchor |
| angustus -a -um | narrow, confined |
| animadverto -ere -verti -versum 3 | notice, observe |
| antequam | before |
| *antrum -i 2 n | cave |
| *appello -ere appuli appulsum 3 | drive, bring to |
| aperio -ire aperui apertum 4 | open, reveal, disclose |
| aquila -ae 1 | eagle, standard |
| ara -ae 1 | altar |
| arbor arboris 3 f | tree |
| arcesso -ere -ivi -itum 3 | summon, send for |
| argentum -i 2 n | silver, money |
| at | but |
| attonitus -a -um | astonished, thunder-struck |
| augeo -ere auxi auctum 2 | increase, exaggerate |
| **aura -ae 1 f | air, wind |
| aut | or, either |

## B

| | |
|---|---|
| *baculum -i 2 n | wand |
| beneficium -i 2 n | kindness, favour, service |
| bis | twice |
| bona -orum 2 n | goods |

## C

| | |
|---|---|
| *caecus -a -um | blind |
| caedes caedis 3 f | slaughter, killing, murder |
| campus -i 2 m | plain, field |
| cano -ere cecini cantum 3 | sing, sound play (of trumpets etc) |
| **carcer carceris 3 m | prison |
| carmen carminis 3 n | song |

| | |
|---|---|
| carus -a -um | dear |
| causa -ae 1 f | cause, reason, case; +gen. for the sake of |
| caveo -ere cavi cautum 2 | beware (of), take care |
| cedo -ere cessi cessum 3 | yield, give up; (in compounds) go |
| centurio centurionis 3 m | centurion |
| cerno -ere crevi cretum 3 | see, perceive, decree |
| certamen certaminis 3 n | contest, battle, struggle |
| certiorem facio | Inform |
| certus -a -um | certain, sure, fixed |
| cingo -ere cinxi cinctum 3 | surround |
| circumspicio -ere conspexi conspectum 3½ | look around |
| civitas civitatis 3 f | citizenship, state, city, tribe |
| clades -is 3 f | disaster, loss, defeat |
| clam | secretly |
| cohors cohortis 3 f | cohort, company |
| colo -ere colui cultum 3 | cultivate, worship, honour |
| committo -ere -misi -missum 3 | commit, fight, begin (battle) |
| *commoveo -ere -movi -motum 2 | move entirely |
| comparo -are 1 | prepare, provide, obtain, compare |
| condemno -are 1 | convict, condemn |
| condo -ere -didi -ditum 3 | found, establish, hide |
| confero -ferre -tuli -latum | collect, compare, contribute, bestow |
| confido -ere confisus sum +dat. | trust, believe, have confidence |
| *coniungo -ere -iunxi -iunctum 3 | bind together |
| consisto -ere constiti constitum 3 | halt, stand, stand firm |
| consulo -ere consului consultum 3 | consult, consider, advise |
| contendo -ere contendi contentum 3 | hurry, march, contend, fight |
| *converto -ere -verti -versum 3 | turn around |
| *copia -ae 1 f | abundance |
| corripio -ere corripui correptum 3 | seize, carry off |
| cotidie | every day, daily |
| crimen criminis 3 n | accusation, charge, crime |
| culpa -ae 1 f | fault blame |
| cunctus -a -um | all, whole |
| cupidus -a -um +gen. | eager (for), greedy |
| curo -are 1 | care for, cure (+gerundive = get s.th. done) |
| *cursus -us 4 m | course |

## D

| | |
|---|---|
| debitus -a -um | owed |
| decipio -ere decepi deceptum 3 | deceive |
| defessus -a -um | tired |
| denique | at last, finally, in short |
| *depello -ere -puli -pulsum 3 | drive away |
| *depono -ere deposui depositum 3 | lay down |
| desino -ere desivi desitum 3 | cease |
| despero -are 1 | despair |
| dexter -ra -rum | right, on the right, right hand |
| dextra -ae 1 f | right hand, right side |
| dignitas dignitatis 3 f | dignity |

| | | | |
|---|---|---|---|
| dignus -a -um +*abl.* | worthy (of), deserving (of) | frumentum -i 2 n | corn, grain |
| diligens -tis | careful, diligent | fuga -ae 1 f | flight, escape |
| dimitto -ere dimisi dimissum 3 | dismiss, scatter | fundo -ere fudi fusum 3 | pour, shed, rout |
| disco -ere didici 3 | learn | furor -is 3 m | rage, fury, passion, madness |
| disiicio -ere -ieci -iectum 3½ | cast asunder | | |
| dissimilis -e | different | **G** | |
| dives divitis | rich | | |
| divitiae divitiarum 1 f pl. | riches, wealth | genus generis 3 n | race, descent, birth, kind |
| divido -ere divisi divisum 3 | divide, separate | *gigas gigantis 3 m | giant |
| doleo -ere dolui 2 | hurt, be in pain, lament | gratia -ae 1 f | favour, thanks, esteem |
| dolor -is 3 m | pain, sorrow, anger | gratias ago -ere egi | thank, give thanks |
| dolus -i 2 m | trick, fraud | graviter | seriously |
| dubito -are 1 | doubt, hesitate | | |
| dubius -a –um | doubtful, wavering | **H** | |
| durus -a -um | hard, harsh, rough | | |
| | | haud | not |
| **E** | | *herba -ae 1 f | grass |
| | | hiberna hibernorum 2 n pl | winter quarters |
| *ebrius -a -um | drunk | hiems hiemis 3 f | winter, storm |
| efficio -ere effeci effectum 3 | carry out, accomplish | hinc | from here, hence, henceforth |
| egeo -ere egui + *gen. or abl.* | need, be in want of, lack | honor honoris 3 m | honour, esteem, glory |
| emitto -ere emisi emissum 3 | send out | hospes hospitis 3 m | guest, host |
| eo | thither | huc | here, to this place |
| eques equitis 3 m | knight, horseman, *pl.* cavalry | *humanus -a -um | human |
| erga +*acc.* | towards | humus -i 2 f | ground, earth |
| ergo | therefore | | |
| erro -are 1 | wander | **I** | |
| etsi | although | | |
| **evanesco -ere evanui 3 | vanish | idoneus -a -um | suitable, convenient |
| *evenio -ire eveni | come out, happen | ignis ignis 3 m | fire |
| excipio -ere excepi exceptum 3 | receive, take, welcome | ignoro -are 1 | do not know, be ignorant, |
| excito -are 1 | wake, rouse, excite | | misunderstand |
| *excogito -are 1 | devise | *impello -ere -puli -pulsum 3 | strike; push forward |
| exemplum -i 2 n | example, precedent | illic | there |
| exilium -i 2 n | exile | impedio -ire impedivi impeditum 4 | delay, hinder, prevent |
| exitium -i 2 n | ruin, destruction | impetus impetus 4 m | attack |
| extra +*acc.* | outside, beyond | incendium -i 2 n | fire |
| | | incipio -ere incepi inceptum 3½ | begin |
| **F** | | incito -are 1 | urge on, arouse, encourage |
| | | inde | from there, thereupon, next |
| facinus facinoris 3 n | crime, outrage, deed | infero inferre intuli illatum | inflict, bring to, cause, carry |
| fallo -ere fefelli falsum 3 | deceive, cheat, escape one's notice | | against |
| fama -ae 1 f | rumour, fame, glory | infra +*acc.* | below |
| familia -ae 1 f | family, household | ingenium -i 2 n | character, ability |
| feliciter | happily, favourably | inimicus -i 2m | (personal) enemy |
| fere | nearly, about | iniquus -a –um | unfair, unjust, unfavourable |
| ferrum -i 2 n | iron, sword | initium -i 2 n | beginning |
| fides fidei 5 f | trust,faith, confidence, loyalty | iniuria -ae 1 | injustice, injury, wrong |
| fido -ere fisus sum 3 | trust, rely upon | inopia -ae 1 f | shortage, lack, poverty |
| finis finis 3 m | end, boundary, *pl.* territory | inquam inquit inquiunt | say |
| fio fieri factum | become, be made, happen | insidiae insidiarum 1 f | ambush, trap, trick |
| flamma -ae 1 f | blaze, flame, passion | insignis -e | distinguished, glorious |
| fodio -ere fodi fossum 3½ | dig | inspicio -ere inspexi inspectum 3 | look at, inspect, examine |
| foedus foederis 3 n | treaty, agreement | instruo -ere instruxi instructum 3 | draw up, prepare, equip, supply |
| fortasse | perhaps | *interim | meanwhile |
| fortuna -ae 1 f | fate, luck, fortune (good or bad) | interior | inner |
| fossa -ae 1 f | ditch, trench | intermitto -ere -misi -missum 3 | place between |
| frango -ere fregi fractum 3 | break, crush | intra +*acc.* | between, among, inside, within |
| frigus frogoris 3n | cold | invitus -a -um | unwilling, reluctant |

| | | | |
|---|---|---|---|
| ita vero | yes | nascor -i natus 3 | am born |
| iudex iudicis 3 m & f | judge, juror | natura -ae 1 f | nature |
| iungo -ere iunxi iunctum 3 | join, unite, fasten | necesse | necessary |
| iustus -a -um | right, just lawful, complete | negligo -ere neglexi neglectum 3 | neglect, disregard |
| iuvo -are iuvi iutum 1 | help | nego -are 1 | say no, deny, refuse, say that ... not |

**L**

| | | | |
|---|---|---|---|
| | | negotium -i 2 n | business |
| | | nobilis -e | noble, famous |
| labor | work, toil, trouble | noceo -ere nocui +dat. 2 | hurt, harm |
| *lac lactis 3 n | milk | nondum | not yet |
| lacrima -ae 1 f | tear | novi | know |
| laedo -ere laesi laesum 3 | hurt, injure, harm | numerus -i 2 m | number |
| latus lateris 3 n | side, wing | | |
| latus -a -um | wide | **O** | |
| laus laudis 3 f | praise | | |
| legatus -i 2 m | (legionary) commander, ambassador, envoy | ob + acc. | because of, on account of |
| | | obliviscor -i oblitus sum 3 +gen. | forget |
| levis -e | light, slight | obses obsidis 3 c | hostage |
| lex legis 3 f | law | obsideo -ere obsedi obsessum 2 | besiege, blockade |
| libens libentis | willing, glad | obviam eo +dat. | meet, go to meet, oppose, resist |
| libenter | willingly, with pleasure | occasio occasionis 3 f | opportunity, occasion |
| liber -a -um | free | occupo -are 1 | seize, take possession of, occupy |
| libertas libertatis 3 f | freedom | oculus -i 2 m | eye |
| licet -ere licuit +dat. | it is allowed | odi odisse | hate v. |
| littera -ae 1 f (usually pl. with sing. meaning) | letter | odium -i 2 n | hate n. |
| | | odio est +dat. | Be hated by |
| litus litoris 3 n | sea-shore, beach | officium -i 2 n | duty, task, function |
| longe | long, a long way off | omitto -ere omisi omissum 3 | neglect, disregard, make no mention of |
| *lotus -i 2 f | lotus fruit | omnino | altogether, at all, entirely |
| **luctor -ari 1 | wrestle, struggle | onus oneris 3 n | burden, load |
| | | opera -ae 1 f | work, effort, attention, trouble |
| **M** | | operam do dare dedi 1 | I take pains, give attention (to) |
| | | oportet -ere oportuit 2 | be necessary, ought, must |
| *magicus -a -um | magic | opportunus -a -um | suitable, opportune |
| mando -are 1 | commit, entrust, command | (ops) opis 3 f | help; pl. resources, riches |
| mane | in the morning, early | opus est esse fuit +abl. | there is need of |
| *matrimonium -i 2 n | marriage | opprimo -ere oppressi oppressum 3 | attack |
| mens mentis 3 f | mind | | |
| mensis mensis 3 m | month | ora orae 1 f | coast |
| metus metus 4 m | fear | oratio orationis 3 f | speech |
| minor -ari minatus 1 | threaten | ordo ordinis 3 m | rank, order, line |
| mirabilis -e | strange, wonderful | orior oriri ortus 4 | rise, start, originate |
| modo | just now, only | orno -are 1 | adorn, decorate, provide, equip |
| moenia orum 2 n | city walls, city | os oris 3 n | mouth, face |
| monstro -are 1 | show, point out, indicate, instruct | otium -i 2 n | leisure, idleness, peace |
| | | *ovis ovis 3 f | sheep |
| *monstrum -i 2 n | monster | | |
| morbus -i 2 m | sickness, disease | **P** | |
| moror -ari moratus 1 | delay | | |
| **mortalis -e | mortal | palam | openly |
| mos moris 3 m | habit, custom, (pl.) character, morals | *palus -i 2 m | stake |
| | | par paris | equal |
| mulier -is 3 f | woman | parco -ere peperci +dat. | spare |
| multitudo multitudinis 3 f | crowd, multitude | pareo -ere parui +dat. 2 | obey |
| munio -ire munivi munitum 4 | fortify, defend, guard | pario -ere peperi partum | win, acquire, gain, secure |
| munus muneris 3 n | service, duty, present | passim | in all directions, far and wide |
| muto -are 1 | change, alter | passus -us 4 m | pace |
| | | paulatim | gradually, little by little |
| **N** | | paulisper | for a short while |
| | | paulum, paulo | a little, somewhat |

| | | | |
|---|---|---|---|
| pauper pauperis | poor | quisque | each, each one, every |
| pedes peditis 3 m | infantry | quisquis quicquid | whoever, whatever |
| perdo -ere perdidi perditum 3 | destroy, lose | quoad | as long as, until |
| perficio -ere perfeci perfectum 3½ | bring about, complete, perfect | quoniam | since |
| | | quotiens | how often? as often as |
| **perflo -are 1 | blow through | | |
| peritus -a -um +*gen.* | skilled (in) | **R** | |
| permitto -ere permisi permissum 3 | hand over, entrust, permit, allow | | |
| | | ratio rationis 3 f | account, reckoning, manner, reason |
| **perscribo -ere -scripsi -scriptum 3 | relate in writing | | |
| pilum -i 2 n | javelin | recens recentis | recent, fresh |
| placet -ere placuit +*dat.* | it pleases, suits, it is resolved | recito -are 1 | recite, read aloud |
| | | rectus -a -um | straight, direct, right, proper |
| *placidus -a –um | tame | recipio -ere recepi receptum 3 | regain, receive, welcome |
| plebs plebis 3 f | the people, common people | reficio -ere refeci refectum 3 | repair, restore, refresh |
| | | reliqui -ae -a | the rest, the other |
| plerique pleraeque pleraque | most, the majority | repente | suddenly |
| *poculum -i 2 n | drinking-cup | *repono -ere reposui repositum 3 | place back |
| polliceor -eri pollicitus sum 2 | promise | res publica –ae | state, republic |
| pons pontis 3 m | bridge | responsum -i 2 n | answer |
| populus -i 2 m | people, nation | restituo -ere restitui restitutum 3 | restore, give back |
| *porcus -i 2 m | pig | retineo -ere retinui retentum 2 | hold back, restrain, keep |
| posco -ere poposci 3 | demand, ask for | ripa -ae 1 f | bank |
| postremus -a -um | last | *ruo -ere rui rutum 3 | rush |
| postulo -are 1 | demand, ask | *rupes -is 3 f | rock, cliff |
| potens potentis | powerful | rursus | back, again |
| potestas potestatis 3 f | power, authority, opportunity | rus ruris 3 n | country |
| potior -iri potitus sum +*gen. or abl.* | seize, get possession of | **S** | |
| potius | rather, more | | |
| praebeo -ere praebui praebitum 2 | provide, give, show, offer | *saccus -i 2 m | bag |
| praeda -ae 1 f | booty, plunder | sacerdos sacerdotis 3 m & f | priest, priestess |
| praeficio -ere praefeci praefectum 3½ | put in charge of | salus salutis 3 f | health, safety, greeting |
| praesidium -i 2 n | protection, garrison, fortification | sapientia -ae 1 f | wisdom |
| | | *saxum -i 2 n | rock, large stone |
| praesum +*dat.* | be in charge of | secundus -a –um | following, next, second, favourable |
| praeter +*acc.* | beyond, except, besides | | |
| praeterea | besides, moreover, in addition | sedes sedis 3 f | seat, temple, home |
| | | semel | once |
| praetor praetoris 3 m | praetor | senatus senatus 4 m | senate |
| **premo -ere pressi pressum 3 | press | sententia -ae 1 f | opinion, judgement, sentence |
| pretium -i 2 n | price, value | **sermo sermonis 3 m | talk, conversation |
| prior prioris | previous, former | sicut | just as, like, as, as if |
| prius | before, previously | silentium -i 2 n | silence |
| priusquam | before, until | similis simile | similar, like |
| procul | far away, distant | sinister -ra –rum | left, on the left, unfavourable |
| prodo -ere prodidi proditum 3 | betray, surrender | sinistra -ae 1 f | left hand, left side |
| provincia -ae 1 f | province | sino -ere sivi situm 3 | allow, permit |
| publicus -a -um | public, common | sive, seu | or if, whether |
| pudor pudoris 3 m | shame, modesty, honour, disgrace | sol solis 3 m | sun, sunlight |
| | | solum | only |
| | | solvo -ere solvi solutum (navem) 3 | set sail |
| **Q** | | somnus -i 2 m | sleep |
| | | **sonorus -a –um | sounding, sonorous |
| quasi | as if, just as, nearly | sonus -i 2 m | sound |
| queror -i questus sum 3 | complain | soror sororis 3 f | sister |
| quidem | indeed, in fact, however | *sortior -iri 4 | cast lots |
| ne ... quidem | not ... even | spatium -i 2 n | space |
| quies quietis 3 f | rest, peace, quiet | *spelunca -ae 1 f | cave |
| quisquam | anyone, anything | | |

| | |
|---|---|
| sperno -ere sprevi spretum 3 | despise, reject, scorn |
| spolium -i 2 n | booty, spoil(s) |
| statuo -ere statui statutum 3 | fix, determine, decide, arrange |
| studium -i 2 n | eagerness, study, devotion |
| *subiaceo -ere -iacui 3½ | lie under |
| sumo -ere sumpsi sumptum 3 | take, take up |
| supersum -esse -fui | be left, remain, survive |
| superus -a -um | upper, higher |
| suscipio -ere suscepi susceptum 3½ | take up, undertake, begin, bear |
| suspicor -ari 1 | mistrust, suspect |

## T

| | |
|---|---|
| tacitus -a -um | quiet, silent, in silence |
| tango -ere tetigi tactum 3 | touch |
| tantum | only |
| tectum -i 2 n | roof, house |
| tego -ere texi tectum 3 | cover, protect, hide |
| telum -i 2 n | weapon, javelin, missile |
| **tenuis -e | thin, fine |
| tego -ere texi tectum 3 | cover, protect, hide |
| tergum -i 2 n | back, rear |
| terror terroris 3 m | terror, panic |
| timor timoris 3 m | fear, anxiety |
| tumultus tumultus 4 m | uproar, disturbance, civil war |
| **turbo turbinis 3 m | whirlwind |

## U

| | |
|---|---|
| ubique | everywhere |
| ullus -a -um | any |
| ultimus -a -um | furthest, last, utmost |
| una | together |
| undique | from / on all sides |
| usque | all the way, right up to, continuously |
| usus -us 4 m | use, experience, practice |
| uter utra utrum? | which (of two)? |
| uterque utraque utrumque | each of (two), both |
| utor uti usus +abl. 3 | use, enjoy |
| *uter utris 3 m | skin bag |

## V

| | |
|---|---|
| valeo -ere valui 2 | be strong, have influence |
| **vastus -a -um | empty, desolate |
| -ve | or |
| veho -ere vexi vectum 3 | carry, bear, convey |
| vel | or, either |
| velut | just as, like, as as if |
| *venter ventris 3 m | stomach |
| vereor -eri veritus 2 | fear |
| vero | indeed, in fact, however |
| vesper -is 3 or -i 2 m | evening |
| vestis vestis 3 f | clothes |
| veto -are vetui vetitum 1 | forbid, order ... not |
| vetus veteris | old |
| victor victoris 3 m | victor, conqueror |
| *vimen -inis 3 n | osier, pliant twig |

| | |
|---|---|
| vincio -ire vinxi vinctum 4 | bind |
| vinc(u)lum -i 2 n | band, cord, noose |
| vis pl. vires 3 f | force, violence; (pl.) strength, forces |
| vito -are 1 | avoid |
| vix | hardly, scarcely, with difficulty |

# Chapter 44      Ritchie's Fabulae Latinae The Odyssey

This original version  of Fabulae Latinae contains a further two hundred words not previously met. These underlined words are to be found in the word list on page 151. This brings the total number of words met in this course to around 1,200. These more or less cover the thousand words most commonly found in Latin literature.  Assembled by computer-based methods, they represent some 68% of all Latin words. There are a few constructions in these pages that will be met in the AS and A2 syllabus, but they should not impede understanding of the story.

### 1. HOMEWARD BOUND

Urbem Troiam a Graecis decem annos obsessam esse satis <u>constat</u>; de hoc enim bello Homerus, maximus poetarum Graecorum, Iliadem opus notissimum scripsit. Troia tandem per insidias capta, Graeci longo bello fessi domum redire <u>maturaverunt</u>. Omnibus rebus igitur ad <u>profectionem</u> paratis navis deduxerunt, et tempestatem idoneam <u>nacti</u> magno cum gaudio solverunt. Erat inter primos Graecorum Ulixes quidam, vir summae virtutis ac <u>prudentiae</u>, quem dicunt nonnulli dolum <u>istum</u> <u>excogitasse</u> quo Troiam captam esse constat. Hic regnum insulae Ithacae obtinuerat, et paulo antequam cum reliquis Graecis ad bellum profectus est, puellam <u>formosissimam</u>, nomine Penelopen, in matrimonium duxerat. Nunc igitur cum iam decem annos quasi in exsilio consumpsisset, magna <u>cupiditate</u> patriae et uxoris videndae <u>ardebat</u>.

### 2. THE LOTUS-EATERS

Postquam tamen pauca milia passuum a litore Troiae progressi sunt, tanta tempestas subito coorta est ut nulla navium cursum tenere posset, sed aliae alias in partis disicerentur. Navis autem qua ipse Ulixes vehebatur vi tempestatis ad <u>meridiem</u> delata decimo die ad litus Libyae appulsa est. <u>Ancoris</u> iactis Ulixes constituit nonnullos e sociis in terram exponere, qui aquam ad navem referrent et qualis esset natura eius regionis cognoscerent. Hi igitur e navi egressi <u>imperata</u> facere parabant. Dum tamen <u>fontem</u> quaerunt, quibusdam ex incolis obviam facti ab iis <u>hospitio</u> accepti sunt. Accidit autem ut maior pars <u>victus</u> eorum hominum in <u>miro</u> quodam <u>fructu</u> quem lotum appellabant consisteret. Quam cum Graeci <u>gustassent</u>, patriae et sociorum statim obliti <u>confirmaverunt</u> se semper in ea terra mansuros, ut <u>dulci</u> illo cibo in <u>perpetuum</u> <u>vescerentur</u>.

### 3. THE RESCUE

Ulixes cum ab hora septima ad vesperum exspectasset, veritus ne socii sui in periculo <u>versarentur</u>, nonnullos e reliquis misit, ut quae causa esset morae cognoscerent. Hi igitur in terram <u>expositi</u> ad <u>vicum</u> qui non longe aberat se contulerunt; quo cum venissent, socios suos quasi vino ebrios reppererunt. Tum ubi causam veniendi docuerunt, iis persuadere conabantur ut secum ad navem redirent. Illi tamen resistere ac manu se defendere coeperunt, saepe clamitantes se numquam ex eo loco abituros. Quae cum ita essent, nuntii re infecta ad Ulixem redierunt. His rebus cognitis ipse cum omnibus qui in navi relicti erant ad locum venit; et socios suos frustra hortatus ut sua sponte redirent, manibus eorum post terga vinctis invitos ad navem reportavit. Tum ancoris sublatis quam celerrime e portu solvit.

### 4. THE ONE-EYED GIANT

Postquam ea tota nocte remis contenderunt, postridie ad terram ignotam navem appulerunt. Tum, quod naturam eius regionis ignorabat, ipse Ulixes cum duodecim e sociis in terram egressus loca explorare constituit. Paulum a litore progressi ad speluncam ingentem pervenerunt, quam habitari senserunt; eius enim introitum et natura loci et manu munitum esse animadverterunt. Mox, etsi intellegebant se non sine periculo id facturos, speluncam intraverunt; quod cum fecissent, magnam copiam lactis in vasis ingentibus conditam invenerunt. Dum tamen mirantur quis in ea sede habitaret, sonitum terribilem audiverunt, et oculis ad portam tortis monstrum horribile viderunt, humana quidem specie et figura, sed ingenti magnitudine corporis. Cum autem animadvertissent monstrum unum oculum tantum habere in media fronte positum, intellexerunt hunc esse unum e Cyclopibus, de quibus famam iam acceperant.

### 5. THE GIANT'S SUPPER

Cyclopes autem pastores erant quidam qui insulam Siciliam et praecipue montem Aetnam incolebant; ibi enim Volcanus, praeses fabrorum et ignis repertor, cuius servi Cyclopes erant, officinam suam habebat. Graeci igitur simul ac monstrum viderunt, terrore paene exanimati in interiorem partem speluncae refugerunt et se ibi abdere conabantur. Polyphemus autem (sic enim Cyclops appellabatur) pecus suum in speluncam compulit; deinde, cum saxo ingenti portam obstruxisset, ignem in media spelunca fecit. Hoc facto, oculo omnia perlustrabat, et cum sensisset homines in interiore parte speluncae esse abditos, magna voce exclamavit: "Qui homines estis? Mercatores an latrones?" Tum Ulixes respondit se neque mercatores esse neque praedandi causa venisse; sed a Troia redeuntis vi tempestatum a recto cursu depulsos esse. Oravit etiam ut sibi sine iniuria abire liceret. Tum Polyphemus quaesivit ubi esset navis qua vecti essent; sed Ulixes cum sibi maxime praecavendum esse bene intellegeret, respondit navem suam in rupis coniectam omnino fractam esse. Polyphemus autem nullo responso dato duo e sociis manu corripuit, et membris eorum divulsis carnem devorare coepit.

### 6. A DESPERATE SITUATION

Dum haec geruntur, Graecorum animos tantus terror occupavit ut ne vocem quidem edere possent, sed omni spe salutis deposita mortem praesentem exspectarent.

Polyphemus, postquam <u>fames</u> hac tam horribili cena depulsa est, humi <u>prostratus</u> somno se dedit. Quod cum vidisset Ulixes, tantam occasionem rei gerendae non omittendam <u>arbitratus</u>, in eo erat ut <u>pectus</u> monstri gladio <u>transfigeret</u>. Cum tamen nihil <u>temere</u> agendum existimaret, constituit explorare, antequam hoc faceret, qua ratione ex spelunca <u>evadere</u> possent. At cum saxum animadvertisset quo introitus obstructus erat, nihil sibi <u>profuturum</u> intellexit si Polyphemum interfecisset. Tanta enim erat eius saxi magnitudo ut ne a decem quidem hominibus <u>amoveri</u> posset. Quae cum ita essent, Ulixes hoc <u>conatu</u> <u>destitit</u> et ad socios rediit; qui cum intellexissent quo in loco res essent, nulla spe salutis oblata de fortunis suis desperare coeperunt. Ille tamen ne animos <u>demitterent</u> vehementer hortatus est; <u>demonstravit</u> se iam antea e multis et magnis periculis evasisse, neque dubium esse quin in tanto <u>discrimine</u> di auxilium laturi essent.

## 7. A PLAN FOR VENGEANCE

Orta luce Polyphemus iam e somno excitatus idem quod <u>hesterno</u> die fecit; correptis enim duobus e reliquis viris carnem eorum sine mora devoravit. Tum, cum saxum amovisset, ipse cum pecore suo ex spelunca progressus est; quod cum Graeci viderent, magnam in spem se post paulum evasuros venerunt. Mox tamen ab hac spe repulsi sunt; nam Polyphemus, postquam omnes oves exierunt, saxum in locum restituit. Reliqui omni spe salutis deposita <u>lamentis</u> lacrimisque se dediderunt; Ulixes vero, qui, ut <u>supra</u> demonstravimus, vir magni fuit consilii, etsi intellegebat rem in discrimine esse, <u>nondum</u> omnino desperabat. Tandem, postquam diu haec toto animo cogitavit, hoc consilium cepit. E <u>lignis</u> quae in spelunca reposita erant palum magnum <u>delegit</u>. Hunc summa cum <u>diligentia</u> <u>praeacutum</u> fecit; tum, postquam sociis quid fieri vellet ostendit, <u>reditum</u> Polyphemi exspectabat.

## 8. A GLASS TOO MUCH

Sub vesperum Polyphemus ad speluncam rediit, et eodem modo quo antea cenavit. Tum Ulixes utrem vini <u>prompsit</u>, quem forte (id quod ei erat saluti) secum attulerat; et postquam magnum poculum vino <u>complevit</u>, monstrum ad bibendum <u>provocavit</u>. Polyphemus, qui numquam antea vinum gustaverat, totum poculum statim <u>exhausit</u>; quod cum fecisset, tantam <u>voluptatem</u> <u>percepit</u> ut iterum et tertium poculum <u>repleri</u> iusserit. Tum, cum quaesivisset quo nomine Ulixes appellaretur, ille respondit se Neminem appellari; quod cum audivisset, Polyphemus ita locutus est: "Hanc, tibi gratiam pro tanto beneficio referam; te postremum omnium devorabo." Hoc cum dixisset, cibo vinoque gravis <u>recubuit</u> et brevi tempore somno oppressus est. Tum Ulixes sociis convocatis, "Habemus," inquit, "quam petiimus facultatem; ne igitur tantam occasionem rei gerendae omittamus."

## 9. THE BLINDING OF POLYPHEMUS

Hac oratione habita, postquam extremum palum igni calefecit, oculum Polyphemi dormientis ferventi ligno perfodit; quo facto omnes in diversas speluncae partis se abdiderunt. At ille subito illo dolore oculi e somno excitatus clamorem terribilem sustulit, et dum per speluncam errat, Ulixem manu prehendere conabatur; cum tamen iam omnino caecus esset, nullo modo hoc efficere potuit. Interea reliqui Cyclopes clamore audito undique ad speluncam convenerunt, et ad introitum adstantes quid Polyphemus ageret quaesiverunt, et quam ob causam tantum clamorem sustulisset. Ille respondit se graviter vulneratum esse et magno dolore adfici. Cum tamen postea quaesivissent quis ei vim intulisset, respondit ille Neminem id fecisse; quibus rebus auditis unus e Cyclopibus: "At si nemo," inquit, "te vulneravit, haud dubium est quin consilio deorum, quibus resistere nec possumus nec volumus, hoc supplicio adficiaris." Hoc cum dixisset, abierunt Cyclopes eum in insaniam incidisse arbitrati.

## 10. THE ESCAPE

Polyphemus ubi socios suos abiisse sensit, furore atque amentia impulsus Ulixem iterum quaerere coepit; tandem cum portam invenisset, saxum quo obstructa erat amovit, ut pecus in agros exiret. Tum ipse in introitu consedit, et ut quaeque ovis ad hunc locum venerat, eius tergum manibus tractabat, ne viri inter ovis exire possent. Quod cum animadvertisset Ulixes, intellexit omnem spem salutis in dolo magis quam in virtute poni. Itaque hoc consilium iniit. Primum tris quas vidit pinguissimas ex ovibus delegit, quas cum inter se viminibus coniunxisset, unum ex sociis suis ventribus earum ita subiecit ut omnino lateret; deinde ovis hominem secum ferentis ad portam egit. Id accidit quod fore suspicatus erat. Polyphemus enim postquam terga ovium manibus tractavit, eas praeterire passus est. Ulixes ubi rem tam feliciter evenisse vidit, omnis socios suos ex ordine eodem modo emisit; quo facto ipse novissimus evasit.

## 11. OUT OF DANGER

Iis rebus ita confectis, Ulixes veritus ne Polyphemus fraudem sentiret, cum sociis quam celerrime ad litus contendit; quo cum venissent, ab iis qui navi praesidio relicti erant magna cum laetitia excepti sunt. Hi enim cum anxiis animis iam tris dies continuos reditum eorum exspectavissent, eos in aliquod periculum magnum incidisse (id quidem quod erat) suspicati, ipsi auxiliandi causa egredi parabant. Tum Ulixes non satis tutum arbitratus in eo loco manere, quam celerrime profisisci constituit. Iussit igitur omnis navem conscendere, et ancoris sublatis paulum a litore in altum provectus est. Tum magna voce exclamavit: "Tu, Polypheme, qui iura hospiti spernis, iustam et debitam poenam immanitatis tuae solvisti." Hac voce audita Polyphemus ira vehementer commotus ad mare se contulit, et ubi navem paulum a litore remotam esse intellexit, saxum ingens manu correptum in eam partem coniecit unde vocem venire sensit. Graeci autem, etsi non multum afuit quin <u>submergerentur</u>, nullo <u>damno</u> accepto cursum tenuerunt.

## 12. THE COUNTRY OF THE WINDS

Pauca milia passuum ab eo loco progressus Ulixes ad insulam Aeoliam navem appulit. Haec patria erat ventorum, "Hic vasto rex Aeolus antro luctantis ventos tempestatesque sonoras imperio premit ac vinclis et carcere frenat." *(Virgil Aenid Book I Lines 51-3)*

 Ibi rex ipse Graecos hospitio excepit, atque iis persuasit ut ad recuperandas viris paucos dies in ea regione <u>commorarentur</u>. Septimo die cum socii e laboribus se recepissent, Ulixes, ne anni tempore a <u>navigatione</u> <u>excluderetur</u>, sibi sine mora proficiscendum statuit. Tum Aeolus, qui sciebat Ulixem cupidissimum esse patriae videndae, ei iam profecturo magnum saccum e <u>corio</u> confectum dedit, in quo ventos omnis praeter unum <u>incluserat</u>. Zephyrum tantum solverat, quod ille ventus ab insula Aeolia ad Ithacam naviganti est secundus. Ulixes hoc donum libenter accepit, et gratiis pro tanto beneficio actis saccum ad <u>malum</u> <u>adligavit</u>. Tum omnibus rebus ad profectionem paratis meridiano fere tempore e portu solvit.

## 13. THE WIND-BAG

Novem dies secundissimo vento cursum tenuerunt, iamque in <u>conspectum</u> patriae suae venerant, cum Ulixes <u>lassitudine</u> confectus (ipse enim <u>gubernabat</u>) ad quietem capiendam recubuit. At socii, qui iam dudum mirabantur quid in illo sacco inclusum esset, cum ducem somno oppressum viderent, tantam occasionem non omittendam arbitrati sunt; credebant enim aurum et argentum ibi esse celata. Itaque spe lucri adducti saccum sine mora solverunt, quo facto venti "velut agmine facto qua data porta ruunt, et terras turbine perflant." *(Virgil Aenid Book I Lines 82-83)*

Hic tanta tempestas subito <u>coorta</u> est ut illi cursum tenere non possent sed in eandem partem unde erant profecti <u>referrentur</u>. Ulixes e somno excitatus quo in loco res esset statim intellexit; saccum solutum, Ithacam post tergum relictam vidit. Tum vero ira vehementer <u>exarsit</u> sociosque <u>obiurgabat</u> quod cupiditate pecuniae adducti spem patriae videndae <u>proiecissent</u>.

## 14. A DRAWING OF LOTS

Brevi spatio intermisso Graeci insulae cuidam appropinquaverunt in qua Circe, filia Solis, habitabat. Quo cum navem appulisset, Ulixes in terram frumentandi causa egrediendum esse statuit; nam cognoverat frumentum quod in navi haberent iam <u>deficere</u>. Sociis igitur ad se convocatis quo in loco res esset et quid fieri vellet ostendit. Cum tamen omnes memoria tenerent quam crudeli morte necati essent ii qui <u>nuper</u> e navi egressi essent, nemo <u>repertus</u> est qui hoc negotium suscipere vellet. Quae cum ita essent, res ad controversiam deducta est. Tandem Ulixes <u>consensu</u> omnium socios in duas partis divisit, quarum alteri Eurylochus, vir summae virtutis, alteri ipse praeesse. Tum hi inter se <u>sortiti</u> sunt uter in terram egrederetur. Hoc facto, Eurylocho <u>sorte</u> evenit ut cum duobus et viginti sociis rem susciperet.

### 15. THE HOUSE OF THE ENCHANTRESS

His rebus ita constitutis ii qui sortiti erant in interiorem partem insulae profecti sunt. Tantus tamen timor animos eorum occupaverat ut nihil dubitarent quin morti obviam irent. Vix quidem poterant ii qui in navi relicti erant lacrimas tenere; credebant enim se socios suos numquam post hoc tempus visuros. Illi autem <u>aliquantum</u> itineris progressi ad villam quandam pervenerunt summa <u>magnificentia</u> aedificatam, cuius ad <u>ostium</u> cum adiissent, <u>cantum</u> dulcissimum audiverunt. Tanta autem fuit eius vocis <u>dulcedo</u> ut nullo modo retineri possent quin ianuam <u>pulsarent</u>. Hoc facto ipsa Circe <u>foras</u> exiit, et summa cum <u>benignitate</u> omnis in hospitium invitavit. Eurylochus insidias sibi comparari suspicatus <u>foris</u> exspectare constituit, sed reliqui rei <u>novitate</u> <u>adducti</u> intraverunt. Cenam magnificam omnibus rebus instructam invenerunt et <u>iussu</u> dominae libentissime <u>accubuerunt</u>. At Circe vinum quod servi <u>apposuerunt</u> <u>medicamento</u> quodam <u>miscuerat</u>; quod cum Graeci bibissent, gravi somno subito oppressi sunt.

### 16. THE CHARM

Tum Circe, quae artis <u>magicae</u> summam <u>scientiam</u> habebat, baculo aureo quod gerebat capita eorum tetigit; quo facto omnes in porcos subito <u>conversi</u> sunt. Interea Eurylochus <u>ignarus</u> quid in aedibus ageretur ad ostium sedebat; postquam tamen ad solis <u>occasum</u> anxio animo et <u>sollicito</u> exspectavit, solus ad navem regredi constituit. Eo cum venisset, <u>sollicitudine</u> ac timore tam <u>perturbatus</u> fuit ut quae vidisset vix dilucide narrare posset. Ulixes autem satis intellexit socios suos in periculo versari, et gladio correpto Eurylocho imperavit ut sine mora viam ad istam domum demonstraret. Ille tamen multis cum lacrimis Ulixem <u>complexus</u> <u>obsecrare</u> coepit ne in tantum periculum se committeret; si quid gravius ei accidisset, omnium salutem in summo discrimine futuram. Ulixes autem respondit se neminem invitum secum adducturum; ei licere, si mallet, in navi manere; se ipsum sine ullo praesidio rem suscepturum. Hoc cum magna voce dixisset, e navi <u>desiluit</u> et nullo sequente solus in viam se dedit.

### 17. THE COUNTERCHARM

Aliquantum itineris progressus ad villam <u>magnificam</u> pervenit, quam cum oculis perlustrasset, statim intrare statuit; intellexit enim hanc esse eandem domum de qua Eurylochus <u>mentionem</u> fecisset. At cum in eo esset ut <u>limen</u> intraret, subito ei obviam stetit adulescens forma pulcherrima aureum baculum gerens. Hic Ulixem iam domum intrantem manu corripuit et, "Quo ruis?" inquit. "Nonne scis hanc esse Circes domum? Hic inclusi sunt amici tui ex humana specie in porcos conversi. Num vis ipse in eandem calamitatem venire?" Ulixes simul ac vocem audivit, deum Mercurium agnovit; nullis tamen precibus ab instituto consilio deterreri potuit. Quod cum Mercurius sensisset, herbam quandam ei dedit, quam contra carmina multum valere dicebat. "Hanc cape," inquit, "et ubi Circe te baculo tetigerit, tu stricto gladio impetum in eam vide ut facias." Mercurius postquam finem loquendi fecit, "mortalis visus medio sermone reliquit, et procul in tenuem ex oculis evanuit auram." *(Virgil Aenid Book IV Lines 277-8)*

## 18. THE ENCHANTRESS IS FOILED

Brevi intermisso spatio Ulixes ad omnia pericula subeunda paratus ianuam pulsavit, et foribus patefactis ab ipsa Circe benigne exceptus est. Omnia eodem modo atque antea facta sunt. Cenam magnifice instructam vidit et accumbere iussus est. Mox, ubi fames cibo depulsa est, Circe poculum aureum vino repletum Ulixi dedit. Ille etsi suspicatus est venenum sibi paratum esse, poculum exhausit; quo facto Circe postquam caput eius baculo tetigit, ea verba locuta est quibus socios eius antea in porcos converterat. Res tamen omnino aliter evenit atque illa speraverat. Tanta enim vis erat eius herbae quam Ulixi Mercurius dederat ut neque venenum neque verba quicquam efficere possent. Ulixes autem, ut ei praeceptum erat, gladio stricto impetum in eam fecit et mortem minitabatur. Circe cum artem suam nihil valere sensisset, multis cum lacrimis eum obsecrare coepit ne sibi vitam adimeret.

## 19. MEN ONCE MORE

Ulixes autem ubi sensit eam timore perterritam esse, postulavit ut socios suos sine mora in humanam speciem reduceret (certior enim factus erat a deo Mercurio eos in porcos conversos esse); nisi id factum esset, se debitas poenas sumpturum ostendit. Circe his rebus graviter commota ei ad pedes se proiecit, et multis cum lacrimis iure iurando confirmavit se quae ille imperasset omnia facturam. Tum porcos in atrium immitti iussit. Illi dato signo inruerunt, et cum ducem suum agnovissent, magno dolore adfecti sunt quod nullo modo eum de rebus suis certiorem facere poterant. Circe tamen unguento quodam corpora eorum unxit; quo facto sunt omnes statim in humanam speciem reducti. Magno cum gaudio Ulixes suos amicos agnovit, et nuntium ad litus misit, qui reliquis Graecis socios receptos esse diceret. Illi autem his rebus cognitis statim ad domum Circaeam se contulerunt; quo cum venissent, universi laetitiae se dediderunt.

## 20. AFLOAT AGAIN

Postridie eius diei Ulixes ex hac insula quam celerrime discedere in animo habebat. Circe tamen cum haec cognovisset, ex odio ad amorem conversa omnibus precibus eum orare et obtestari coepit ut paucos dies apud se moraretur; qua re tandem impetrata tanta beneficia in eum contulit ut facile ei persuasum sit ut diutius maneret. Postquam tamen totum annum apud Circen consumpserat, Ulixes magno desiderio patriae suae motus est. Sociis igitur ad se convocatis quid in animo haberet ostendit. Ubi tamen ad litus descendit, navem suam tempestatibus tam <u>adflictam</u> invenit ut ad navigandum paene <u>inutilis</u> esset. Hac re cognita omnia quae ad navis <u>reficiendas</u> usui essent comparari iussit, qua in re tantam diligentiam omnes <u>adhibebant</u> ut ante tertium diem opus perfecerint. At Circe ubi omnia ad profectionem parata esse vidit, rem <u>aegre</u> ferebat et Ulixem vehementer obsecrabat ut eo consilio desisteret. Ille tamen, ne anni tempore a navigatione excluderetur, maturandum sibi existimavit, et tempestatem idoneam nactus navem solvit. Multa quidem pericula Ulixi subeunda erant antequam in patriam suam perveniret, quae tamen hoc loco longum est perscribere.

# List of words in Ritchie's Fabulae Latinae not previously met
## Number indicates first occurrence of word

**A**

| | | |
|---|---|---|
| abdo ere abdidi abditum 3 | remove | 5 |
| accumbo ere accubui 3 | lie down | 15 |
| adduco -ere adduxi adductum 3 | bring | 15 |
| adficio -ere adfeci affectum 3½ | influence | 9 |
| adhibeo -ere adhibui 2 | apply | 20 |
| adligo -are 1 | tie to | 12 |
| aegre | with difficulty | 20 |
| afflictus -a -um | damaged | 20 |
| agnosco -ere agnovi 3 | recognize | 17 |
| aliquantum | considerably | 15 |
| aliter | otherwise | 18 |
| amentia -ae 1 | madness | 10 |
| amoveo -ere amovi 2 | move away | 6 |
| animadverto -ere -verti -versum 3 | perceive | 4 |
| ancora -ae 1 | anchor | 2 |
| anxius -a -um | anxious | 11 |
| appello -are | name | 5 |
| appono -ere apposui appositum 3 | place near | 15 |
| arbitror-ari 1 | think | 6 |
| ardeo -ere arsi arsum 2 | burn | 1 |
| auxilior -ari 1 | help | 11 |

**B**

| | | |
|---|---|---|
| beneficium -i 2 n | benefit | 20 |
| benignitas benignitatis 3 f | kindness | 15 |

**C**

| | | |
|---|---|---|
| calamitas calamitatis 3 f | calamity | 17 |
| calefacio -ere -feci -factum 3½ | make warm | 9 |
| cantus -us 4 m | song | 15 |
| caro carnis 3 f | flesh | 5 |
| clamito -are 1 | cry loudly | 3 |
| commoror -ari 1 | delay | 12 |
| compello -ere compuli compulsum 3 | drive, compel | 5 |
| complector -i complexus 3 | embrace | 16 |
| compleo -ere -plevi -pletum 2 | fill up | 8 |
| conatus -us 4 m | attempt | 6 |
| confirmo -are 1 | strengthen | 2 |
| conicio -ere conieci coniectum 3½ | throw | 5 |
| conscendo -ere -scendi -scensum 3 | ascend | 11 |
| consido -ere -sedi -sessum 3 | sit down | 10 |
| consensus -us 4 m | agreement | 14 |
| conspectus -us 4 m | sight | 13 |
| constat | it is well-known | 1 |
| controversia -ae 1 f | dispute | 14 |
| coorior -iri -ortus 4 | arise | 13 |
| corium -i 2 n | leather | 12 |
| cupiditas cupiditatis 3 f | desire | 1 |

**D**

| | | |
|---|---|---|
| damnum -i 2 n | damage | 11 |
| dedo -ere dedidi deditum 3 | give up | 19 |
| deficio -ere -feci -fectum 3½ | fail | 14 |
| deligo -ere delegi delectum 3 | choose | 7 |
| demitto -ere -misi -missum 3 | send down | 6 |
| demonstro -are 1 | show | 6 |
| desiderium -i 2 n | desire | 20 |
| desilio -ere -silui -sultum 3½ | leap down | 16 |
| desisto -ere -stiti -stitum 3 | cease | 6 |
| devoro -are 1 | devour | 5 |
| diligentia -ae 1 f | carefulness | 20 |
| Dilucide | clearly | 16 |
| discrimen discriminis 3 n | danger; difference | 6 |
| diversus -a -um | turned in different directions | 9 |
| divello -ere divelli divulsus 3 | tear asunder | 5 |
| dulcedo dulcedinis 3 f | sweetness | 15 |
| dulcis -e | sweet | 2 |

**E**

| | | |
|---|---|---|
| evado -ere evasi evasum 3 | escape | 6 |
| examinatus -a -um | deprived of breath | 5 |
| exardesco -ere -arsi -arsum 2 | burn up | 13 |
| excludo -ere -clusi -clusum 3 | shut out | 12 |
| excogito -are 1 | devise | 1 |
| exhaurio -ire -hausi -hausum 3½ | empty | 8 |
| exploro -are 1 | explore | 4 |
| expono -ere -posui -positum 3 | set out | 3 |
| extremus —a -um | outermost | 9 |

**F**

| | | |
|---|---|---|
| faber fabri 2 m | worker | 5 |
| fames famis 3 f | hunger | 6 |
| fervens ferventis | glowing hot | 9 |
| figura -ae 1 f | form | 4 |
| fons fontis 3 m | spring, fountain | 2 |
| foras | out of doors | 15 |
| foris | out of doors | 15 |
| foris foris 3 f | door | 18 |
| formosus -a -um | beautifully formed | 1 |
| fraus fraudis 3 f | deceit | 11 |
| frons frontis 3 f | forehead | 4 |
| fructus -us 4 m | fruit | 2 |

**G**

| | | |
|---|---|---|
| guberno -are 1 | steer | 13 |
| gusto -are 1 | taste | 2 |

## H

| | | |
|---|---|---|
| herba -ae 1 f | grass | 17 |
| hesternus -a -um | relating to yesterday | 7 |
| horribilis -e | horrible | 4 |
| hospitium -i 2 n | hospitality | 2 |

## I

| | | |
|---|---|---|
| ignarus -a -um | ignorant of | 16 |
| ignotus -a -um | unknown | 4 |
| immanitas immanitatis 3 f | savageness | 11 |
| imperatum -i 2 n | that which has been commanded | 2 |
| impetro -are 1 | accomplish | 20 |
| incido -ere -cidi 3 | fall in | 9 |
| includo -ere -clusi -clusum 3 | shut in | 12 |
| incolo -ere -colui -cultum 3 | inhabit | 5 |
| infectus -a -um | unfinished | 3 |
| insania -ae 1 f | madness | 9 |
| instituto -ere -stitui -stitutum 3 | arrange | 17 |
| introitus -us 4 m | entrance | 4 |
| inutilis -e | useless | 20 |
| iste -a -ud | this / that | 4 |
| ius iuris 3 n | right, law | 11 |
| iusiurandum iurisiurandi n | oath | 19 |
| iussum -i 2 n | command | 15 |

## L

| | | |
|---|---|---|
| laetitia -ae 1 f | happiness | 11 |
| lamentum -i 2 n | wailing | 7 |
| lassitudo lassitudinis 3 f | weariness | 13 |
| lateo -ere latui 2 | be concealed | 10 |
| latro latronis 3 m | brigand | 8 |
| lignum -i 2 n | wood | 7 |
| limen liminis 3 n | threshold | 17 |

## M

| | | |
|---|---|---|
| magicus -a -um | magical | 16 |
| magnificentia -ae 1 f | magnificence | 15 |
| magnificus -a -um | magnificent | 17 |
| magnitudo magnitudinis 3 f | greatness | 4 |
| malus -i 2 m | mast | 12 |
| maturo -are 1 | hasten | 1 |
| medicamentum -i 2 n | medicine | 15 |
| membrum -i 2 n | limb | 5 |
| mentio mentionis 3 f | mention | 17 |
| meridies meridiei 5 m | midday | 2 |
| minitor -ari 1 | threaten | 18 |
| mirus -a -um | wonderful | 2 |
| misco -ere miscui mixtum 2 | mix | 15 |

## N

| | | |
|---|---|---|
| nanciscor -i nactus 3 | obtain | 1 |
| navigatio navigationis 3 f | sailing | 12 |

| | | |
|---|---|---|
| novitas novitatis 3 f | newness | 15 |
| nuper | lately | 14 |

## P

| | | |
|---|---|---|
| pastor pastoris 3 m | shepherd | 5 |
| patefacio -ere -feci -factum 3½ | open | 18 |
| pectus pectoris 3 n | breast | 6 |
| pecus pectoris 3 n | herd | 5 |
| percipio -ere -cepi -ceptum 3½ | perceive | 8 |
| perfodio -ere -fodi -fossum 3½ | pierce through | 9 |
| perlustro -are 1 | examine | 5 |
| perpetuus -a -um | continuous | 2 |
| perturbatus -a -um | confused | 16 |
| pinguis -e | fat | 10 |
| praeacutus -a -um | pointed | 7 |
| praecaveo | take precaution | 5 |
| praecipio -ere -cepi -ceptum 3½ | receive in advance | 18 |
| praecipue | especially | 5 |
| praedor ari 1 | plunder | 5 |
| praesens presentis | in person | 6 |
| praeses presidis | protecting | 5 |
| praetereo -ire -ii -itum | pass over | 10 |
| prehendo -ere prehendi prehensum 3 | seize hold of | 9 |
| profectio profectionis 3 f | departure | 1 |
| proiicio -ere -ieci -iectum 3½ | throw down | 13 |
| promo -ere prompsi promptum 3 | bring forth | 8 |
| prostratus -a -um | lying on the ground | 6 |
| prosum prodesse profui | be useful | 6 |
| proveho -ere -vexi -vectum 3 | carry forward | 11 |
| provoco -are 1 | call forth | 8 |
| prudentia -ae 1 f | prudence | 1 |
| pulso -are 1 | strike | 15 |

## R

| | | |
|---|---|---|
| recumbo -ere -cubui 3 | lie backwards | 8 |
| reditus -us 4 m | coming back | 7 |
| reduco -ere -duxi -ductum 3 | bring back | 19 |
| refero -ferre -tuli -latum | carry back | 8 |
| reficio -ere -feci -fectum 3½ | make again | 20 |
| refugio -ere -fugi -fugitum 3½ | flee away | 5 |
| remus -i 2 m | oar | 4 |
| reperio -ire reperi repertum 4 | find | 14 |
| repertor repertoris 3 m | discoverer | 5 |
| repleo -ere -plevi -plevi 2 | fill up | 8 |
| reporto -are 1 | bring back | 3 |
| rupes -is 3 f | rock | 5 |

## S

| | | |
|---|---|---|
| scientia -ae 1 f | knowledge | 16 |
| sollicitudo sollicitudinis 3 f | anxiety | 16 |
| sollicitus -a -um | disturbed | 16 |
| sonitus -us 4 m | sound | 4 |
| sors sortis 3 f | lot | 14 |

| | | |
|---|---|---|
| sortior -iri sortitus 4 | cast lots | 14 |
| species specie 5 f | sight | 4 |
| spons spontis 3 f | free-will | 3 |
| stringo -ere strinxi strictum 3 | unsheathe | 17 |
| submergo -ere -mersi -mersum 3 | sink | 11 |
| supplicium supplicii 2 n | torture, punishment | 9 |
| suspicor -ari 1 | suspect | 10 |

**T**

| | | |
|---|---|---|
| temere | rashly | 6 |
| terribilis -e | terrible | 4 |
| torqueo -ere torsi tortum 2 | twist | 4 |
| tracto -are 1 | handle | 10 |
| transfigo -ere -fixi -fixum 3 | transfix | 6 |

**U**

| | | |
|---|---|---|
| ungo -ere unxi unctum 3 | anoint | 19 |
| unguentum -i 2 n | ointment | 19 |
| universus -a -um | entire | 19 |

**V**

| | | |
|---|---|---|
| vas  vasis *pl.* vasa -orum | vase | 4 |
| venenum -i 2 n | poison | 18 |
| verso -are 1 | turn | 3 |
| victus -us 4 m | food | 2 |
| vicus -i 2 m | village | 3 |
| voluptas voluptatis 3 f | pleasure | 8 |

# Chapter 45       Passages of English for translation

## 1 The Trojan Horse

The Trojans saw a huge wooden horse standing near the walls. Some shouted: 'The Greeks have departed but have left us a gift.' Others shouted: 'It's a trick. Don't trust the Greeks.' King Priam himself ordered his soldiers to drag the horse from the shore to the middle of the city. In the middle of the night while all the Trojans were sleeping, Ulixes' men came out of the horse, killed the Trojan soldiers guarding the horse and ran as quickly as possible to the gates to open them. For the rest of the Greeks had returned to Troy and were now waiting near the gates of the city. The gates were opened by one of the Ulixes' soldiers. When the Trojans saw the Greeks advancing towards them they were so terrified that many fled. Those that remained were easily overcome by the Greeks. Menelaus rushed to the palace of King Priam, killed him and his son, Paris, and after ten years finally saw his wife again. After a lot of gold and money had been taken and the city set on fire, the Greeks then set sail home.

## 2 The Ciconians

While Ulixes and his companions were returning to Ithaca, a fierce storm arose which drove them to the land of the Cicones. When they reached the shore, Ulixes ordered his men to hurry to the town to look for food and water. When the men reached the town, they found many inhabitants. Some were working, some were sleeping, and others were playing. The Greeks attacked the wretched inhabitants, took a lot of food and wine and returned as quickly as possible to the ships. As they were now very tired, they didn't want to leave. So they sat down near the boats and ate and drank for many hours and finally fell asleep. In the middle of the night the angry Ciconians arrived and immediately began to throw spears and arrows against the Greeks sleeping near the ships. The Greeks were so tired that they were unable to resist the Ciconians. Ulixes ordered his men to hurry to the ships as quickly as they could but many Greeks perished there in the land of the Cicones.

## 3 The Lotus-Eaters

Ulixes and his brave companions sailed for many days and finally arrived at the island of the lotus-eaters. While he and his companions remained near the ships, Ulixes sent three sailors to the centre of the island to look for food and water. When the men arrived at the centre of the town, they found the inhabitants sitting on the ground. Some were drinking the juice of the lotus fruit, others were sleeping. They all seemed very happy. One of the lotus-eaters gave the three Greeks some lotus juice. They liked the juice so much that they no longer wanted to return to Ithaca; they said they wanted to stay with the inhabitant of this island. Ulixes was now so worried because the three men had not returned after many hours that he decided to go alone to the town himself. There he saw his three companions drinking with the inhabitants. Without delay they were led back to the boats by their angry leader. When they arrived there, Ulisses ordered his men to leave at once.

## 4 Polyphemus

After sailing for a few days the Greeks arrived at the land of the Cyclops. Ulixes wanted to explore the island. While they were in a large cave, Polyphemus, the son of Neptune himself, suddenly arrived with his goats. The huge monster, who had only one eye, caught sight of the Greeks and immediately seized two of them, threw them against the wall of the cave, ate them and fell asleep. At first light the Cyclops went out with his sheep to the fields. But the Greeks could not escape because Polyphemus had put a huge stone at the entrance to the cave. While he was away in the fields, Ulixes devised a plan and he ordered his men to look for a large stake in the cave. When they had found a stake it was carried by two men to the fire which was in the middle of the cave. Then Ulixes prepared the head of the stake with his sword and then ordered his men to put it into the flames. When it was hot, Ulixes ordered his men to hide the stake.

When Polyphemus finally returned to the cave, again he took two of Ulixes' men and ate them. Now Ulixes gave Polyphemus some wine. The Cyclops liked the wine and asked Ulxes: 'What is your name?' 'My name is Nobody' replied Ulixes. Soon Polyphemus fell asleep. Ulixes ordered his men to take the stake and push it into the eye of Polyphemus. The giant cried out most fiercely. By chance two other Cyclops who lived near this cave heard the cries and hastened as quickly as they could. They asked: 'O Polyphemus, why are you shouting like this? Who has harmed you?' When Polyphemus replied: 'Nobody has harmed me' his two friends went away, laughing.

## 5 Aeolus

When the Greeks had sailed for four days they finally reached a small island. Aeolus, the keeper of the winds, was king of this island. He received Ulixes and his companions in a very friendly way and asked his six sons and daughters to give the Greeks food and wine. They remained on the island for five days and when they were leaving, Aeolus gave Ulixes a bag in which he had put all the winds except the west wind, which would carry them to Ithaca. But he warned Ulixes not to open this bag while they were in the boat.

While they were sailing to Ithaca, the exhausted Ulixes finally fell asleep. When the bag was opened by one of Ulixes' companions, the winds immediately escaped. Within a few hours the ships were driven back by a terrible storm to the island of King Aeolus.

When they arrived at the island, Ulixes asked by the king Aeolus what had happened said that his men had opened the bag. When he asked for help a second time, the king was so angry that he didn't want to give help to the Greeks so that they could return to Ithaca quickly. So the miserable Greeks departed on a long and dangerous journey without the help of king Aeolus.

## 6 The Laestrygonians

As they sailed the wretched Greeks were driven by fierce storms to another island. When they arrived at the island, Ulixes ordered three of his men to go to the town to look for food and water. While they were walking to the town they saw a huge girl sitting near the road. She led them to her parents, the king and queen of the island. But these Laestrygonians, a race of giants, did not receive the Greeks well. King Antiphates grabbed and killed one of the men. The other two men however were able to escape and ran as quickly as they could to their friends who were waiting in the ships. But the inhabitants threw such enormous rocks at the Greek ships that they were alost all destroyed. After many men had perished, Athena, the friend of Ulixes, sent a mist so that Ulixes and a few of his companions could escape.

## 7 Circe on the island of Aeaea

The tired Greeks driven by strong winds for many days finally arrived at a certain island named Aeaea.  When they arrived at the island, Ulixes sent his friend Eurylochus and some men to the middle of the island to look for food and wine. Soon they came to a palace and saw a lady with a beautiful voice, named Circe. She asked them to come into the palace to drink some wine. Almost all the Greeks wanted to go in. Eurylochus was so terrified of this lady that he didn't want to go in.

While the men were eating and drinking, suddenly Circe changed all the men into pigs with her magic stick. When Eurylochus saw this awful deed, terrified he immediately ran to Ulixes who was waiting near the boat with the other Greeks. Ulixes himself made up his mind to go alone to Circe's palace. While he was on the way, Mercury, the messenger of the gods, gave him a magic flower so that Circe could not change him into a pig. Ulixes ordered her to change his men into humans again. When Circe recognized that this man was Ulixes she immediately promised to do what he has asked. When the pigs had been changed into humans again, everyone was happy and Ulixes, although he had a wife and son waiting for him in Ithaca, decided to stay with Circe for one year.

## 8 The Land of the Dead and The Sirens

Circe told Ulixes that he had to sail to the land of the dead, named Tartarus. There Teiresias, the blind prophet, warned Ulixes not to listen to the Sirens and not to eat the sacred cows of Hyperion. Before leaving this land, Ulixes saw again his mother and many heroes from Troy.

The Greeks returned to the island of Circe to get food and water for the journey to Ithaca. Circe herself too warned Ulixes about some of the dangers and gave him some wax so that he and his men would not hear the beautiful voices of the Sirens.

Next they came to the island of the Sirens, strange birds with beautiful human voices. Sailors who approached the island always perished on the rocks which were in the sea. When Ulixes caught sight of this island, he ordered his men to put wax into their ears. Then he ordered Eurylochus to tie him to the mast of the ship because he wanted to hear the voices of the Sirens. When Ulixes heard the beautiful voices of the Sirens he ordered Eurylochus to set him free but because he had put the wax into his ears he was unable to hear Ulixes. In this way the Greeks were able to sail safely.

## 9 Scylla and Charybdis and the Sun god's cattle

Next they had to sail through the Straits of Sicily. On the left lay Scylla, the six headed monster and on the right lay Charybdis, a huge whirlpool. As they were afraid to approach Charybdis, the Greeks sailed near the land on the left. Suddenly Scylla awoke and snatched six sailors from Ulixes' ship.

After six brave sailors had thus been killed the Greeks approached the island of Hyperion, the sun god. The men wanted to get off the boat to look for food. Ulixes had been warned and the danger and told his men not to approach the sacred cows. When they came to land Ulixes immediately departed to get to know the island. His stupid companions immediately killed one of the cows and took it to the fire to prepare it. While they were eating the cow, Ulixes came back. Very angry, he ordered his comrades to sail away as quickly as possible. Soon Jupiter sent lightning to the Greeks' boat and destroyed it. All the men perished except Ulixes, who was able to get hold of the mast and escape.

Holding on to the mast, Ulixes was able to escape from the whirlpool, named Charybdis. The waves carried him for several days. Finally he arrived, half-dead at the island of Calypso, a beautiful goddess with a human voice.

## 10 Calypso

When Calypso caught sight of the half-dead Ulixes on the shore, she gave him food and water. Then she led him to her palace and fell in love with him so much that she forced Ulixes to stay with her for seven years. He was not happy, however, because he wanted to see his wife and son again. Finally Mercury, the messenger of the gods, instructed by Athene, came and ordered Calypso to set Ulixes free. And so the goddess gave Ulixes an axe. With this axe he was able to build a raft. He left the island of Calypso and sailed for many days on a calm sea. By chance, at that time Neptune, the father of Polyphemus, was returning from Ethiopia and caught sight of Ulixes on his raft. He immediately sent such a wild storm from the sky that the raft was destroyed and Ulixes fell into the sea. Ino, a sea nymph, arrived and gave him a magic vest with which to save himself. In this way Ulixes finally arrived finally at the island of Phaeacia.

## 11 Phaeacia

The goddess Athena, the friend of Ulixes, ordered Nausicaa, the daughter of king Alcinous, to go to the river with two maid servants to wash some clothes. While they were playing on the shore, Ulixes saw Nausicaa and asked who she was. Nausicaa said she was the daughter of king Alcinous and that her parents would help him. She showed him how to get to the palace. When he arrived at the palace the king and the queen received him kindly. After telling the king and queen about the Trojan War and his difficult journey to Ithaca, the king ordered his servants to prepare a ship. The next day they took Ulixes in a boat to Ithaca.

## 12 Return to Ithaca

Athena came to Ulixes, changed him into an old man and told him to go to Eumaeus, who still looked after his pigs. When Ulixes reached Eumaeus' house, he told Ulixes that there were suitors in his palace who wanted to marry his wife, Penelope. By chance, Ulixes' son Telemachus arrived. Athena took away the old man's mask from Ulixes and Telemachus recognized who this old man was.

The next day many suitors tried to do what Penelope had asked. But no suitor was able to. Finally Ulixes, still appearing as an old man, said he wanted to try. When he had strung the bow he sent an arrow through the row of twelve axes and suddenly threw off his mask. With the help of his son, Telemachus, and Eumaeus, he quickly killed all the suitors. Finally now after twenty years, Penelope threw herself into the arms of her husband. Both gods and humans finally were able to live in peace.

# Vocabulary by Chapter

## Chapter 1

| | | | |
|---|---|---|---|
| ago -ere egi actum 3 | do, act drive | doceo -ere docui doctum 2 | teach |
| emo -ere emi emptum 3 | buy | invito 1 | invite |
| traho -ere traxi tractum 3 | drag | vendo -ere vendidi venditum 3 | sell |
| vivo -ere vixi victum 3 | live | | |

## Chapter 2

| | | | |
|---|---|---|---|
| amor -is 3 m | love | animus -i 2 m | spirit, soul, mind |
| ars artis 3 f | art, skill | canis -is 3 c | dog |
| caput -itis 3 n | head | castra -orum 2 n | camp |
| cena -ae 1 f | dinner, meal | consilium -i 2 n | plan, idea, advice |
| consul -is 3 m | consul | cura -ae 1 f | care, worry |
| domina -ae 1 f | mistress | epistula -ae 1 f | letter |
| forum -i 2 n | forum, market-place | hortus -i 2 m | garden |
| ianua -ae 1 f | gate | imperator -is 3 m | emperor, general, leader |
| leo leonis 3 m | lion | libertus -i 2 m | freedman |
| mercator -is 3 m | merchant | pax pacis 3 f | peace |
| porta -ae 1 f | gate | senator -is 3 m | senator |
| signum -i 2 n | sign, signal, standard | silva -ae 1 f | wood, forest |
| taberna -ae 1 f | inn, shop | tempus temporis 3 n | time |
| victoria -ae 1 f | victory | vita -ae 1 f | life |

## Chapter 3

| | | | |
|---|---|---|---|
| ecce! | look! | minime | very little, least, no |
| qualis? | of what sort? | quantus | how big? how much? |
| quo? | to where? | quo modo? | how? |
| quot? | how many? | salve! | hello! |
| satis | enough | umquam | ever |
| vale! | farewell! goodbye! | | |

## Chapter 4

| | | | |
|---|---|---|---|
| ac, atque | and | centum | a hundred |
| interea | meanwhile | lente | slowly |
| nec, neque | neither | paene | almost, nearly |
| mille *pl.* milia | thousand | | |

## Chapter 6

| | | | |
|---|---|---|---|
| annus -i 2 m | year | dies diei 5 m | day |
| domus -us 4 f | house | duo duae, duo | two |
| hora -ae 1 f | hour | mensis -is 3 m | month |
| nox noctis 3 f | night | res rei 5 f | thing |
| tres, tria | three | | |

**Chapter 7**

| | | | |
|---|---|---|---|
| custos -odis 3 m | guard | ferox ferocis | fierce, ferocious |
| fidelis -e | faithful | gravis -e | heavy, serious |
| lentus -a -um | slow | nolo nolle nolui | not want, refuse |
| stultus -a -um | stupid, foolish | summus -a -um | highest, greatest, top (of) |
| vehementer | violently, loudly | volo velle volui | want |

**Chapter 9**

| | |
|---|---|
| convenio -ire -veni -ventum 4 | come together, gather, meet |
| credo -ere credidi creditum *(+dat.)* 3 | believe, trust |
| custodio 4 | guard |
| interficio -ere interfeci interfectum 3½ | kill |
| peto -ere petivi petitum 3 | make for, seek, beg/ask for |
| relinquo -ere reliqui relictum 3 | leave |

**Chapter 10**

| | | | |
|---|---|---|---|
| fero ferre tuli latum | carry | nullus -a -um | not any, no |
| qui quae quod | who, which | totus -a -um | whole |

**Chapter 11**

| | |
|---|---|
| accido -ĕre accedi 3 | happen |
| ascendo -ĕre ascendi ascensum 3 | climb |
| descendo -ĕre -cendi -censum 3 | go/ come down |
| lacrimo 1 | weep, cry |
| procedo -ĕre -cessi -cessum 3 | advance, proceed |
| quaero -ĕre quaesivi quaesitum 3 | search for, look for, ask |
| resisto -ĕre restiti *(+dat.)* 3 | resist |
| sedeo -ēre sedi sessum 2 | sit |
| surgo -ĕre surrexi surrectum 3 | get up, stand up, rise |
| taceo -ēre tacui 2 | be silent, be quiet |

**Chapter 12**

| | | | |
|---|---|---|---|
| alius -ia -iud | other, another, else | alter -a -um | the other, another, the second of two |
| celer -is -e | quick, fast | ipse ipse ipsum | himself, herself, itself, themselves |

**Chapter 13**

| | | | |
|---|---|---|---|
| nisi | unless, except | si | if |

**Chapter 18**

| | | | |
|---|---|---|---|
| domus -us 4 f | home, house | manus -us 4 f | hand |

**Chapter 19**

| | |
|---|---|
| cognosco -ĕre cognovi cognitum 3 | get to know, find out |
| intellego -ĕre intellexi intellectum 3 | understand realise |
| nescio -ire nescivi nescitum 4 | not know |
| scio -ire scivi scitum 4 | know |
| sentio -ire sensi sensum 4 | feel, notice |

## Chapter 20

| | |
|---|---|
| promitto -ĕre promisi promissum 3 | promise |
| nego 1 | say ... not, deny |

## Chapter 21

| | | | | | |
|---|---|---|---|---|---|
| talis -e | such | tantus -a -um | so great, such a great | tot | so many |

## Chapter 23

| | | | |
|---|---|---|---|
| ne | that ... not | ut | in order that |

## Chapter 24

| | | | |
|---|---|---|---|
| adeo | so much, so greatly | tam | so |

## Chapter 25

| | |
|---|---|
| persuadeo -ere persuasi *(+dat.)* 2 | persuade |

## Chapter 30

| | | | |
|---|---|---|---|
| captivus -i 2 m | captive, prisoner | diligens diligentis | careful |
| iaceo -ĕre iacui 2 | lie | impero *(+dat.)* 1 | order, command |
| nonnulli -ae -a | some, several | praemium -i 2 n | prize, reward, profit |
| princeps principis 2 m | chief, emperor | quando? | when? |
| rapio -ĕre rapui raptum 3 | seize, grab | reddo -ĕre reddidi redditum | give back, restore |
| unde? | from where? | | |

## Chapter 31

| | | | |
|---|---|---|---|
| celo 1 | hide | coepi coepisse | began |
| cogito 1 | think, consider | cogo -ĕre coegi coactum 3 | force, compel |
| dirus -a -um | dreadful | faveo -ēre favi fautum *(+dat.)*2 | favour, support |
| gens gentis 3 f | family, tribe, race, people | incendo -ĕre incendi incensum 3 | burn, set on fire |
| inimicus -i 2 m | enemy | libenter | willingly, gladly |
| oro 1 | beg | plenus -a -um | full |
| puto 1 | think | scelus sceleris 2 n | crime |
| spero 1 | hope | | |

## Chapter 32

| | | | |
|---|---|---|---|
| ante *(+acc.)* | before | antea | before(hand) |
| antequam | before | benignus -a -um | kind |
| brevis -e | short, brief | dum | while, until |
| imperium -i 2 n | order, command | maritus -i 2 m | husband |
| pello -ere pepuli pulsum 3 | drive | post *(+acc.)* | after |
| postea | afterwards | postquam | after |
| primo | at first | postridie | on the next day |
| rumpo -ere rupi ruptum 3 | break, burst | simul | at the same time |
| simulac | as soon as | tempestas -atis 3 f | storm |
| verto -ere verti versum 3 | turn | | |

## Chapter 33

| | |
|---|---|
| alii … alii | some … others |
| apud *(+acc.)* | among, with, at the house of |
| autem | but, however |
| cado -ĕre cecidi casum 3 | fall |
| conficio ĕre confeci confectum 3 | finish, wear out |
| enim | for |
| gaudium -i 2 n | joy, pleasure |
| idem eadem idem | the same |
| labor -is 3 m | work |
| magis | greatly |
| multo | much |
| pes pedis 3 m | foot |
| poena -ae 1 f | punishment |
| poenas do 1 | pay penalty, am punished |
| quidam quaedam quoddam | one, a certain, some |
| sanguis sanguinis 3 m | blood |
| scelestus -a -um | wicked |
| tollo -ere sustuli sublatum 3 | raise, lift up, hold up |
| verus -a -um | true, real |

## Chapter 34

| | |
|---|---|
| infelix infelicis | unlucky, unhappy |
| legio legionis 3 f | legion |
| opprimo -ĕre oppressi oppressum 3 | crush, overwhelm |
| pervenio -ire -veni -ventum 4 | reach, arrive at |
| proximus -a -um | nearest, next to |
| regnum -i 2 n | kingdom |

## Chapter 35

| | |
|---|---|
| aufero auferre abstuli ablatum | take away, carry off, steal |
| exercitus -us 4 m | army |
| malo malle malui | prefer |
| offero offerre obtuli oblatum | offer |
| portus -us 4 m | harbour, port |
| refero referre rettuli relatum | bring / carry back, report, tell |
| spes spei 5 f | hope |
| vultus -us 4 m | face, expression |

## Chapter 36

| | | | |
|---|---|---|---|
| conor 1 | try | egredior -i egressus 3½ | go out |
| hortor 1 | encourage | ingredior -i ingressus 3½ | enter |
| loquor -i locutus 3 | speak | miror 1 | wonder at, admire |
| morior -i mortuus 3½ | die | patior -i passus 3½ | suffer, endure |
| precor 1 | pray (to), beg | proficiscor -i profectus 3 | set out |
| progredior -i progressus 3½ | advance | regredior -i regressus 3½ | go back, return |
| sequor -i secutus 3 | follow | | |

## Chapter 37

| | | |
|---|---|---|
| audeo -ēre ausus sum 2 | dare | gaudeo -ēre gavisus sum 2 be pleased, rejoice |
| soleo -ēre solitus sum | be accustomed | |

## Chapter 38

| | | |
|---|---|---|
| appareo -ere apparui 2 | appear | ut *(+indic.)* as |

# Answers to selected Exercises

**Exercise 1.1**

1. My master never invites my friend.
2. The wild wind are driving the wretched sailors away from the island.
3. My sister never buys gold.
4. The strong soldier is now dragging the general's body from the battle.
5. The old man is sellind all the gold today.
6. The father is teaching his little son to run in the field.
7. That old man is now living near the sea.
8. The bad master wants to sell the dead horse.
9. Nobody invites that miserable young man.
10. 'What are you doing in the field?' says the angry master.'I'm working' replies the terrified slave.

**Exerice 1.2**

1. Surely your master always used to greet the companion?
2. The wild winds were by chance driving all the ships from the island.
3. 'My friend, did you used to buy Greek slaves?'
4. The tired soldier was now dragging the general's body from the battle.
5. The old man was selling all the weapons to his friend.
6. 'Were you teaching your companion how to fight with a sword?'
7. No one was wanting to buy this tired horse.
8. 'Why were you selling this dead horse?'
9. My friends used to invite this very beautiful young lady.
10. 'What were you doing in the house?' says the angry master. 'We were working' answer the slaves.

**Exercise 1.3**

1. Tomorrow my friends will invite these beautiful young ladies.
2. Surely you will live in the island?
3. Will the wild wind drive our ships from the island?
4. The man will soon sell three of the books to his companion.
5. Surely you won't sell this bad food to the old man?
6. My friends, will you sell those Greek slaves?
7. Surely your brother will invite his own companions?
8. Surely you won't teach the little boy to fight with the sword?
9. Will the Trojans drag the huge horse into the town?
10. Will you greet the bad man in the street?

**Exercise 1.4**

1. Yesterday my friends invited their dear companions.
2. Who bought this wild horse?
3. A very wild wind drove all of our ships from the island.
4. The man sold ten books to his companion.
5. The wretched farmer and his sons had to live on poor food for a long time.
6. My companion, why did you buy these bad books?
7. The brother lived happily in that island for a long time.
8. Surley you didn't teach those slaves to fight with a sword?
9. Then the Trojans dragged the huge horse into the town.
10. I didn't greet that woman in the street.

**Exercise 1.5**

1. My friends had already invited me before the war.
2. The man was sad because he had bought a bad horse.
3. The winds had driven all our ships to the island.
4. The man left at once when he had sold the ten books.
5. We had sold the bad weapons before the battle.
6. I had also invited my companion before I left for my house yesterday.
7. Why had you not invited your brother?
8. The master had never taught those slaves to fight with swords.
9. Before the Greeks returned, the Trojans had already dragged the huge horse into the town.
10. I had never greeted those women in the street.

**Exercise 2.1**

1. I have never seen a more beautiful woman in my life.
2. The freedman invited all his companions to dinner yesterday.
3. The sad young man sent many letters to his angry mistress.
4. The merchant used to sell many pieces of Greek art in the forum.
5. The huge fierce dog was standing in front of the shop door.
6. The man gave his wife some advice but in vain for she was not listening.
7. The brave inhabitant killed the wild lion with a sword.
8. Two dogs were sleeping in the freedman's garden.
9. The merchant used to buy and sell famous works of art.
10. The lions caught sight of the inhabitants in the forest.

**Exercise 2.3**

1. The wretched general sent a dog's head to the enemy.
2. The young man was writing a love letter with the greatest of care.
3. The senator gave a dinner for all his friends.
4. The senators finally gave the victory sign.
5. The general wanted to see the standard.
6. The mistress did not send a letter to the freedman for she did not have time.
7. The emperor ordered his own soldiers to enter through the camp gate.
8. I have in mind to sell my dog.
9. Finally there was peace through all the lands.
10. The master spent all his time on his own fields.

**Exercise 2.5E**

1. The merchant had in mind to sell many Greek works of art.
2. The bold emperor killed the fierce lion with a sword.
3. The senators invited the emperor to dinner yesterday.
4. After the battle many soldiers finally deserted.
5. The emperor had a famous victory in mind.
6. The leader prepared the plan with great care.
7. Three fierce dogs were standing near the shop door.
8. 'The slaves are now serving the main course' said the senator.
9. The general had never seen a larger town in his life.
10. The enemy suddenly attacked the Roman camp.

**Exercise 3.1**

1. Why did the emperor sell the dog?
2. What did the merchant buy?
3. What frightened the senator?
4. Surely you have time to invite your companion?
5. Did the men drag the lion's body into the forum?
6. Slave, you surely didn't drive the wild dogs into the house?
7. Where are the best wine shops?
8. 'Where is my dinner?' the man shouted to his terrified wife.
9. 'Why did the soldiers desert? Asked the emperor.
10. 'Where is the dog?' asked the emperor. 'He's sleeping in front of the door' replied his son.

**Exercise 3.2**

1. 'How many dogs does the master have?' 'Five.'
2. 'Slave, where have you run from?' 'From the town.'
3. 'Hello, sailor, how did you come to the island?' 'In that ship.'
4. 'Freedman, have you ever seen a larger market-place?' 'Never.'
5. 'Soldier, what's your general like?' 'Very brave.'
6. 'What's that river like?' 'Very deep.'
7. The general never used to say more words than were necessary.
8. 'My son, do you have enough time?' 'No.'
9. 'How big is the enemy camp?' 'Very big.'
10. 'I have seen enough, now goodbye!' said the emperor.
11. 'Look, this is the Roman forum. Have you ever seen a larger one?'
12. 'Where did your father go?' 'Home.'

**Exercise 4.9**

1. These wretched boys are being wounded by the savage dogs.
2. Almost all the boys and girls are praised by the teacher.
3. How many letters are being read by the mistress?
4. Meanwhile the rest of the ships are being driven to the island by the harsh wind.
5. A few slaves are often punished by the bad master.
6. This very good wine is being slowly drunk by the sailors.
7. How are the Greek sailors being beaten by a hundred Roman soldiers?
8. That soldier is never chosen by his leader.
9. The enemy camp is being attacked for a long time by one thousand Romans.
10. We are neither captured nor wounded by the angry soldiers.

**Exercise 4.10E**

1. The very beautiful Helen is being captured by Paris.
2. This large city is being bravely defended by a thousand Trojans.
3. These brave men are neither killed nor wounded by the Greeks.
4. This huge horse is being dragged to the centre of the town by the Trojans.
5. The most wretched Helen is finally freed by the very brave Menelaus.
6. The tired Trojans are easily overcome by these very strong Greeks.
7. How is the gold taken by those fortunate Greeks?
8. The hundred Greek ships are now being destroyed.
9. How much wine is being drunk by the tired Greeks?
10. Almost the whole of the camp is destroyed by the cruel enemy.

**Exercise 5.3**

1. The very beautiful Helen was being taken by Paris.
2. The small city was being bravely defended by a hundred citizens.
3. The Roman soldiers were not being beaten by the tired enemy.
4. How was the huge horse being dragged by the Trojans?
5. The fortunate wife was finally being freed by her brave husband.
6. The Trojans were being beaten by the bold Greeks.
7. What kind of wine was being taken by the lucky Greeks?
8. Land was finally caught sight of by the happy sailors.
9. After the battle the food was being consumed by our soldiers.
10. How many dogs were being driven from the city by the savage citizens?

**Exercise 5.4E**

1. The slave often used to be punished by his master.
2. All the pupils used to be praised by the wise teachers.
3. Almost all the books were being read by all the boys.
4. How many ships were being driven by the savage wind?
5. How were the slaves being punished by the queen?
6. The best wine was being drunk by the sailors.
7. The Greek sailors were being overcome by the bold soldiers.
8. How was the dead horse being dragged by the slaves and the boys?
9. All the enemy were being killed by the cruel soldiers.
10. The slaves were neither punished nor praised by the noble master.

**Exercise 6.3**

1. Surely the wretched mistresses were not being wounded by the harsh soldiers?
2. The pupils will be praised tomorrow by the wise teachers.
3. How many books will be bought by the merchants?
4. The remaining ships will be destroyed by the fierce winds within five days.
5. A few slaves will be punished on the third day by the bad queen.
6. How many hours will they remain in front of the camp gate?
7. The Greek sailors will be beaten by the bold soldiers within two hours.
8. Surely the wretched inhabitants will soon be killed by the lions?
9. The guards will be killed by the cruel soldiers in the forum within three hours.
10. The Roman soldiers will neither be overcome nor wounded by the tired enemy.

**Exercise 6.4E**

1. In how many days will the slaves be led back to Rome?
2. The small city will be defended for two days by the brave citizens?

3. The good slaves will not be punished by the noble emperor.
4. The huge horse will be built within six days by the Greeks.
5. The fortunate wife will be freed by the brave husband.
6. The Trojans will be beaten by the bold Greeks on the second night.
7. A lot of gold will be taken by the lucky Greeks.
8. How will the shop door be destroyed by the young men?
9. All the food will be bought tomorrow by the merchant.
10. The arrows and spears will be bought by these merchants.

**Exercise 7.3**
1. Surely you want to read these books?
2. That freedman wanted to lead a happy life with his wife near the forest.
3. Why weren't you wanting to do this?
4. How many soldiers wanted to cross the river and enter the enemy camp?
5. Do you want to make this man a god?
6. This man didn't want to be a farmer.
7. How do you want to go to Rome?
8. Have you ever wanted to go to that house?
9. The poet wanted to live in Rome for a long time.
10.  Why don't you want to write the letter?

**Exercise 7.4**
1. The angry chief was shouting loudly in the middle of the battle.
2. Many ships were being driven to the island by the heavy winds.
3. Surely you want to invite that faithful young man to dinner?
4. Companions, do you want to fight against the Trojans?
5. The Romans treated the republic well for a long time.
6. We were able to overcome the enemy by the efforts of all the citizens.
7. 'We shall always be faithful to you' shouted the soldiers.
8. At night the Romans quickly pitched camp at the top of the mountain.
9. The fierce lion finally caught sight of the stupid and slow soldier in the forest.
10. The boys ran as quickly as possible to the top of the mountain.

**Exercise 7.5E**
1. Will the victory be soon announced by the emperor?
2. How can this very slow boy get to the middle of the city within two days?
3. At that time he was crueller than the other emperors.
4. Why is this slave shouting loudly like this?
5.  Three guards were drinking wine in the emperor's garden.
6. 'What type of lion escaped?' 'Both big and very fierce.'
7. The faithful soldiers didn't want to leave.
8. The stupid soldiers had in mind to desert.
9. It's time to invite those senators to dinner.
10. The faithful soldier by chance received a very serious wound.

**Exercise 8.2**
1. The letter was received on the third day.
2. The woman's beautiful voice was heard by the young man.
3. The general's spears were taken by the slave.
4. The rest of the slaves have already been gathered in the middle of the town.
5. The boy was caught sight of by his father.
6. War was decided upon by the king.
7. The heavy food was eaten yesterday.
8. The town was defended for a long time by the citizens.
9. The walls were destroyed by the young men.
10. These words were said by the king.
11. The standards were captured yesterday.
12. How was the water drunk?
13. These things were quickly done.
14. A few arrows were thrown into the town.
15. This gold was found in rome.
16. This soldier was ordered to leave.
17. A very bad leader was chosen by the king.

18. Nineteen soldiers were sent to the city.
19. The horses were moved at the fourth hour.
20. The wretched slave was klled at the second hour.
21. The doors were destroyed yesterday.
22. The rest of the dead dogs were dragged from the forum.
23. The Romans were ruled for a long time by kings.
24. A small part of the book was written by three pupils.
25. All the books were handed over by the pupil.
26. That young man was caught sight of in Rome yesterday.

**Exercise 8.3E**
1. The enemy camp was taken at the second hour.
2. The water was quickly drunk by the horse.
3. All the spears were taken by the young man.
4. The soldiers have already been collected together by their leader.
5. Meanwhile the enemy was defeated.
6. War was finally decided upon by the chief.
7. The food has already been eaten by the horse.
8. The city was bravely defended by the citizens.
9. The very beautiful house was destroyed by the guards.
10. These words were said by the sad leader.
11. Those soldiers were led to Rome.
12. He became man.
13. These things were done well.
14. All the spears have already been thrown against the enemy.
15. This gold was found yesterday under the house.
16. This soldier was ordered to leave.
17. The best leader was chosen by the soldiers.
18. Seven guards were sent to the sea.
19. The weapons were moved yesterday by the bold boy.
20. The chief was killed at the third hour.
21. The gold was put there yesterday.
22. The soldiers were led back to the river.
23. This shop was destroyed yesterday.
24. This letter was written by a famous poet.
25. The wretched slaves were handed over by the master.
26. War was waged for a long time.

**Exercise 9.1**
1. The signal had been given at first light.
2. The merchant's voice had been heard by the girl.
3. The chief's weapons had been taken by the slave.
4. All the slaves had now been gathered together in the city.
5. The boy had now been caught sight of by his mother.
6. War had been decided upon by the chief.
7. The food had been eaten yesterday by the horses.
8. The walls had been defended for a long time by the citizens.
9. The camp gate had been destroyed by the enemy.
10. These bad words had been said by the king.

**Exercise 9.2E**
1. The horse had been moved at the fifth hour.
2. The chief had been killed at the second hour.
3. This shop had been destroyed yesterday.
4. The leader had been invited to dinner by the emperor.
5. The Britons had been ruled for a long time by the Romans.
6. This book had been written by a famous poet.
7. All the slaves had been handed over by the leader.
8. My companion had been seen yesterday in the town.

**Exercise 9.3**
1. The boys are chasing the dogs along the road.
2. The soldiers guard the camp for a long time.

3. I never desert my friends.
4. A faithful soldier does not kill his chief.
5. The mistress is looking for the money.
6. The wretched farmer is looking for the road.
7. The father leaves his son at home.

**Exercise 9.4E**
1. The farmer is looking for his stupid son.
2. The tired guards are building the walls.
3. The chief catches sight of his wife in the forum.
4. The soldiers kill the slave.
5. Harsh winds are driving the ships.
6. The wretched slaves are chasing the dogs.
7. The leaders leave the soldiers in the city.

**Exercise 9.9**
1. The boys were left in the forum by their parents.
2. All the young men assembled in the middle of the city.
3. The freedman's wife had been greeted by the emperor.
4. The slave was killed by the soldiers.
5. The ships had been driven by the harsh winds.
6. The dog had been chased by the wretched slaves.
7. The soldiers were left in the city by their leader.
8. The soldiers trust their wise leader.
9. The young man left the girl at the top of the hill.
10. The walls had been guarded by the guards for a long time.

**Exercise 9.10E**
1. The citizens did not trust their new leader.
2. The walls was being guarded for a long time by the young men.
3. The young man was invited to dinner by the emperor's wife.
4. Why was the slave killed?
5. How was the ship destroyed?
6. The dog was chased by the slaves.
7. The women had been left in  the city by the soldiers.
8. I always trust my friends.
9. The old men will meet tomorrow in the villa.
10. How many soldiers went slowly to the river?

**Exercise 10.1**
1. I took many books.
2. The pupils were taking the books to the teacher.
3. How are you bringing the money?
4. The husband brought gifts for his wife.
5. The leader had already brought all the weapons.
6. The slave brings the food.
7. The slaves will bring the king the letter.
8. This merchant always brings good food.
9. Why are you not bringing the money?
10. What type of wine did your friends bring?

**Exercise 10.2E**
1. The merchant brought all the books to the forum.
2. The pupil was bringing the teacher three books.
3. The mistress brought the letter yesterday.
4. The boy's father brought the teacher many gifts.
5. The chief had already brought all the swords.
6. At that time the winds were carrying the ships to Italy.
7. The mother did not bring her daughter any presents.
8. Companion, how much money have you brought me?
9. To where are you carrying this little dog?
10. I shall not take those swords.

**Exercise 10.5**

1. The old man had lived all his life in Rome.
2. Almost the whole city in which I used to live was destroyed in the war.
3. The whole place in which the boys are playing is very beautiful.
4. This part of the city which all the citizens like is very beautiful.
5. I have given many gifts to that woman whose daughter is very beautiful.
6. I often used to see that boy whom the teacher punished in the town with his friends.
7. Slave, take these books to the teacher who is now in the town.
8. Have you seen the young man I fought with yesterday?
9. The enemy the Romans fought with quickly escaped.
10. These are the girls I often used to play with.

**Exercise 10.6E**

1. The forces which were tired didn't want to fight.
2. Those books the very famous poet wrote are very beautiful.
3. The bar in which the merchants were drinking is very famous.
4. Pompey, to whom the citizens had given the name Magnus, was greeted by everybody.
5. I used to give many gifts to the man whose daughters are very beautiful.
6. I caught sight of the boys the master punished at the top of the hill.
7. Boys, take these books to the teacher who is sleeping in the villa.
8. Comrades, have you seen the young men I fought with yesterday?
9. When two legions were beaten by the slaves, Crassus ordered every tenth soldier to be killed by their colleagues.
10. I sold the books to the merchants who were in the forum yesterday.

**Exercise 10.9**

1. We don't like those who praise the consul.
2. Don't believe those who say these things!
3. That which is difficult often brings rewards.
4. Those young men always watch those women who are very beautiful.
5. We were not able to capture those who were running quickly.

**Exercise 11.1**

1. The troops were descending the hill slowly.
2. At that time all the soldiers were going up to the top of the hill.
3. The wretched woman was crying in front of the shop because she no longer had any money.
4. The wretched boys were sitting in the garden and were quiet.
5. The inhabitants were proceeding through the forest with great care because they were looking for the lions.
6. No one will be able to resist this fierce young man.
7. I always get up at the sixth hour.
8. What happened in the forum yesterday?
9. It's often easier to go up a hill than come down.
10. The wife was always silent in front of the emperor.

**Exercise 11.2E**

1. The fierce dog suddenly got up and chased the terrified boy.
2. The freeman lived in Rome for two years.
3. How can we resist the enemy?
4. The citizens looked for the wild dogs in the streets.
5. The wretched man was crying in front of the bar in which he had caught sight of his wife.
6. Soldiers, proceed to the city as quickly as possible!
7. It is time to be quiet and listen to the king.
8. There were heavy winds yesterday.
9. Why were the maids sitting in the garden?
10. The arrow went into the soldier's body and the leader was unable to take it out.

**Exercise 12.1**

1. I caught sight of the other consul in the middle of the forum.
2. The freedman took a quick horse because he wanted to reach the town before his friend.
3. Meanwhile the leader left other troops at the top of the hill.
4. Surely the king himself didn't bring his wife dinner?
5. Did the maids prepare another dinner?
6. Some women were laughing, others were sleeping.
7. I myself drove these dogs from the garden yesterday.

8. How did these young men resist the soldiers?
9. How many books did the teacher himself take?
10. Some soldiers were killed, others received serious wounds.

**Exercise 12.2E**
1. Meanwhile the other soldiers left as quickly as possible.
2. The master himself was sleeping but no slave fled.
3. The father however finally chose his other son.
4. The king himself neither drank wine nor ate any food.
5. The queen herself drove these dogs out of the garden.
6. Some men were eating, others were drinking.
7. I saw the king himself in that place.
8. These things were done yesterday.
9. What happened to you yesterday?
10. The swift young men were able to capture almost all the dogs.

**Exercise 13.1**
1. If you trust this freedman you are very stupid.
2. The young man will be sad unless he see his girlfriend.
3. If the boy killed this lion he was very brave.
4. If the leader ordered this he was cruel.
5. If we find the road within two hours, we will be able to reach home today.
6. If you have the teacher's books give them to me at once!
7. If you caught sight of the king you were fortunate.
8. If the master said these words he was wise.
9. If you kill the lions the inhabitants will no longer be terrified.
10. If we soon have peace the citizens will trust our leader.

**Exercise 13.2E**
1. If you have the leader's weapons give them to me at once!
2. If you trust those merchants you are very stupid.
3. If we soon have peace the citizens will be happy.
4. If you drive those wild dogs out of the garden at once the mistress will be happy.
5. If the soldiers caught sight of the leader himself they were fortunate.
6. If the slave did this punish him at once!
7. If you stay at home I shall not buy you a present.
8. If you have driven the wild dogs out of the garden you did well.
9. If you want peace, prepare the country for war.

**Exercise 13.4**
1. The companion said to his brother 'Although I have lived in Rome for a long time, I have never seen that senator.'
2. The Romans were easily able to enter the enemy camp because no one was guarding the walls.
3. After sleeping for six hours the old man got up and immediately went out.
4. Although they had wanted to flee yesterday, the soldiers now were defending themselves bravely against the enemy.
5. What will happen if the slaves can kill their masters in this way?
6. The mother was very sad because her daughter had left for Rome.
7. After reaching the enemy camp, the messenger looked for the leader.
8. After receiving the beautiful gift the boy smiled a lot.
9. If the lion kills that inhabitant the others will leave at one.
10. Although the slave was faithful the cruel master resolved to punish him very harshly.
11. Very many men travelled to Rome yesterday because they wanted to see the famous senator.
12. After the messenger announced these things to the emperor, he himself gave the signal.
13. The gods were very angry because men were no longer giving them gifts.
14. Although he lived in Rome for many years, the freedman never saw the emperor.
15. If you give us some money we will be able to buy some gifts in this shop.
16. Although he continued to live in a very beautiful house for many years the old man was always miserable.
17. After hearing this the man praised his companion because of the help.
18. Although the young man looked for the slave-girls for a long time he was not able to find them.
19. The merchant said 'If I buy this garden I shall be able to make wine.'
20. Although they didn't have any money the old men went to the bar.

**Exercise 14.1**
1. After they had been set free by their noble master the fortunate slaves were happy.

2. After the soldier had been made leader by his comrades the soldier behaved well.

3. The old men escaped as quickly as possible after they had been left by their comrades.

4. After the king had been warned about the danger by his companions he resolved to behave well.

5. The father searched for his captured son in all parts of the country.

6. Although they had been wounded by the enemy the soldiers continued guarding the walls.

7. The body of Augustus was brought to Rome and without delay burnt in the forum.

8. The wretched slaves, ordered to work by their master, immediately fled to the bar.

9. Almost all the citizens, wounded by the enemy, fled from the city.

10. After the town had been attacked for a long time it was finally captured.


**Exercise 14.2E**

1. The wind drove the ship that had been destroyed to the island.

2. The farmer for a long time chased all the dogs that had been left in the field.

3. The chief immediately took all the weapons that had been taken to the town.

4. After the wise queen had been warned by her daughter she fled immediately.

5. These temples which had been built in two months were quickly destroyed.

6. The enemy destroyed the walls which had been bravely guarded by the citizens.

7. The enemy finally captured the soldiers who had been defeated in the battle.

8. The huge horse which had been left near the walls was dragged into the city.

9. The ships that had almost been destroyed finally reached Britain.

10. I read within three days the other books that had been praised by the teacher.


**Exercise 15.1**

1. The chief caught sight of almost all the soldiers as they were leaving the town.

2. As the young man had less money he was more miserable.

3. The very bad men were laughing as they took our money.

4. The citizens loved the chief as he behaved well.

5. The boys were safe as they slept in the villa.

6. The leader praised the soldiers as they guarded the temple for the whole night.

7. The soldiers were taken shouting to the ship.

8. The soldiers were killed fighting bravely in the fierce battle.

9. The mother caught sight of her sons as they played in the street.

10. I caught sight of that merchant selling the master's books.


**Exercise 15.2E**

1. The guard caught sight of the freedmen rushing into the town.

2. The boys were terrified as they watched the savage lion.

3. The bad young men were laughing as they took all the money.

4. The citizens drove from the city the king who was behaving badly.

5. The girls were not safe as they slept in the villa.

6. The king praised the guards as they remained the whole night on the wall.

7. The slaves shouting loudly were taken to the general's villa.

8. The hundred soldiers were finally killed as they fought bravely.

9. The brother caught sight of his sister as she played in the garden.

10. The father saw his son sleeping in front of the bar door.


**Exercise 16.1**

1. About to read the book the mistress sat down.

2. By chance we caught sight of the young man as he was about to throw himself into the river.

3. I caught sight of the boy as he was about to take the money.

4. The emperor about to punish the tired slaves ordered his little son to leave.

5. The general was about to give the sign for battle.

6. The boys were about to drive the dog from the garden.

7. When her daughter arrived, the mother was about to buy some gold.

8. When the Romans were about to pitch camp strong winds suddenly arrived.

9. What happened to you as you were about to leave Rome?

10. I warned my father about the old man who was about to take the money.


**Exercise 16.2E**

1. You should not eat such heavy food when you about to sleep.

2. About to relate the words of the general the senator ordered everyone to be quiet.

3. About to attack the city the soldiers were waiting for the general's signal.

4. About to announce a famous victory the emperor finally got up.

5. I greeted my companion as he was about to go into his house.
6. The senator was about to get up.
7. By chance I caught sight of the slave as he was about to hide the money in the wood.
8. Maid, what were you about to do when I caught sight of you?
9. Savage winds destroyed the ships as they were about to leave for Rome.
10. Slaves, what were you about to do when the master returned?

**Exercise 17.1**
1. The general did not want to be heard by the soldiers.
2. The shouts cannot be heard.
3. The citizens do not want to be captured.
4. The dogs could not be driven into the field.
5. The dog did not want to be driven.
6. The woman was not wanting to be caught sight of.
7. The general ordered this food to be consumed.
8. The leader ordered the wall to be defended bravely.
9. The king had ordered the city to be defended.
10. The chief will not order the town to be destroyed.
11. The soldiers did not want to be led along the street.
12. The leader immediately ordered wage to be waged with the enemy.
13. These spears cannot be thrown into the town.
14. The gold will not be able to be found.
15. The leader ordered the slaves to be killed.
16. The teacher ordered all the books to be read.
17. The king ordered the messenger to be sent to Rome.
18. The master will order the slave to be killed.
19. The leader didn't want the gold to be shown to the king.
20. The soldier didn't want to be put in that place.
21. The horse doesn't want to be led by the boy.
22. The king ordered the gold to be searched for in that place.
23. The horses did not want to be led back to the city.
24. The Romans no longer wanted to be ruled by kings.
25. The boys did not want to be left in Rome.
26. The poet didn't want this book to be read.

**Exercise 18.1**
1. The senator invited the leader to his house yesterday.
2. These senators stayed at home for three days.
3. The leader left home at first light.
4. There was a serious wound in the soldier's hand.
5. The town is now in the hands of the enemy.
6. The arrow went into the messenger's hand.
7. The old man was holding a book in one hand, and a letter in the other.
8. The arrow was taken out from the soldier's hand with great care.
9. the senator has two houses: one is in Rome, the other is near the sea.
10. Your life is in my hands.

**Exercise 19.1**
1. I know that the teacher's house is small.
2. The poet writes that the emperor rules well.
3. Do you think that the king is praised?
4. Have you heard that the emperor is in the city?
5. These citizens say that the enemy is approaching the city.
6. The leader always answers that the soldiers do not know these things.
7. The old man is finding out that his horses are no longer in the field.
8. Do you know that the merchants are in the forum?
9. The king understands that the gold is no longer in the villa.
10. Very many men say that the queen has beautiful hands.

**Exercise 19.2**
1. Who knew that the man was at home?
2. The poet narrated that the emperor ruled well.
3. Surely you didn't believe that Rome was an island?

4. I heard that many troops were approaching the city.
5. Those citizens were saying that the enemy were fleeing.
6. The general always used to say that his own soldiers didn't know these things.
7. The old man shouted that the slaves were being handed over to the soldiers.
8. Surely you knew that that man was a senator?
9. The king found out that the city was already in enemy hands.
10. Very many women said the the king had very small hands.

**Exercise 20. 1**
1. Then the old man noticed that two of the dogs had left.
2. The brother announced that the town had been captured by the enemy.
3. Almost all the citizens now know that the emperor has died.
4. All the pupils knew that the teacher had written a very well-known book.
5. The slave replied to his master that the horses had been captured by the enemy.
6. For a long time I used to believe that the king had been killed by these men.
7. My brother told me that the general had left at first light.
8. The king announced that all the ships had been destroyed before the battle.
9. The general announced that three soldiers had escaped from enemy hands.
10. Who didn't know that the emperor was wise?

**Exercise 20.2**
1. I said that I hadn't done this very bad thing.
2. Who announced that you had destroyed the walls?
3. Did the soldiers tell you that they had done these bad things?
4. Surely the young men didn't announce that they had been beaten by the little boys?
5. The slave often used to say to me that he couldn't find his master's gold.
6. The man promised his wife that he would buy some gold in the forum.
7. The general announced that his own troops would move camp at first light.
8. The guard said that the soldier had not escaped.
9. The parents wrote that they were staying in the city.
10. Why do you say that you yourself have done this?

**Exercise 20.3E**
1. The chief used to say that he wanted to save the republic.
2. Who announced that you had reached the town?
3. Surely the general didn't tell you that he had done these bad things?
4. Surely the young men announced that they had overcome the boys?
5. The bad boys often used to tell us that they had wounded the dogs.
6. The soldiers promised that they would fight as bravely as possible.
7. The allies shouted in a loud voice that they wanted to wage a new war against the enemy.
8. The guards said that the enemy had not fled.
9. The boys said that they had not done these very bad things.
10. Why do they say that you yourself did this bad thing?

**Exercise 21.1**
1. There were as many boys as girls.
2. The man had as much money as his wife.
3. Boys are like they have always been.
4. The freedman had as large a house as the senator.
5. There were as many men as women in the shop.
6. The son had as much money as his father.
7. The enemy had as large a camp as the Romans.
8. We have as many books as you.
9. He who can understand this is wise.
10. He is just as you wrote him to be.

**Exercise 22.1**
1. The wretched boy had no food; I wanted to prepare an excellent dinner for him.
2. The leader saw that the soldiers were fighting bravely; after the victory they were sent to the king.
3. I noticed that the dogs were sleeping in the garden; I ordered them to be driven away after the dinner.
4. Yesterday I bought a beautiful gift for the senator; when he received it he was very happy.
5. Your sister was in the forum yesterday; when I saw her, I greeted her at once.
6. The consul had four sons; of these one was a soldier.

7. The messenger announced the emperor's words; when the citizens heard them they were angry.

8. I sent a letter to my brother yesterday; when he received it he was happy.

9. I gave the teacher two books; when he saw them he laughed.

10. The merchant sold me the books; so I gave him the money.

## Exercise 23.1

1. The citizens hurried to the middle of the city to see the queen.
2. The Romans fought bravely to overcome the enemy.
3. The slaves escaped quickly lest they be punished by their master.
4. The young men drove the dogs into the field to kill them there.
5. The soldiers gathered in the town to choose another leader.
6. The soldiers fled at once lest they be captured by the enemy.
7. The citizens left the city as quickly as possible to escape from the enemy.
8. The citizens and the soldiers built a huge wall to defend the city.
9. The boy went to the town with his father to avoid being on his own in the house.
10. The master decided to travel to the forum so that he could see for himself the new slaves.

## Exercise 23.2E

1. The consul hurried to the forum to see his companion.
2. The citizens quickly gathered to catch sight of the new slaves.
3. The enemy quickly escaped to avoid being defeated by us.
4. The farmers drove the rest of the dogs out of the town so that the citizens would not be terrified.
5. The soldiers ran to the town centre to see the general again.
6. The guards fled at once in order not to be killed by the enemy.
7. Almost all the citizens left the city to escape from the enemy.
8. The soldiers used to eat a lot of good food to have strong bodies.
9. The girl remained in the house to be alone.
10. All the spears and arrows were taken to the house so that the leader could defend himself.

## Exercise 23.4

1. The father sent his son to Rome to work with his brother there.
2. The leader ordered the best soldiers to hurry to the city to defend it bravely.
3. The teacher showed the best books to the pupils so that they would write better.
4. The master praised the slave so that he would run more quickly.
5. The leader said these words to the soldiers so that they would fight more boldly.
6. The king himself came to the city in order that the soldiers would defend the wall more bravely.
7. The king sent the soldiers to the fields in order that the farmers work more safely.
8. The leader sent the soldiers to the town to destroy the walls.
9. The father punished his son very savagely so that he would work better.
10. The leader handed over the best weapons to the soldiers in order that they could carry out the matter more easily.

## Exercise 24.1

1. There were so many dogs in the forum that the merchants left.
2. The wound was so serious that the general had to stay at home for a long time.
3. The boy was driving the dogs so violently that his father was angry.
4. The emperor was so wise that he could easily understand the enemy's plan.
5. The slave was working with such care that his master praised him.
6. The lion was so quick that the inhabitants could not kill him.
7. The enemy wounded many Romans so seriously that they could not resist them.
8. There were so many dogs in the garden that the mistress didn't want to leave the house.
9. The freedman built the house in such a way that his wife didn't want to live there.
10. The winds were so strong that the whole camp was destroyed.

## Exercise 25.1

1. The wise teacher advised his pupils to read the best books.
2. My father asked the young men to leave the city centre.
3. Surely the citizens didn't persuade you to throw the weapons into the river?
4. The general himself persuaded all the soldiers to remain in the city.
5. Surely the leader asked you to defend the city?
6. Why did your father advise you to cross the river?
7. Who asked you drive the dogs out of the forum?
8. The leader asked the bold soldiers to attack the enemy camp at the third hour.
9. The teacher persuaded the pupils to behave well.

10. The angry king asked the slaves to prepare the food.

**Exercise 25.2E**
1. The father advised his son not to read the very bad books.
2. The teacher persuaded the boys to write well.
3. Surely the leader asked you to attack the town?
4. The queen herself persuaded her son to remain in the city.
5. Surely the king asked you to remain in the city?
6. How did the guard persuade you to throw yourself into the river?
7. Who asked you to bring the dogs food?
8. The master asked the slaves to prepare food for the horses.
9. The guard asked the soldiers to leave the town centre.
10. After warning one soldier with words, the general persuaded the others to fight.

**Exercise 26.1**
1. When he was finally an old man, the merchant lived a happy life.
2. As the enemy were slowly approaching, the soldiers were preparing to flee.
3. Since the king didn't want to do this, the citizens were very angry.
4. Since he was little, this boy didn't want to fight with those young men.
5. Although he was very small this brave boy was preparing to fight with those young men.
6. As he was neither brave nor strong, nobody loved that chief.
7. As the winds were wild, the ships were driven to the island.
8. As the slaves were running quickly no one was able to catch them.
9. As the guards were leading the wretched man to his death, the emperor suddenly arrived.
10. As he was very angry, the boy's father went immediately to the teacher.

**Exercise 26.2E**
1. As they read the books, the boys were laughing.
2. As their friend approached, the companions stood in the middle of the road.
3. As he thought there was danger, the leader didn't want to enter that house.
4. The enemy destroyed this temple although it was very beautiful and most sacred.
5. As the slave used to work well, the master often warmly praised him.
6. As they were driven by savage winds, those ships were not able to reach the island.
7. As the enemy were at hand, the terrified citizens hurried to the sea.
8. Although he was working in the fields, the farmer did not see the horses.
9. As they fought bravely in the battle, the bold soldiers received many serious wounds.
10. As they were sailing slowly towards Italy, two of these ships were destroyed.

**Exercise 27.1**
1. When they had caught sight of the young men, the old men fled to the mountains.
2. As they made a very long journey, the soldiers were very tired.
3. When you had fought bravely, you were praised by both the king and the general.
4. When all his soldiers had fled, the general gave himself up to the enemy.
5. When he had read the book of the famous poet, the pupil wanted to read another book.
6. When he had heard the words of the messenger, the king was very afraid.
7. When he had sat down, the guard killed the king at once with his sword.
8. When they had fought bravely in the battle, the soldiers were praised by their leader.
9. When they had fled the danger, the leader punished the wretched soldiers most harshly.
10. When a part of the town had been captured by the enemy, very many terrified citizens fled.

**Exercise 27.2E**
1. Master, surely you were angry when you found out that your villa had been destroyed?
2. When they had fought bravely in the battle, the soldiers were not praised by their leader.
3. The leader warmly praised the brave guards when they had remained near the walls.
4. When he had eaten heavy food, the old man didn't want to go out.
5. When all the women had arrived they were greeted by the men.
6. As I had received a serious wound, I was no longer able to climb the hill.
7. The citizens were happy when they had understood the emperor's new plan.
8. When they had been warned of the danger, the soldiers chose another road through the forest.
9. The master was very angry when he found out that one of his slaves had been dragged from the villa.
10. When he had understood that the man was not an enemy, the emperor decided to free him.

**Exercise 28.1**

1. I asked the boys whether they had seen the new teacher.
2. The master asked the slave where the horse was.
3. The father wanted find out why his son had left.
4. The leader didn't know where the soldiers had hurried to.
5. Did you hear how many ships were approaching?
6. The leader knew why the messenger had arrived.
7. Do you know who had taken all the books?
8. Only the senator didn't know what had happened.
9. The farmer asked what the wind was like.
10. At that time the emperor found out how the enemy had won.
11. The emperor asked the general why he had done this.
12. The man was asked who he was.
13. The leader asked the soldier what he felt.
14. When she found out what the maid was preparing, the mistress returned home.
15. The citizens were terrified as they did not understand what had happened.

**Exercise 28.2E**

1. Surely you understood how the temple had been destroyed?
2. I did not understand what had happened.
3. Did you hear how much money that man had?
4. I never understood what the teacher was saying.
5. I didn't know where my wife wanted to go.
6. The leader asked the soldier where he had left the horses.
7. I didn't hear what type of villa the freedman had bought.
8. The leader wanted to know why the soldiers had left at first light.
9. The senator asked how many soldiers were drinking in the bar.
10. The boy finally found out what his father had done.
11. The girl asked her mother what she should do.
12. The old man didn't know what he should eat.
13. I told nobody what had happened at home.
14. I hadn't made up my mind where to go.
15. Asked who she was, the terrified girl said nothing.

**Exercise 29.1**

1. The master is here today, but his wife is away.
2. The other river is deep.
3. By chance the brave soldier was killed.
4. I have a large house where I live with my dear children.
5. And so I made this journey again yesterday.
6. Do the job like this, stupid!
7. The happy slave was taken to his master's house.
8. The freedman's children were carrying nine books to the new gate.
9. After returning home, the master shouted loudly.
10. The king's affairs frighten me.

**Exercise 29.2E**

1. We are at the top of the mountain.
2. Suddenly the freedman gets up and immediately stands near the door with his children.
3. The boy frightens the dog, but is afraid of the lion.
4. The citizens finally handed over the horse to the consul which had been dragged into the town centre.
5. After defeating the enemy, the emperor lived for a long time in Rome.
6. The new leader has three books and nine children.
7. Finally I took the ninth book.
8. 'Take me to your master!' said the freedman.
9. In this way the Romans finally won.
10. The children are dear to the master.

**Exercise 30.1**

1. If the captives have thrown the prizes into the river they are stupid.
2. The chief ordered the careful slaves to bring all the prizes home.
3. I often asked my father to give me back the gold.
4. Several soldiers praised his courage in a loud voice.

5. I didn't know where the captives had come from.
6. The emperor ordered all the soldiers to return the arms at once.
7. When did the emperor reach the forum?
8. Nobody knew when the emperor had arrived.
9. The careful chieftain himself used to read all the letters he had received.
10. Some wretched slaves that had been immediately captured by the soldiers were dragged to the king.

**Exercise 30.2E**
1. If you don't return the prizes at once, I shall be angry.
2. The wretched boy begged his mother not to give the prizes back to the merchant.
3. When did you buy these careful slaves?
4. Several captives were lying at the top of the hill eating food and drinking wine.
5. In this way the chieftain taught the legions that had been very often prepared to be defeated how to win.
6. At that time the chieftain gave orders to the general that the soldiers attack the town.
7. Asked who he was and where he had come from, the man replied 'I am a Roman citizen.'
8. The general didn't know when those soldiers had left Rome.
9. Have you ever seen a more careful slave than this one?

**Exercise 31.1**
1. The emperor was hoping to reach Rome within two days.
2. The senator believed that his own slaves had begun to build the wall.
3. My companion said that he would not support my enemy.
4. The slaves were forced to work for a long time in the field.
5. Some people think that these senators are careful.
6. The leader thought that he himself could lead the Roman troops.
7. My friend willingly supported that senator.
8. The emperor hid these dreadful deeds from his wife for a long time.
9. Some people believed that the emperor himself had set fire to the city.
10. The merchant was hoping to sell all the gold to these women.
11. The old man believed that he would never see his daughter.
12. The freedman believed that he would lead a happier life near the sea.
13. I promise to kill the very fierce lion.
14. The king promised the citizens that he would make a great city.
15. The woman was very sad because she thought she would never see her daughter.

**Exercise 31.2E**
1. Freedman, when did you begin to build this house?
2. The wretched old man was forced to sell all the gold.
3. The father continued thinking about this thing for a few hours then suddenly left.
4. This young man comes from a very famous family and hopes to be a consul within a few years.
5. The senator begged me to support his companion.
6. The freedman carried out many crimes in Rome.
7. When did you hide these prizes in the garden?
8. The chieftain didn't know when his son had arrived in Rome.
9. The chieftain knew that nobody would do such things.
10. The freedman hoped to go to Rome and live happily.
11. I hope that these merchants will soon leave the city.
12. The young man promised to work for many hours.
13. The father said that he would take all the books.
14. I shall never support the enemy of my companion.
15. These stupid people decided set fire to the forest.

**Exercise 32.1**
1. While the senators were thinking about this matter, a large crowd of citizens assembled in the forum.
2. After her husband left, the wife began to think about her wretched life.
3. As soon as the leader understood that the enemy was approaching the town, he sent a letter to the emperor.
4. Greeted kindly in this way by the senator, the citizens turned back from the forum.
5. The freedman was miserable. For, when he was an old man, he saw his town captured by the enemy.
6. Many years after the emperor finally received the highest command.
7. The Roman soldiers were entering the camp; at the same time the enemy general was preparing to flee.
8. After the dreadful storm had driven all the ships from the island, the leader no longer believed that he would win.
9. While the soldiers were arriving at the house of the villa, the master took a bold plan.
10. Many senators supported his enemy because Caesar had the command.

**Exercise 32.2E**

1. As soon as he heard about the victory the emperor sent a letter to the senators.
2. At first the soldiers fought bravely, but within a few hours they were beaten by the enemy.
3. By chance the Roman troops broke a way through the enemy; in this way they were able to defeat them.
4. Then the senator turned to his companion and smiled kindly.
5. That emperor had a short command because of his many dreadful crimes.
6. The chief resolved to be fierce in war and generous in peace.
7. The wife by chance caught sight of her husband drinking in the bar with a beautiful woman; she never trusted him afterwards.
8. While the wife was burning the letter she had received, the husband suddenly returned home.
9. As soon as the flames had consumed the body of the emperor, heavy winds arrived.
10. At that time several Romans believed that there were many savage tribes in that land.

**Exercise 33.1**

1. The senator caught sight of a certain enemy standing near the shop door.
2. The general had to remain at home for four days because of the deep wound in his foot.
3. Caesar's father lifted his son up and said 'I accept him'.
4. This is an onerous task; I will not be able to complete it on my own.
5. The enemy entered the town at night and took all the weapons.
6. A lot of blood was falling from the wound; the soldier however felt nothing.
7. I am supporting this kindly senator much rather than that wicked one.
8. When the emperor heard that the Romans had defeated the enemy he was full of joy.
9. In tears a certain companion approached the freedman
10. I have to complete these difficult matters before night.

**Exercise 33.2E**

1. Some men were doing the same job, others were lying in the garden.
2. The freedman remained at home for three hours; for he had eaten some heavy food.
3. Joy was short with the leader; for on the next day he heard that his daughter would not be returning.
4. The same families always carry out these crimes.
5. The prince was looking for a life full of joy.
6. Several citizens think that the new chief is very wicked.
7. So much blood had fallen from his foot that he could no longer walk.
8. With very great care the two soldiers lifted onto his horse the leader who had been seriously wounded in the foot.
9. While the wretched slave was being led away by the guards, a certain companion approached him.
10. Some men were looking at some women and other men other women.

**Exercise 34.1**

1. The little boy was afraid to leave because there were several dogs in the street.
2. The danger was so great that the citizens were afraid that the enemy would capture the city.
3. How willingly he invites everyone to his house!
4. Fearing that his son was in danger, the father left at once for the forum.
5. The man feared that those wicked men would come to attack his house.
6. Fearing that his unfortunate son would be killed by the lion the father shouted out at the top of his voice.
7. A part of the ninth legion finally reached the nearest camp two hours before night.
8. The slaves were punished for their wicked crimes.
9. After so many years the Roman citizens were afraid that one man would bring back a kingdom.
10. Fearing that her husband would return before night, his wife burnt the letters she had received.

**Exercise 34.2E**

1. Fearing that the emperor would find this out, the leader hid the book.
2. At that time many citizens feared that the enemy would attack within a few days.
3. Fearing that the tribes would gather there the emperor sent two legions to Germany.
4. The noise was so great that several citizens were afraid to go to the forum.
5. The freedman was afraid that those soldiers would come to take his wife.
6. The maid was afraid that her master would not leave.
7. Fearing that his troops would be overcome by the enemy, the leader begged the emperor for help.
8. After this dreadful crime several people were afraid that all the slaves would be punished.
9. Fearing that the enemy would soon be arriving at the city gates, the citizens hid all the gold.
10. Stay with me as long as you can, my friend!

**Exercise 35.1**

1. Thinking that man was the king, the stupid freedman offered him a beautiful gift.
2. After the enemy took all the weapons away, the citizens were forced to flee.
3. As they were sailing slowly to the harbour, two of these ships were destroyed by the savage storm.
4. Several men shouted that the chief had handed the port over to the enemy.
5. Where have you taken my books and letter to, slave?
6. Full of hope the emperor ordered the general to lead the army into battle.
7. Exhausted by the serious wounds the leader stayed at home for six months.
8. The mother saw in the expression of the little boy that he had hope.
9. After the slaves had reported these things to their master, his son were very miserable.
10. The freedman preferred to live a happy life near the sea than on the wretched island.

**Exercise 35.2E**

1. The son was of such hope that his father believed that he would be consul within a few years.
2. The father took the books away lest his son read them.
3. The old man very much preferred to stay at home than to go to the bar.
4. The emperor put all hope of victory in the courage of his own soldiers.
5. The slave preferred to be punished than to flee.
6. At first light the emperor full of hope led the army out the camp.
7. The old man understood by the expression of the dog that it was sad.
8. Thinking that the emperor would arrive within a few hours, the general led the legion to the river.
9. Certain messengers are reporting that the Romans have already captured the city.
10. When the head of Pompey was brought to him, Caesar wept.

**Exercise 36.1**

1. As the boys knew that the journey was difficult they didn't want to set out.
2. The consul spoke for a long time to the senators then finally sat down tired.
3. Several believe that the Romans will enter the war within two years.
4. The old men spoke for two hours then left.
5. The nine soldiers set out; however they all died on the journey.
6. The soldier suffered many serious wounds; he finally died.
7. We followed the legion for three hours then we returned to the town.
8. The leader said that the soldiers would set out within two hours and return before night.
9. How cruelly you have suffered for so many years!
10. While the soldiers were advancing towards the door of the house, the master had a bold plan.

**Exercise 36.2E**

1. Although the chieftain was dead, very many citizens were afraid of his body.
2. The soldiers hope to leave at the second hour and return tomorrow.
3. The fourth farmer will go into the house within two hours.
4. The angry women had spoken for two hours about their husbands crimes.
5. The queen finally returned and suddenly died in the house.
6. The parents were enduring the wild cries of the little girls.
7. We admired the emperor because he sang well.
8. The emperor suffered many serious wounds.
9. Almost all the troops advanced to the river and soon returned.
10. Within three days the king will try to set out on a long journey.

**Exercise 36.5**

1. We heard the leader encouraging the soldiers.
2. Boy, did you see the slave trying to do his job?
3. We caught sight of the soldiers as they left the town.
4. We escaped from the women as they talked in a loud voice in the house.
5. By chance we saw the troops as they were setting out for the mountain.
6. The Romans chased the enemy as they tried to escape.
7. Don't believe men saying these things!
8. The enemy suddenly attacked the troops as they were setting out.
9. The son greeted his father as he came in.
10. The guards drove back the men as they were advancing towards the town.

**Exercise 36.7**

1. After Sulla had died, Caesar immediately returned to Rome.
2. After he had often tried to escape but in vain, the slave decided to stay in the town.

3. After speaking for many hours the old men finally went off home.
4. Having set off on a long journey the soldiers were now very tired.
5. Having set off at dawn the troops reached the river within three hours.
6. Having followed the men across the hills the young men finally caught sight of them near the river.
7. The master savagely punished the boy who had been trying to take the prizes.
8. The soldiers led back the man who had endured many savage things.
9. Our soldiers attacked the enemy as they were trying to attack the city.
10. A crowd of women who had set out from the city at dawn walked for five hours.

**Exercise 36.9E**
1. As the enemy were at hand, the army advanced towards the sea.
2. The crowd of young men who had set out from the town at dawn walked for three hours.
3. Boys, did you see the old man trying to do his job?
4. The men killed almost all the soldiers who were trying to attack the town.
5. The leader caught sight of people as they were leaving the town.
6. The teacher very harshly punished the boys who had been trying to destroy the prizes.
7. Although they knew that this journey was difficult, the boys wanted to set out.
8. After following the young men across the sea, the sailors finally caught sight of them on the island.
9. Almost all the citizens caught sight of the defeated leader as he returned to the city.
10. Having set out at dawn the women reached the river within a few hours.
11. The Greek leader decided to attack the enemy as they were trying to escape.
12. Having set out three hours beforehand, the soldiers quickly reached the place.
13. Do not speak about this matter with the senators!
14. After speaking for many hours the husbands were home.
15. The soldiers suddenly attacked with many weapons the men as they set out.
16. The maid having tried in vain to drive the dogs returned home.
17. The daughter greeted her mother as she entered the temple.
18. Having suffered many serious wounds the soldiers finally died.
19. The guard chased the man as he was proceeding to the town.
20. Although they were being driven by fierce winds, those ships were able to enter the port.

**Exercise 36.12**
1. Hail, emperor, we who about to die salute you.
2. As he was about to set off from Rome, the leader spoke to the senators.
3. As he was about to speak to the senators the emperor got up.
4. About to be punished, the captives threw themselves at the feet of the emperor.
5. About to follow her son to the top of the hill, the mother decided to drink a lot of water.
6. About to return home the husband bought a beautiful gift for his wife.
7. As he was about to go into the bar the man by chance caught sight of his companion.
8. About to enter into war the emperor ordered a hundred ships to be built.
9. About to set off from home the husband said 'Goodbye' to his wife.
10. About to speak to the citizens the emperor first smiled.

**Exercise 37.1**
1. The man dared to say to the senators that the emperor was cruel.
2. Who dared to carry out such a great crime?
3. The leader himself hoped the soldiers would dare to attack the town.
4. He alone dared to advance through the forest.
5. At that time nobody dared to address the senators.
6. The anger of the citizens was so great that the senator didn't dare to speak to them.
7. The leader was very pleased because his soldiers had beaten the enemy.
8. Very pleased because they had received the presents, the boys returned home.
9. Don't take away these gifts which are normally offered to the gods.
10. If one slave had killed their own master, the Romans used to kill all his slaves.

**Exercise 37.2E**
1. Who will dare to speak like this before the senators?
2. The father was hoping that his son would dare to cross the deep river.
3. So great was the courage of that soldier that he alone dared to climb the hill.
4. The mother was very pleased because her son had received so many prizes.
5. The senator dared to say to his companions that the general was leading the army badly.
6. I used to see the same merchants in the forum.
7. Who will dare to enter the enemy camp on his own at night?

8. At that time nobody dared to set out for Rome.
9. Very pleased that his son had received so many gifts the father returned home.
10. She alone dared to advance along the road.

**Exercise 38.1**
1. That man had been elected senator a few days before.
2. This man is now called Augustus by all the citizens.
3. The wretched leader had to remain a captive on the island for three years.
4. The leader was reported as dead yesterday by a certain messenger.
5. That consul, as reported by several people, will soon leave.
6. After the death of his very dear dog, the old man always seemed sad.
7. That woman remained a maid with the emperor for many years.
8. This soldier was thought to be braver than all his comrades.
9. The king seemed to everybody to be careful.
10. There was a savage storm yesterday, as you had often warned me.

**Exercise 38.2E**
1. Why was this maid reported to be careful?
2. This man always appeared wise among the senators.
3. Surely this unlucky soldier will not be chosen leader by his comrades?
4. The maid of that woman stayed with me for nine years.
5. The emperor was reported as dead yesterday by certain citizens.
6. That senator had been elected consul a few days before.
7. After the victory of the army the emperor did not appear sad.
8. This woman was thought to behave more kindly than her husband.
9. Neither Crassus nor Pompey wanted to appear greater than the other.
10. After the victory Crassus and Pompey were made consuls.

**Exercise 39.1**
1. The emperor made a very bold plan to serve his country from danger.
2. The frightened slaves were preparing everything to drive back the fierce young men.
3. Soldiers were sent to kill all the slaves.
4. The citizens hurried to the forum to catch sight of the famous leader.
5. When Caesar entered the Circus Maximus all the senators rose to greet him.
6. The emperor sent soldiers to save the city.
7. Many citizens came to the city centre to hear the queen.
8. Many ships were sent to Greece to capture the slaves.
9. The messenger was sent yesterday to warn the citizens about the danger.
10. The Sabines came to Rome to snatch the women.

**Exercise 39.2E**
1. The emperor sent his leader to destroy the city.
2. Several brave soldiers were sent to kill all the lions.
3. Many citizens came together at the city centre to listen to the queen.
4. The young men hurried to the forum to catch a sight of the beautiful women.
5. The man returned home to look for the money.
6. The old man entered the bar to drink some wine.
7. When will you make a plan to drive all the dogs from the town?
8. The terrified citizens were preparing their weapons to drive the enemy back.
9. The father came to Rome to buy some slaves.
10. Since he had enough money, the freedman came to Rome to buy some gold.

**Exercise 40.3**
1. When he had eaten a lot of heavy food, the master went to the garden to sleep.
2. When they found out that the cruel emperor had died most citizens were happy.
3. When the senators had praised this plan, the old man finally sat down.
4. With his sword hidden the naughty man went to the forum.
5. As the master's dinner had been prepared the maid went out into the garden.
6. When he had seen the wound on the soldier's foot, the leader got off his horse.
7. After his dear dog had been killed in the street the wretched old man continued to live alone.
8. When this letter had been received the young man cried for a long time.
9. When the emperor's name had been heard, most citizens made a noise.
10. Having put down their weapons, they slowly approached the door.

**Exercise 40.4**

1. With this done everyone went away.
2. Once he had been seen, soldiers who had previously been terrified now began to fight more bravely.
3. Once the girl had been save from danger everyone returned home happy.
4. With the master thus dead, all the slaves were sad.
5. With few towns putting up resistance Caesar with his legions soon reached Rome.
6. He pushed the door and went into the villa.
7. With these things done, the senators departed.
8. With all the citizens watching, the ships set off for Troy.
9. After hearing these words the girls were very sad.
10. With the city captured, the leader left.

**Answers to the Captions**

| | | | | | |
|---|---|---|---|---|---|
| Ch. 1: 4,2 | Ch.2: 3,4 | Ch. 3: 2,5 | Ch. 4: 4,3 | Ch. 5: 3,3 | Ch. 6: 4,5 |
| Ch. 7: 4,3,5,2 | Ch. 8: 5,4,3,4 | Ch. 9: 4,3,1,5 | Ch. 10: 3,1,5,3 | Ch.11: 5,5 | Ch.12: 1,1 |
| Ch. 13: 3,2 | Ch.14: 3,5,4 | Ch. 15: 3,3,5,4 | Ch. 16: 1,2 | Ch.17: 4 | Ch.18: 5 |
| Ch. 19: 1,2 | Ch.20: 4,4 | Ch. 21: 5,2 | Ch. 22: 5,1 | Ch.23: 4,4 | Ch.24: 3,1 |
| Ch. 25: 3,3,3,4 | Ch.26: 4,5 | Ch. 27: 4,1 | Ch. 28: 2,1 | Ch. 30: 5,4 | Ch. 31: 4,1 |
| Ch. 32: 3,2 | Ch.33: 2,1 | Ch: 34: 3,5 | Ch. 35: 4,5 | Ch. 36: 1,4 | Ch. 37: 3,5 |
| Ch. 38: 2 | Ch.39: 2,1 | Ch. 40: 4,5 | | | |

# GRAMMAR SUMMARY

## Nouns

| declension | 1 | 2 | 2 | 2 | 2 |
|---|---|---|---|---|---|
| gender | feminine | masculine | masculine | masculine | neuter |
| **singular** | | | | | |
| nominative. | puella | servus | puer | ager | bellum |
| vocative | puella | serve | puer | ager | bellum |
| accusative | puellam | servum | puerum | agrum | bellum |
| genitive | puellae | servi | pueri | agri | belli |
| dative | puellae | servo | puero | agro | bello |
| ablative | puella | servo | puero | agro | bello |
| **plural** | | | | | |
| nominative | puellae | servi | pueri | agri | bella |
| vocative | puellae | servi | pueri | agri | bella |
| accusative | puellas | servos | pueros | agros | bella |
| genitive | puellarum | servorum | puerorum | agrorum | bellorum |
| dative | puellis | servis | pueris | agris | bellis |
| ablative | puellis | servis | pueris | agris | bellis |

| declension | 3 | 3 | 3 neut. | 4 | 5 |
|---|---|---|---|---|---|
| **singular** | | | | | |
| nominative | rex | civis | nomen | exercitus | res |
| vocative | rex | civis | nomen | exercitus | res |
| accusative | regem | civem | nomen | exercitum | rem |
| genitive | regis | civis | nominis | exercitus | rei |
| dative | regi | civi | nomini | exercitui | rei |
| ablative | rege | cive | nomine | exercitus | re |
| **plural** | | | | | |
| nominative | reges | cives | nomina | exercitus | res |
| vocative | reges | cives | nomina | exercitus | res |
| accusative | reges | cives | nomina | exercitus | res |
| genitive | regum | civium | nominum | exercituum | rerum |
| dative | regibus | civibus | nominibus | exercitibus | rebus |
| ablative | regibus | civibus | nominibus | exercitibus | rebus |

# Adjectives

**bonus -a -um**     **good**

|  | masculine | feminine | neuter |
|---|---|---|---|
| **singular** | | | |
| nominative | bonus | bona | bonum |
| vocative | bone | bona | bonum |
| accusative | bonum | bonam | bonum |
| genitive | boni | bonae | boni |
| dative | bono | bonae | bono |
| ablative | bono | bona | bon |
| **plural** | | | |
| nominative | boni | bonae | bona |
| vocative | boni | bonae | bona |
| accusative | bonos | bonas | bonos |
| genitive | bonorum | bonarum | bonorum |
| dative | bonis | bonis | bonis |
| ablative | bonis | bonis | bonis |

**miser -a -um**     **miserable**

|  | masculine | feminine | neuter |
|---|---|---|---|
| **singular** | | | |
| nominative | miser | misera | miserum |
| vocative | miser | misera | miserum |
| accusative | miserum | miseram | miserum |
| genitive | miseri | miserae | miseri |
| dative | misero | miserae | misero |
| ablative | misero | misera | misero |
| **plural** | | | |
| nominative | miseri | miserae | misera |
| vocative | miseri | miserae | misera |
| accusative | miseros | miseras | misera |
| genitive | miserorum | miserarum | miserorum |
| dative | miseris | miseris | miseris |
| ablative | miseris | miseris | miseris |

**sacer -ra -rum**     **sacred**

|  | masculine | feminine | neuter |
|---|---|---|---|
| **Singular** | | | |
| nominative | sacer | sacra | sacrum |
| vocative | sacer | sacra | sacrum |
| accusative | sacrum | sacram | sacrum |
| genitive | sacri | sacrae | sacri |
| dative | sacro | sacrae | sacro |
| ablative | sacro | sacra | sacro |
| **plural** | | | |
| nominative | sacri | sacrae | sacra |
| vocative | sacri | sacrae | sacra |
| accusative | sacros | sacras | sacros |
| genitive | sacrorum | sacrarum | sacrorum |
| dative | sacris | sacris | sacris |
| ablative | sacris | sacris | sacris |

**laetior -ius**          happier

**singular**
| | | | |
|---|---|---|---|
| nominative | laetior | laetior | laetius |
| vocative | laetior | laetior | laetius |
| accusative | laetiorem | laetiorem | laetius |
| genitive | laetioris | laetioris | laetioris |
| dative | laetiori | laetiori | laetiori |
| ablative | laetiore | laetiore | laetiore |

**plural**
| | | | |
|---|---|---|---|
| nominative | laetiores | laetiores | laetiora |
| vocative | laetiores | laetiores | laetiora |
| accusative | laetiores | laetiores | laetiora |
| genitive | laetiorum | laetiorum | laetiorum |
| dative | laetioribus | laetioribus | laetioribus |
| ablative | laetioribus | laetioribus | laetioribus |

**tristis, triste**          sad, gloomy

**singular**
| | | | |
|---|---|---|---|
| nominative | tristis | tristis | triste |
| vocative | tristis | tristis | triste |
| accusative | tristem | tristem | triste |
| genitive | tristis | tristis | tristis |
| dative | tristi | tristi | tristi |
| ablative | tristi | tristi | tristi |

**plural**
| | | | |
|---|---|---|---|
| nominative | tristes | tristes | tristia |
| vocative | tristes | tristes | tristia |
| accusative | tristes | tristes | tristia |
| genitive | tristium | tristium | tristium |
| dative | tristibus | tristibus | tristibus |
| ablative | tristibus | tristibus | tristibus |

**ingens, ingens**          huge

**singular**
| | | | |
|---|---|---|---|
| nominative | ingens | ingens | ingens |
| vocative | ingens | ingens | ingens |
| accusative | ingentem | ingentem | ingens |
| genitive | ingentis | ingentis | ingentis |
| dative | ingenti | ingenti | ingenti |
| ablative | ingenti | ingenti | ingenti |

**plural**
| | | | |
|---|---|---|---|
| nominative | ingentes | ingentes | ingentia |
| vocative | ingentes | ingentes | ingentia |
| accusative | ingentes | ingentes | ingentia |
| genitive | ingentium | ingentium | ingentium |
| dative | ingentibus | ingentibus | ingentibus |
| ablative | ingentibus | ingentibus | ingentibus |

**celer -is -e**          fast, swift

| | | | |
|---|---|---|---|
| nominative | celer | celeris | celere |
| vocative | celer | celeris | celere |
| accusative | celerem | celerem | celere |
| genitive | celeris | celeris | celeris |
| dative | celeri | celeri | celeri |
| ablative | celeri | celeri | celeri |

**plural**

| | | | |
|---|---|---|---|
| nominative | celeres | celeres | celeria |
| vocative | celeres | celeres | celeria |
| accusative | celeres | celeres | celeria |
| genitive | celerum | celerum | celerum |
| dative | celeribus | celeribus | celeribus |
| ablative | celeribus | celeribus | celeribus |

**hic, haec, hoc        this**

**singular**

| | | | |
|---|---|---|---|
| nominative | hic | haec | hoc |
| accusative | hunc | hanc | hoc |
| genitive | huius | huius | huius |
| dative | huic | huic | huic |
| ablative | hoc | hac | hoc |

**plural**

| | | | |
|---|---|---|---|
| nominative | hi | hae | haec |
| accusative | hos | has | haec |
| genitive | horum | harum | horum |
| dative | his | his | his |
| ablative | his | his | his |

**ille, illa, illud = that**

**singular**

| | | | |
|---|---|---|---|
| nominative | ille | illa | illud |
| accusative | illum | illam | illud |
| genitive | illius | illius | illius |
| dative | illi | illi | illi |
| ablative | illo | illa | illo |

**plural**

| | | | |
|---|---|---|---|
| nominative | illi | illae | illa |
| accusative | illos | illas | illa |
| genitive | illorum | illarum | illorum |
| dative | illis | illis | illis |
| ablative | illis | illis | illis |

**is, ea, id   that; he she, it**

**Singular**

| | | | |
|---|---|---|---|
| nominative | is | ea | id |
| accusative | eum | eam | id |
| genitive | eius | eius | eius |
| dative | ei | ei | ei |
| ablative | eo | eā | eo |

**plural**

| | | | |
|---|---|---|---|
| nominative | ei, ii | eae | ea |
| accusative | eos | eas | ea |
| genitive | eorum | earum | eorum |
| dative | eis, iis | eis, iis | eis |
| ablative | eis, iis | eis, iis | eis, iis |

**ipse ipsa ipsum**     -self

**singular**

| | | | |
|---|---|---|---|
| nominative | ipse | ipsa | ipsum |
| accusative | ipsum | ipsam | ipsum |
| genitive | ipsius | ipsius | ipsius |
| dative | ipsi | ipsi | ipsi |
| ablative | ipso | ipsa | ipso |

**plural**

| | | | |
|---|---|---|---|
| nominative | ipsi | ipsae | ipsa |
| accusative | ipsos | ipsas | ipsa |
| genitive | ipsorum | ipsarum | ipsorum |
| dative | ipsis | ipsis | ipsis |
| ablative | ipsis | ipsis | ipsis |

**solus -a -um**     alone

| | | | |
|---|---|---|---|
| nominative | solus | sola | solum |
| accusative | solum | solam | solum |
| genitive | solius | solius | solius |
| dative | soli | soli | soli |
| ablative | solo | sola | solo |

**unus -a -um**     one

| | | | |
|---|---|---|---|
| nominative | unus | una | unum |
| accusative | unum | unam | unum |
| genitive | unius | unius | unius |
| dative | uni | uni | uni |
| ablative | uno | una | uno |

**totus -a -um**     whole

**singular**

| | | | |
|---|---|---|---|
| nominative | totus | tota | totum |
| accusative | totum | totam | totum |
| genitive | totius | totius | totius |
| dative | toti | toti | toti |
| ablative | toto | tota | toto |

**plural**

| | | | |
|---|---|---|---|
| nominative | toti | totae | tota |
| accusative | totos | totas | tota |
| genitive. | totorum | totarum | totorum |
| dative | totis | totis | totis |
| ablative | totis | totis | totis |

**alius -a -iud**     other

**singular**

| | | | |
|---|---|---|---|
| nominative | alius | alia | aliud |
| accusative | alium | aliam | aliud |
| genitive | alius | alius | alius |
| dative | alii | alii | alii |
| ablative | alio | alia | alio |

**plural**

| nominative | alii | aliae | alia |
|---|---|---|---|
| accusative | alios | alias | alia |
| genitive | aliorum | aliarum | aliorum |
| dative | aliis | aliis | aliis |
| ablative | aliis | aliis | aliis |

Note:

In place of alius in the gen sing. **alterius** is often used

### idem eadem idem  the same

**singular**

| nominative | idem | eadem | idem |
|---|---|---|---|
| accusative | eundem | eandem | idem |
| genitive | eiusdem | eiusdem | eiusdem |
| dative | eidem | eidem | eidem |
| ablative | eodem | eadem | eodem |

**plural**

| nominative | eidem | eaedem | eadem |
|---|---|---|---|
| accusative | eosdem | easdem | eadem |
| genitive | eorundem | earundem | eorundem |
| dative | eisdem | eisdem | eisdem |
| ablative | eisdem | eisdem | eisdem |

# Pronouns

### qui quae quod    who which

**singular**

| nominative | qui | quae | quod |
|---|---|---|---|
| accusative | quem | quam | quod |
| genitive | cuius | cuius | cuius |
| dative | cui | cui | cui |
| ablative | quo | qua | quo |

**plural**

| nominative | qui | quae | quae |
|---|---|---|---|
| accusative | quos | quas | quae |
| genitive | quorum | quarum | quorum |
| dative | quibus | quibus | quibus |
| ablative | quibus | quibus | quibus |

| nominative | ego | tu | nos | vos |
|---|---|---|---|---|
| vocative | - | tu | - | vos |
| accusative | me | te | nos | vos |
| genitive | mei | tui | nostri / nostrum | vestri / vestrum |
| dative | mihi | tibi | nobis | vobis |
| ablative | me | te | nobis | vobis |

# Verbs

## active

| | 1 | 2 | 3 | 4 | 3½ | irreg. |
|---|---|---|---|---|---|---|
| **present** | | | | | | |
| I | amo | moneo | rego | audio | capio | sum |
| you *(sing.)* | amas | mones | regis | audis | capis | es |
| he, she, it | amat | monet | regit | audit | capit | est |
| we | amamus | monemus | regimus | audimus | capimus | sumus |
| you *(pl.)* | amatis | monetis | regitis | auditis | capitis | estis |
| they | amant | monent | regunt | audiunt | capiunt | sunt |
| **future** | | | | | | |
| I | amabo | monebo | regam | audiam | capiam | ero |
| You *(sing.)* | amabis | monebis | reges | audies | capies | eris |
| he, she, it | amabit | monebit | reget | audiet | capiet | erit |
| we | amabimus | monebimus | regemus | audiemus | capiemus | erimus |
| you *(pl.)* | amabitis | monebitis | regetis | audietis | capietis | eritis |
| they | amabunt | monebunt | regent | audient | capient | erunt |
| **imperfect** | | | | | | |
| I | amabam | monebam | regebam | audiebam | capiebam | eram |
| you *(sing.)* | amabas | monebas | regebas | audiebas | capiebas | eras |
| he, she, it | amabat | monebat | regebat | audiebat | capiebat | erat |
| we | amabamus | monebamus | regebamus | audiebamus | capiebamus | eramus |
| you *(pl.)* | amabatis | monebatis | regebatis | audiebatis | capiebatis | eratis |
| they | amabant | monebant | regebant | audiebant | capiebant | erant |
| **perfect** | | | | | | |
| I | amavi | monui | rexi | audivi | cepi | fui |
| you *(sing.)* | amavisti | monuisti | rexisti | audivisti | cepisti | fuisti |
| he, she, it | amavit | monuit | rexit | audivit | cepit | fuit |
| we | amavimus | monuimus | reximus | audivimus | cepimus | fuimus |
| you *(pl.)* | amavistis | monuistis | rexistis | audivistis | cepistis | fuistis |
| they | amaverunt | monuerunt | rexerunt | audiverunt | ceperunt | fuerunt |
| **pluperfect** | | | | | | |
| I | amaveram | monueram | rexeram | audiveram | ceperam | fueram |
| you *(sing.)* | amaveras | monueras | rexeras | audiveras | ceperas | fueras |
| he, she, it | amaverat | monuerat | rexerat | audiverat | ceperat | fuerat |
| we | amaveramus | monueramus | rexeramus | audiveramus | ceperamus | fueramus |
| you *(sing.)* | amaveratis | monueratis | rexeratis | audiveratis | ceperatis | fueratis |
| they | amaverant | monuerant | rexerant | audiverant | ceperant | fuerant |
| **infinitive** | amare | monēre | regĕre | audire | capĕre | esse |
| **imperatives** | | | | | | |
| *sing.* | ama | mone | rege | audi | cape | es |
| *pl.* | amate | monete | regite | audite | capite | este |

## Passive

| | **1** | **2** | **3** | **4** | **3½** |
|---|---|---|---|---|---|
| **present** | amor | moneor | regor | audior | capior |
| | amaris | moneris | regeris | audiris | caperis |
| | amatur | monetur | regitur | auditur | capitur |
| | amamur | monemur | regimur | audimur | capimur |
| | amamini | monemini | regimini | audimini | capimini |
| | amantur | monentur | reguntur | audiuntur | capiuntur |
| **imperfect** | amabar | monebar | regebar | audiebar | capiebar |
| | amabaris | monebaris | regebaris | audiebaris | capiebaris |
| | amabatur | monebatur | regebatur | audiebatur | capiebatur |
| | amabamur | monebamur | regebamur | audiebamur | capiebamur |
| | amabamini | monebamini | regebamini | audiebamini | capiebamini |
| | amabantur | monebantur | regebantur | audiebantur | capiebantur |
| **future** | amabor | monebor | regar | audiar | capiar |
| | amaberis | moneberis | regeris | audieris | capieris |
| | amabitur | monebitur | regetur | audietur | capietur |
| | amabimur | monebimur | regemur | audiemur | capiemur |
| | amabimini | monebimini | regemini | audiemini | capiemini |
| | amabuntur | monebuntur | regentur | audientur | capientur |

| **volo I want** | **present** | **imperfect** | **future** | **perfect** | **pluperfect** |
|---|---|---|---|---|---|
| | volo | volebam | volam | volui | volueram |
| | vis | volebas | voles | voluisti | volueras |
| | vult | volebat | volet | voluit | voluerat |
| | volumus | volebamus | volemus | voluimus | volueramus |
| | vultis | volebatis | voletis | voluistis | volueratis |
| | volunt | volebant | volent | voluerunt | voluerant |
| **infinitive** velle | | | | | |

| **nolo I don't want** | **present** | **imperfect** | **future** | **perfect** | **pluperfect** |
|---|---|---|---|---|---|
| | nolo | nolebam | nolam | nolui | nolueram |
| | non vis | nolebas | noles | noluisti | nolueras |
| | non vult | nolebat | nolet | noluit | noluerat |
| | nolumus | nolebamus | nolemus | noluimus | nolueramus |
| | non vultis | nolebatis | noletis | noluistis | nolueratis |
| | nolunt | nolebant | nolent | noluerunt | noluerant |
| **infinitive** nolle | | | | | |

| **possum I am able** | **present** | **imperfect** | **future** | **perfect** | **pluperfect** |
|---|---|---|---|---|---|
| | possum | poteram | potero | potui | potueram |
| | potes | poteras | poteris | potuisti | potueras |
| | potest | poterat | poterit | potuit | potuerat |
| | possumus | poteramus | poterimus | potuimus | potueramus |
| | potestis | poteratis | poteritis | potuistis | potueratis |
| | possunt | poterant | poterunt | potuerunt | potuerant |
| **infinitive** | posse | | | | |

| eo  I go | present | imperfect | future | perfect | pluperfect |
|---|---|---|---|---|---|
| | eo | ibam | ibo | ii *or* ivi | ieram |
| | is | ibas | ibis | isti, ivisti | ieras |
| | it | ibat | ibit | iit, ivit | ierat |
| | imus | ibamus | ibimus | iimus, ivimus | ieramus |
| | itis | ibatis | ibitis | istis, ivistis | ieratis |
| | eunt | ibant | ibunt | ierunt, iverunt | ierant |

**infinitive** ire
**imperative** **sing.** i  **pl.** ite

**fero**    **I carry**

| active | present | imperfect | future | perfect | pluperfect |
|---|---|---|---|---|---|
| | fero | ferebam | feram | tuli | tuleram |
| | fers | ferebas | feres | tulisti | tuleras |
| | fert | ferebat | feret | tulit | tulerat |
| | ferimus | ferebamus | feremus | tulimus | tuleramus |
| | fertis | ferebatis | feretis | tulistis | tuleratis |
| | ferunt | ferebant | ferent | tulerunt | tulerant |

**infinitive** ferre
**imperative** **sing.** fer **pl.** ferte

| passive | present | imperfect | future | perfect | pluperfect |
|---|---|---|---|---|---|
| | feror | ferebar | ferar | latus sum | latus eram |
| | ferris | ferebaris | fereris | latus es | latus eras |
| | fertur | ferebatur | feretur | latus est | latus erat |
| | ferimur | ferebamur | feremur | lati sumus | lati eramus |
| | ferimini | ferebamini | feremini | lati estis | lati eratis |
| | feruntur | ferebantur | ferentur | lati sunt | lati erant |

# Latin – English word list

|  |  |
|---|---|
| a, ab *(+abl.)* | *from, away from, by* |
| absum, abesse, afui | *be away, absent* |
| ac | *and* |
| accido -ere accidi 3 | *happen* |
| accipio -ere accepi acceptum3 ½ | *receive, accept, take in* |
| ad *(+acc.)* | *to, towards, at* |
| adeo | *so much, so greatly* |
| adsum, adesse, adfui | *be here, present* |
| advenio 4 | *arrive* |
| aedifico 1 | *build* |
| ager -ri 2 m | *field* |
| ago -ere egi actum 3 | *do, act, drive* |
| * agricola -ae 1 m | *farmer* |
| alii … alii | *some…. others* |
| alius -a -ud | *other* |
| alter -a -um | *the other, another* |
| altus -a -um | *high, deep* |
| ambulo 1 | *walk* |
| amicus -i 1 m | *friend* |
| amo 1 | *like, love* |
| amor -is 3 m | *love* |
| ancilla -ae 1 f | *maid-servant, slave-girl* |
| animus -i 2 m | *spirit, soul, mind* |
| annus -i 2 m | *year* |
| ante *(+acc.)* | *before, in front of* |
| antea | *before(hand)* |
| * antequam | *before* |
| appareo -ere apparui 2 | *appear* |
| appropinquo 1 | *approach, come near to* |
| apud *(+acc.)* | *among, with, at house* |
| aqua -ae 1 f | *water* |
| arma -orum 2 n | *weapons* |
| ars artis 3 f | *art, skill* |
| ascendo -ere ascendi ascendum 3 | *climb* |
| atque | *and* |
| audax -acis | *bold* |
| audeo -ere ausus sum 2 | *dare* |
| audio 4 | *hear, listen to* |
| aufero | *take away, carry off, steal* |
| * aurum -i 2 n | *gold* |
| autem | *but, however* |
| auxilium -i 2 n | *help* |
| bellum -i 2 n | *war* |
| bellum gero -ere gessi gestum 3 | *wage war* |
| bene | *well* |
| benignus -a -um | *kind* |
| bibo -ere bibi bibitum 3 | *drink* |
| bonus -a -um | *good* |
| brevis -e | *short, brief* |
| cado -ere cecidi casum 3 | *fall* |
| caelum -i 2 n | *sky* |
| canis -is 3 c | *dog* |
| * canto 1 | *sing* |
| capio -ere cepi captum 3½ | *take, capture* |
| captivus -i 2 m | *captive, prisoner* |
| caput capitis 3 n | *head* |
| * carus -a -um | *dear* |
| castra castrorum 2 n | *camp* |
| celer -is -e | *swift, quick, fast* |
| celeriter | *quickly* |
| celo 1 | *hide* |
| cena -ae 1 f | *dinner, meal* |
| centum | *hundred* |
| ceteri -ae -a | *the rest, the others* |
| cibus -i 2 m | *food* |
| circum *(+acc.)* | *around* |
| civis -is 3 c | *citizen* |
| clamo 1 | *shout* |
| clamor -is 3 m | *shout, shouting, noise* |
| clarus -a -um | *famous, clear* |
| coepi coepisse | *began* |
| cogito 1 | *think, consider* |
| cognosco -ere cognovi cognitum 3 | *force, compel* |
| cogo -ere coegi coactum 3 | *force* |
| * colligo -ere collegi collectum 3 | *collect* |
| comes -itis 3 c | *companion, comrade* |
| conficio -ere confeci confectum 3½ | *finish, wear out* |
| * coniunx -iugis 3 c | *husband, wife* |
| conor -ari 1 | *try* |
| consilium -i 2 n | *plan, idea, advice* |
| conspicio -ere -spexi -spectum 3 ½ | *catch sight of, notice* |
| constituo -ere -i -utum 3 | *decide* |
| consul consulis 3 m | *consul* |
| consumo -ere consumpsi consumptum 3 | *eat* |
| contra *(+acc.)* | *against* |
| convenio 4 | *meet, gather* |
| copiae -arum 1 f | *forces,troops* |
| corpus -oris 3 n | *body* |
| cras | *tomorrow* |
| credo ere credidi creditum 3 *(+dat.)* | *believe, trust* |
| crudelis -e | *cruel* |
| cum | *when, since* |
| cum *(+abl.)* | *with* |
| cupio -ere cupivi cupitum 3½ | *want, desire* |
| cur? | *why* |
| cura -ae 1 f | *care, worry* |
| curro -ere cucurri cursum 3 | *run* |
| custodio -ire -ivi -itum 4 | *guard v.* |
| custos -odis 3 c | *guard* |
| de *(+abl.)* | *down from, about* |
| dea -ae 1 f | *goddess* |
| debeo -ere debui debitum 2 | *owe, ought, should, must* |
| decem | *ten* |
| * decimus -a -um | *tenth* |
| defendo -ere -defendi defensum 3 | *defend* |
| deinde | *then, next* |
| deleo -ere delevi deletum 2 | *destroy* |
| descendo -ere descendi descensum 3 | *go down, come down* |
| deus -i 2 m | *god* |
| dico -ere dixi dictum 3 | *say, tell* |
| dies -ei 5 m | *day* |
| difficilis -e | *difficult* |
| diligens diligentis | *careful* |
| dirus -a -um | *dreadful* |
| discedo -ere discessi discessum 3 | *depart, leave* |
| diu | *for a long time* |
| do -are dedi datum1 | *give* |
| doceo -ere docui doctum 2 | *teach* |
| domina -ae 1 f | *mistress* |
| dominus -i 2 m | *master* |
| domus -us 4 f | *house* |
| donum -i 2 n | *gift, reward* |
| dormio 4 | *sleep* |

|  |  |
|---|---|
| duco -ere duxi ductum 3 | lead, take |
| dum | while, until |
| duo duae duo | two |
| * duodecim | twelve |
| * duodeviginti | eighteen |
| dux ducis 3 c | leader |
| e, ex *(+abl.)* | out of, from |
| ecce! | look! |
| effugio -ere effugi 3 ½ | escape |
| ego | I |
| egredior -i egressus 3½ | go out |
| emo -ere emi emptum 3 | buy |
| enim | for |
| eo ire -ii *or* -ivi itum | go |
| epistula -ae 1 f | letter |
| equus -i 2 m | horse |
| * erro 1 | wander |
| et | and |
| et … et | both .. and |
| etiam | even, also |
| exeo exire exii exitum | go out |
| exercitus -us 4 m | army |
| exspecto 1 | wait for |
| facilis -e | easy |
| facio -ere feci factum 3½ | do, make |
| faveo -ere favi fautum 2 *(+dat.)* | favour, support |
| felix -icis | happy, lucky, fortunate |
| femina -ae 1 f | woman |
| fero ferre tuli latum | bring, carry, bear |
| ferox ferocis | fierce, ferocious |
| * fessus -a -um | tired |
| festino 1 | hurry |
| fidelis -e | faithful, loyal |
| filia -ae 1 f | daughter |
| filius -i 2 m | son |
| flumen -inis 3 n | river |
| forte | by chance |
| fortis -e | brave |
| fortiter | bravely |
| forum -i 2 n | forum, market-place |
| frater -ris 3 m | brother |
| frustra | in vain |
| fugio -ere fugi 3½ | flee |
| fui | see sum |
| gaudeo -ere gavisus sum 2 | be pleased, rejoice |
| gaudium -i 2 n | joy, pleasure |
| gens -tis 3 f | race, tribe, family, people |
| * gero -ere gessi gestum 3 | do, wear |
| gladius -i 2 m | sword |
| Graecus -a -um | Greek |
| gravis -e | heavy, serious |
| habeo -ere habui habitum 2 | have |
| habito 1 | live |
| * hasta -ae 1 f | spear |
| heri | yesterday |
| hic | here |
| hic haec hoc | this; he, she, it |
| hodie | today |
| homo -inis 3 c | man, human being |
| hora -ae 1 f | hour |
| hortor 1 | encourage, urge |
| hortus -i 2 m | garden |
| hostis -is 3 c | enemy pl. |
| iaceo -ere iacui 2 | lie |
| iacio -ere ieci iactum 3½ | throw |

|  |  |
|---|---|
| iam | now, already |
| ianua -ae 1 f | door |
| Ibi | there |
| idem eadem idem | same |
| igitur | therefore, and so |
| ille, illa, illud | that; he, she, it |
| imperator -is 3 m | emperor, general, leader |
| imperium -i 2 n | empire, power command |
| impero 1 *(+dat.)* | order |
| in *(+abl.)* | in, on |
| in *(+acc.)* | into |
| incendo -ere incendi incensum 3 | burn, set on fire |
| * incola -ae 1 c | inhabitant |
| ineo inire inii initum | go in |
| infelix infelicis | unlucky, unhappy |
| ingens ingentis | huge |
| ingredior -i ingressus 3½ | enter |
| inimicus -i 2 m | enemy |
| inquit | (s)he says, said |
| insula -ae 1 f | island, block of flats |
| intellego -ere intellexi intellectum 3 | understand, realize |
| inter *(+acc.)* | between, among |
| interea | meanwhile |
| interficio -ere -feci -fectum 3½ | kill |
| intro 1 | enter |
| invenio -ire inveni inventum 4 | find |
| invito 1 | invite |
| ipse ipsa ipsum | him/her/itself, themselves |
| ira -ae 1 f | anger |
| iratus -a -um | angry |
| is ea id | that; he, she, it |
| ipse -a -um | himself |
| ita | in this way, to such an extent, so |
| Italia -ae | Italy |
| itaque | and so, therefore |
| iter itineris 3 n | journey |
| iterum | again |
| iubeo -ere iussi iussum 2 | order |
| iuvenis iuvenis 3 c | young person |
| labor -is 3 m | task, work |
| laboro 1 | work |
| lacrimo 1 | weep, cry |
| laetus -a -um | happy |
| laudo 1 | praise |
| libenter | willingly, gladly |
| legio legionis 3 f | legion |
| lego -ere legi lectum 3 | read, choose |
| lente | slowly |
| lentus -a -um | slow |
| leo leonis 3 m | lion |
| libenter | willingly, gladly |
| liber -ri 2 m | book |
| liberi 2 m pl | children |
| libero 1 | free |
| libertus -i 2 m | freedman, ex-slave |
| locus -i 2 m | place |
| longus -a -um | long |
| loquor -i locutus 3 | speak |
| * ludo -ere lusi lusum 3 | play |
| lux lucis 3 f | light, daylight |
| magis | more |
| * magister -ri 2 m | master |
| magnopere | greatly |
| magnus -a -um | big, great, large |

|  |  |
|---|---|
| malo malle malui | prefer |
| malus -a -um | bad |
| maneo -ere mansi mansum 2 | remain, stay |
| manus -us 4 f | hand, group of |
| mare maris 3 n | sea |
| maritus -i 2 m | husband |
| mater matris 3 f | mother |
| maxime | very greatly |
| me | me |
| medius -a -um | middle |
| melior melius | better |
| * mensis mensis 3 m | month |
| mercator -is 3 m | merchant |
| meus -a -um | my |
| miles militis 3 c | soldier |
| mille, milia | thousand |
| minime | very little, least, no |
| miror 1 | wonder at, admire |
| miser -a -um | miserable, wretched, sad |
| mitto -ere misi missum 3 | send |
| modus -i 2 m | manner, way, kind |
| moneo -ere monui monitum 2 | warn, advise |
| mons montis 3 m | mountain |
| * mora -ae 1 f | delay |
| morior mori mortuus 3½ | die |
| mors mortis 3 f | death |
| mortuus -a -um | dead |
| moveo -ere movi motum 2 | move |
| mox | soon |
| * mulier mulieris 3 f | woman |
| multo | much |
| multus -a -um | much, many |
| murus -i 2 m | wall |
| nam | for |
| narro 1 | tell, relate |
| nauta -ae 1 m | sailor |
| navigo 1 | sail |
| navis -is 3 f | ship |
| ne | that.. not, lest |
| -ne? | introduces question |
| nec, neque | and not, neither, nor |
| neco 1 | kill |
| * nego | say not |
| nemo gen. nullius | nobody |
| neque … neque | neither … nor |
| nescio nescire nescivi | not know |
| nihil | nothing |
| nisi | unless, except |
| * nobilis -e | noble |
| noli / nolite | do not! |
| nolo nolle nolui | not want |
| nomen nominis 3 n | name |
| non | not |
| nonne | surely? |
| nonnulli -ae -a | some, several |
| * nonus -a -um | ninth |
| nos | we, us |
| noster -ra -rum | our |
| * notus -a -um | well-known |
| novem | nine |
| novus -a -um | new |
| nox noctis 3 f | night |
| nullus -a -um | not any, no |
| num | whether |
| num? | surely not? |
| numquam | never |
| nunc | now |
| nuntio 1 | announce |
| nuntius -i 2 m | messenger, message, news |
| O | o! |
| occido -ere occidi occisum 3 | kill |
| * occupo 1 | seize |
| * octavus -a -um | eighth |
| octo | eight |
| offero offerre obtuli oblatum | offer |
| olim | once, some time ago |
| omnis -e | every, all, whole |
| * oppidum -i 2 n | town |
| opprimo -ere oppressi oppressum 3 | crush, overwhelm |
| oppugno 1 | attack |
| optimus -a -um | best |
| oro 1 | beg |
| ostendo -ere ostendi ostentum 3 | show |
| paene | almost, nearly, scarcely, hardly |
| * parens -tis 3 c | parent |
| paro 1 | prepare |
| pars partis 3 f | part |
| parvus -a -um | small, little |
| pater patris 3 m | father |
| patior -i passus 3½ | suffer, endure; allow |
| patria -ae 1 f | country, homeland |
| pauci -ae -a | few |
| pax pacis 3 f | peace |
| pecunia -ae 1 f | money |
| peior peius | worse |
| pello -ere pepuli pulsum 3 | drive |
| per (+acc.) | through, along |
| pereo perire perii | die, perish |
| periculum -i 2 n | danger |
| persuadeo -ere persuasi 2 + dat. | persuade |
| perterritus -a -um | terrified |
| pervenio -ire perveni perventum 4 | reach, arrive at |
| pes pedis 3 m | foot |
| pessimus -a -um | worst |
| peto ere petivi petitum 3 | look for, seek, beg, attack |
| plenus -a -um | full |
| * poeta -ae 1 m | poet |
| poena -ae 1 f | punishment |
| poenas do | am punished |
| pono -ere posui positum 3 | put, place, put up |
| porta -ae 1 f | gate |
| porto 1 | carry |
| portus -us 4 m | harbour, port |
| possum posse potui | be able, can |
| post (+acc.) | after, behind |
| postea | afterwards |
| postquam | after, when |
| postridie | on the next day |
| praemium -i 2 n. | reward, prize |
| precor -ari 1 | pray (to), beg |
| primo | at first |
| primus -a -um | first |
| princeps principis 3 m | chief, emperor |
| pro (+abl.) | instead of, in front of |
| procedo -ere processi processum 3 | advance, proceed |
| proelium -i 2 n | battle |
| proficiscor -i profectus 3 | set out |

|  |  |
|---|---|
| progredior -i progressus 3½ | advance |
| promitto -ere promisi promissum 3 | promise |
| prope *(+acc.)* | near |
| propter *(+acc.)* | on account of, because of |
| proximus -a -um | nearest, next to |
| puella -ae 1 f | girl |
| puer -i 2 m | boy |
| pugno 1 | fight |
| pulcher -ra -rum | beautiful, handsome |
| punio 4 | punish |
| puto 1 | think |
| quaero -ere quaesivi quaesitum 3 | search for, look for, ask |
| qualis? | what sort of? |
| quam *+superlative adverb* | as ... as possible |
| quam | than |
| quam? quam! | how ... ? how ...! |
| quamquam | although |
| quando? | when? |
| quantus? quanta? quantum? | how big? how much? |
| * quartus -a -um | fourth |
| quattuor | four |
| * quattuordecim | fourteen |
| -que | and |
| qui quae quod | who, which |
| quid? | what? |
| quidam | one, a certain, some |
| * quindecim | fifteen |
| quinque | five |
| * quintus -a -um | fifth |
| quis? quid? | who? what? |
| quo? | to where? |
| quod | because |
| quo modo? | how? |
| quoque | also, too |
| quot? | how many? |
| rapio -ere rapui raptum 3½ | seize, grab |
| reddo -ere reddidi redditum 3 | give back, restore |
| redeo redire redii reditum | go back, come back, return |
| reduco -ere reduxi reductum3 | lead back |
| refero referre rettuli relatum | bring back, report, tell |
| regina -ae I f | queen |
| regnum -i 2 n | kingdom |
| rego -ere rexi rectum3 | rule |
| regredior -i regressus 3½ | go back, return |
| relinquo -ere reliqui relictum 3 | leave, leave behind |
| res -ei 5 f. | thing, matter, event |
| resisto -ere restiti *(+ dative)* | resist |
| respondeo -ere respondi responsum 2 | reply |
| rex regis 3 m | king |
| rideo -ere risi risum 2 | laugh, smile |
| rogo 1 | ask, ask for |
| Romanus -a -um | Roman |
| rumpo -ere rupi ruptum 3 | break, burst |
| * ruo -ere rui rutum 3 | rush |
| sacer -ra -rum | scared |
| saepe | often |
| saevus -a -um | savage, cruel |
| * sagitta -ae 1 f | arrow |
| saluto 1 | greet |
| salve! | hello! |
| sanguis sanguinis 3 m | blood |
| sapiens -tis | wise |
| satis | enough |
| scelestus -a -um | wicked |
| scribo -ere scripsi scriptum 3 | write |
| scio scire scivi scitum 4 | know |
| * scutum -i 2 n | shield |
| se | him/her/itself themselves |
| * secundus -a -um | second |
| sed | but |
| sedeo -ere sedi 2 | sit |
| * sedecim | sixteen |
| semper | always |
| senator -is 3 m | senator |
| senex senis 3 m | old man |
| sentio -ire sensi sensum 4 | feel, notice |
| septem | seven |
| * septendecim | seventeen |
| * septimus -a -um | seventh |
| sequor -i secutus 3 | follow |
| servo 1 | save, protect, keep |
| servus -i 2 m | slave |
| sex | six |
| * sextus -a -um | sixth |
| si | if |
| sic | thus, in this way |
| signum -i 2 n | sign, signal, standard |
| silva -ae 1 f | wood, forest |
| simul | at the same time |
| simulac, simulatque | as soon as |
| sine *(+abl.)* | without |
| * socius -i 2 m | ally |
| soleo -ere solitus sum 2 | be accustomed |
| solus -a -um | alone, lonely, on one's own |
| * soror sororis 3 f | sister |
| specto 1 | watch, look at |
| spero 1 | hope, expect |
| spes -ei 5 f | hope |
| statim | immediately, at once |
| sto -are steti statum 1 | stand |
| stultus -a -um | stupid, foolish |
| sub *(+abl.)* | under, beneath |
| subito | suddenly |
| sum, esse, fui | be |
| summus -a -um | highest, greatest, top (of) |
| * super *(+acc.)* | over |
| supero 1 | overcome, overpower |
| surgo -ere surrexi surrectum 3 | get up, stand up, rise |
| suus -a -um | his, her, its |
| taberna -ae 1 f | shop, inn |
| taceo -ere tacui 2 | be silent, be quiet |
| talis -e | such |
| tamen | however |
| tandem | finally, at last |
| tantus -a -um | so great, such a great |
| te | you |
| tempestas tempestatis 3 f | storm, weather |
| templum -i 2 n | temple |
| tempus temporis 3 n | time |
| teneo -ere tenui tentum 2 | hold |
| terra -ae 1 f | land, earth, ground, country |
| terreo -ere terrui territum 2 | frighten |
| * tertius -a -um | third |
| timeo -ere timui 2 | fear, be afraid |
| tollo -ere sustuli sublatum 3 | raise, lift up, hold up |
| tot | so many |
| totus -a -um | whole, all |

| | | | |
|---|---|---|---|
| trado -ere tradidi traditum 3 | *hand over* | vendo -ere vendidi venditum 3 | *sell* |
| traho -ere traxi tractum 3 | *drag* | venio -ire veni ventum 4 | *come* |
| trans *(+acc.)* | *across* | * ventus -i 2 m | *wind* |
| transeo -ire transii transitum | *go across* | verbum -i 2 n | *word* |
| * tredecim | *thirteen* | verto -ere verti versum | *turn* |
| tres | *three* | vester -ra -rum | *your* |
| tristis -e | *sad* | via -ae 1 f | *street, road, way* |
| tu | *you* | victoria -ae 1 f | *victory* |
| tum | *then* | video -ere vidi visum 2 | *see* |
| turba -ae 1 f | *crowd* | videor -eri visus 2 | *seem, appear* |
| * tutus -a -um | *safe* | * viginti | *twenty* |
| tuus -a -um | *your* | villa -ae 1 f | *(country) house* |
| ubi | *when* | vinco -ere vici victum 3 | *conquer, win, be victorious* |
| ubi? | *where?* | vinum -i 2 n | *wine* |
| umquam | *ever* | vir -i 2 m | *man* |
| * unda -ae 1 f | *wave* | virtus virtutis 3 f | *courage, virtue* |
| unde | *from where* | vita -ae 1 f | *life* |
| * undecim | *eleven* | vivo -ere vixi victum 3 | *live, be alive* |
| * undeviginti | *nineteen* | vivus -a -um | *alive, living* |
| unus -a -um | *one* | voco 1 | *call* |
| urbs urbis 3 f | *town, city* | volo 1 | *want* |
| ut + *subj.* | *that, so that, in order that* | vos | *you (plural)* |
| ut + *indic.* | *as, when* | vox vocis 3 f | *voice, shout* |
| uxor uxoris 3 f | *wife* | vulnero 1 | *wound, injure* |
| vale! valete! | *goodbye! farewell!* | vulnus vulneris 3 n | *wound* |
| validus -a -um | *strong* | vultus -us 4 m | *expression, face* |
| vehementer | *violently, loudly* | | |

# English – Latin word list

| | | | |
|---|---|---|---|
| abandon | relinquo -ere reliqui relictum 3 | at first | primo |
| able | possum posse potui | at last | tandem |
| about | de *(+abl.)* | at once | statim |
| absent am | absum abesse afui | as soon as | simulac, simulatqe |
| accept | accipio -ere accepi acceptum 3 | at the house of | apud *(+acc.)* |
| accustomed be | soleo -ere solitus sum 2 | at the same time | simul |
| across | trans *(+acc.)* | attack | oppugno 1 |
| act | ago -ere egi actum 3 | away from | a, ab *(+abl.)* |
| admire | miror 1 | bad | malus -a -um |
| advance | progredior -i progressus 3½ , | bar | taberna -ae 1 f |
| | procedo -ere processi processum 3 | battle | proelium -i 2 n |
| advice | consilium -i 2 n | be | sum, esse, fui |
| advise | moneo -ere monui monitum 2 | be able | possum posse potui |
| afraid of be | timeo -ere timui 2 | be afraid of | timeo -ere timui 2 |
| affair | res, rei 5 f | be away | absum, abesse, afui |
| after | post *(+acc.)* | be present | adsum, adesse, adfui |
| after | postquam | be wrong | erro 1 |
| afterwards | postea | bear | fero ferre tuli latum |
| again | iterum | beat | vinco -ere vici victum 3 |
| against | contra *(+acc.)* | beautiful | pulcher -ra -rum |
| alive | vivus -a -um | because | quod |
| alive be | vivo -ere vixi victum 3 | before | ante *(+acc.)* |
| all | omnis -e | before | ante, * antequam |
| allow | patior -i passus 3½ | beforehand | antea |
| ally | * socius -i 2 m | beg | oro 1, precor 1 |
| almost | paene | | peto -ere petivi petitum 3, |
| alone | solus -a -um | began | coepi coepisse |
| already | iam | behind | ante *(+acc.)* |
| also | quoque, etiam | believe | credo -ere credidi 3 *(+dat.)* |
| although | quamquam | beneath | sub *(+abl.)* |
| always . | semper | best | optimus -a -um |
| among | inter *(+acc.).*, apud *(+acc.)* | better | melior melius |
| and | et, -que | between | inter *(+acc.)* |
| and so | itaque, igitur | big | magnus -a -um |
| anger | ira -ae 1 f | block of flats | insula -ae 1 f |
| angry | iratus -a -um | blood | sanguis sanguinis 3 m |
| announce | nuntio 1 | body | corpus -oris 3 n |
| another | alius -a -um | bold | audax -acis |
| answer | respondeo -ere respondi responsum 2 | book | liber -ri 2 m |
| appear | appareo -ere apparui 2, videor | both .. and | et … et |
| approach | appropinquo 1 | boy | puer -i 2 m |
| arms | arma armorum 2 n pl | brave | fortis -e |
| army | exercitus -us 4 m | bravely | fortiter |
| around | circum *(+acc.)* | break | rumpo –ere rupi ruptum 3 |
| arrive at | advenio 4 | brief | brevis -e |
| arrogant | superbus -a -um | bright | clarus -a -um |
| arrow | * sagitta -ae 1 f | bring | fero ferre tuli latum |
| art | ars artis 3 f | bring back | refero referre rettuli relatum |
| as | ut | brother | frater -ris 3 m |
| as large as | tantus … quantus | build | aedifico 1 |
| as many as | tot … quot | burn | incendo -ere incendi incensum 3 |
| as… as possible | quam | burst | rumpo -ere rupi ruptum 3 |
| ask | rogo 1, | but | autem |
| | quaero -ere quaesivi quaesitum 3 | but | sed |
| ask for | rogo 1 peto -ere petivi petitum 3 | buy | emo -ere emi emptum 3 |
| at | ad *(+acc.)* | by | a, ab *(+abl.)* |

| | | | |
|---|---|---|---|
| by chance | forte | desire | cupio -ere cupivi cupitum 3½ |
| call | voco 1 | destroy | deleo -ere delevi deletum2 |
| call together | convoco 1 | die | morior mori mortuus 3½ , pereo |
| can | possum posse potui | difficult | difficilis -e |
| captive | captivus -i 2 m | dinner | cena -ae 1 |
| capture | capio -ere cepi captum 3 ½ | do | facio -ere feci factum 3½ , |
| care | cura -ae 1 f | | ago -ere egi actum 3 |
| careful | diligens diligentis | | gero -ere gessi gestum 3 |
| carry | porto 1, fero ferre tuli latum | do not! | noli! nolite! |
| carry back | refeo referre rettuli relatum | do, make | facio -ere feci factum 3 ½ |
| carry off | aufero auferre abstuli ablatum | do, wear | gero -ere gessi gestum 3 |
| catch | capio -ere cepi captum 3½ | dog | canis canis 3 c |
| catch sight of | conspicio -ere -spexi -spectum 3 ½ | door | ianua -ae 1 f |
| a certain | quidam quaedam quoddam | down from | de (+abl.) |
| charge | ruo ruere rui rutum 3 | drag | traho |
| chief | princeps principis 2 m | dreadful | durus -a -um |
| chieftain | princeps principis 3 | drink | bibo -ere bibi bibitum3 |
| children | liberi -orum 2 m | drive | pello -ere pepuli pulsum 3, |
| choose | lego -ere legi 3 | | ago -ere egi actum 3 |
| citizen | civis -is 3 c | earth | terra -ae 1 f |
| city | urbs urbis 3 f | easy | facilis -e |
| clear | clarus -a -um | eat | consumo -ere -sumpsi -sumptum3 |
| climb | ascendo -ere ascendi ascensum 3 | eight | octo |
| collect | * colligo -ere collegi collectum 3 | eighteen | * duodeviginti |
| come | venio 4 | eighth | * octavus -a -um |
| come back | redeo redire redii reditum | else | alius -a -um |
| come down | descendo -ere descendi descensum 3 | emperor | imperator -is 3 m, |
| come near to | appropinquo 1 (+dat.) | | princeps principis 3 m |
| come together | convenio -ire conveni conventum 4 | empire | imperium -i 2 n |
| command | imperium -i 2 n | encourage | hortor -ari hortatus 1 |
| companion | comes -itis 3 c | endure | patior -i passus sum 3½ |
| compel | cogo -ere coegi coactum 3 | enemy pl. | hostis -is 3 c, inimicus -i 2 m |
| conquer | vinco -ere vici victum 3 | enough | satis |
| comrade | comes comitis 3 m | enter | intro 1 |
| consider | cogito 1 | escape | effugio -ere effugi 3 ½ |
| consul | consul -is 3 m | even | etiam |
| country | patria –ae 1 f, terra -ae 1 f | ever | umquam |
| country-house | villa -ae 1 f | every | omnis -e |
| courage | virtus virtutis 3 f | everyone | omnes |
| crime | scelu sceleris 3 n | evil | malus -a -um |
| cross | transeo -ire transii transitum | except | nisi |
| crowd | turba -ae 1 f | expect | exspecto 1 |
| cruel | crudelis –e, saevus | expression | vultus -us 4 m |
| crush | opprimo -ere oppressi oppressum 3 | face | vultus -us 4 m |
| cry | fleo ere flevi 2, lacrimo | faith | fides -ei 5 f |
| danger | periculum -i 2 n | faithful | fidelis -e |
| dare | audeo -ere ausus sum 2 | fall | cado -ere cecidi casum 3 |
| daring | audax audacis | family | gens gentis 3 f |
| daughter | filia -ae 1 f | famous | clarus -a -um |
| day | dies diei 5 m | farewell | vale! valete! |
| daylight | lux lucis 3 f | farmer | * agricola -ae 1 m |
| dead | mortuus -a -um | fast | celer -is -e |
| dear | * carus -a -um | father | pater patris 3 m |
| death | mors mortis 3 f | fatherland | patria -ae 1 f |
| decide | constituo -ere -i -tum 3 | favour | faveo -ere favi fautum (+dat.) |
| deep | altus -a -um | fear | timeo -ere timui 2 |
| defeat | vinco -ere vici victum 3 | feel | sentio -ire sensi sensum 4 |
| defend | defendo -ere -i defensum3 | ferocious | ferox ferocis |
| delay | *mora -ae 1 f | few | pauci |
| depart | discedo -ere discessi discessum 3 | fierce | ferox ferocis |

| | | | |
|---|---|---|---|
| field | ager -ri 2 m | greet | saluto 1 |
| fifth | quintus -a -um | ground | terra |
| fight | pugno 1 | guard n | custos custodis 3 c |
| finally | tandem | guard v | custodio 4 |
| find | invenio -ire inveni 4 | hand | manus -us 4 f |
| find out | cognosco -ere cognovi cognitum 3 | hand over | trado -ere tradidi traditum3 |
| finish | conficio -ere confeci confectum 3 | handsome | pulcher pulchra pulchrum |
| first | primus -a -um | happen | occido -ere accidi 3 |
| five | quinque | happy | laetus -a -um, felix |
| flee | fugio -ere fugi 3 ½ | harbour | portus -us 4 m |
| follow | sequor -i secutus 3 | have | habeo -ere habui habitum 2 |
| food | cibus -i 2 m | he | is, hic, ille |
| foolish | stultus -a -um | head | caput capitis 3 n |
| for | nam, enim | hear | audio 4 |
| for a long time | diu | heaven | caelum -i 2 n |
| force | cogo -ere coegi coactum 3 | heavy | gravis -e |
| forces | copiae -arum 1 f | Hello! | salve! salvete! |
| forest | silva -ae 1 f | help n | auxilium -i 2 n |
| fortunate | felix felicis | her | suus -a -um |
| forum | forum -i 2 n | herself | se |
| four | quattuor | here | hic |
| fourteen | * quattuordecim | here, be | adsum adesse adfui |
| fourth | * quartus -a -um | hide | celo 1 |
| free | libero 1 | high | altus -a -um |
| freedman | libertus -i 2 m | highest | summus -a -um |
| friend | amicus -i 1 m | himself | se |
| frighten | terreo -ere terrui territum 2 | his | suus -a -um |
| from | a, ab *(+abl.)*, de | hold | teneo -ere tenui tentum 2 |
| from where | unde? | hold up | tollo -ere sustuli sublatum 3 |
| full | plenus -a -um | home | domus -us 4 f |
| garden | hortus -i 2 m | homeland | patria -ae 1 |
| gate | porta -ae 1 f | hope v | spero 1 |
| gather | convenio -ire conveni conventum 4 | hope n | spes spei 5 f |
| general | dux ducis 3 m | horse | equus -i 2 m |
| get to know | cognosco -ere cognovi cognitum 3 | hour | hora -ae 1 f |
| get up | surgo -ere surrexi surrectum 3 | house | domus -us 4 f, villa -ae 1 f |
| gift | donum -i 2 n | how… ? | quam? quo modo? |
| girl | puella -ae 1 f | how… ! | quam! |
| give | do -are dedi datum1 | how big? | quantus -a -um? |
| give back | reddo -ere reddidi redditum 3 | how many | quot? |
| gladly | libenter | how much? | quantus a -um |
| go | eo ire ii *or* ivi itum | however | tamen, autem |
| go across | transeo -ire -ii transitum | huge | ingens ingentis |
| go back | redeo redire redii reditum, | human being | homo hominis 3 m |
| | regredior -i regressus 3½ | hurry | festino 1 |
| go forward | progredior -i progressus 3½ | husband | * coniunx -iugis 3 c, maritus -i 2 m |
| go in | ineo inire inii initum | I | ego |
| go down | descendo -ere descendi descensum 3 | idea | consilium -i 2 n |
| go out | exeo exire exii exitum | if | si |
| go towards | adeo adire adii aditum | immediately | statim |
| god | deus -i 2 m | in | in *(+abl.)* |
| goddess | dea -ae 1 f | in front of | pro *(+abl.)*, ante *(+acc.)* |
| gold | * aurum -i 2 n | in return for | pro *(+abl.)* |
| good | bonus -a -um | in this way | sic, ita |
| goodbye | vale! valete! | in vain | frustra |
| grab | capio -ere cepi captum 3½ | inhabitant | * incola -ae 1 c |
| great | magnus -a -um | injure | vulnero 1 |
| greatest | maximus -a -um | inn | taberna -ae 1 f |
| greatly | magnopere | instead of | pro *(+abl.)* |
| Greek | Graecus -a -um | into | in *(+acc.)* |
| | | island | insula -ae 1 f |

|  |  |
|---------|-------|
| Italy | Italia -ae 1 f |
| its | suus -a -um |
| itself | se |
| journey | iter itineris 3 n |
| joy | gaudium -i 2 n |
| keep | servo 1 |
| kill | interficio -ere -feci -fectum 3½ , occido -ere occidi occisum 3 neco 1 |
| kind | benignus -a -um |
| king | rex regis 3 m |
| kingdom | regnum -i 2 n |
| know | scio -ere scivi scitum 4 |
| land | terra -ae 1 f |
| large | magnus -a -um |
| later | postea |
| laugh | rideo -ere risi 2 |
| lead | duco -ere duxi ductum3 |
| lead back | reduco -ere reduxi reductum3 |
| leader | dux ducis 3 m, imperator -is 3 m |
| least | minime |
| leave (depart) | discedo -ere discessi discessum 3 |
| leave(behind) | relinquo -ere reliqui relictum 3 |
| leave (go out) | egredior -i egressus 3½ |
| legion | legio legionis 3 f |
| letter | epistula -ae 1 f |
| lie | iaceo -ere iacui 2 |
| life | vita -ae 1 f |
| lift up | tollo -ere sustuli sublatum 3 |
| light | lux lucis 3 f |
| like | amo 1 |
| lion | leo leonis 3 m |
| listen to | audio 4 |
| little | parvus -a -um |
| live | habito 1, vivo -ere vixi victum 3 |
| living | vivus -a -um |
| lonely | solus -a -um |
| long | longus -a -um |
| look! | ecce! |
| look at | specto 1 |
| look for | peto -ere petivi petitum 3, quaero -ere quaesivi quaesitum 3 |
| loud | magnus -a -um |
| loudly | vehementer |
| love | amo 1 |
| loyal | fidelis -e |
| lucky | felix -icis |
| maid-servant | ancilla -ae 1 f |
| make | facio -ere feci factum 3½ |
| make for | peto -ere petivi petitum 3 |
| man | homo -inis 3 m |
| man | vir -i 2 m, homo hominis 3 m |
| manner | modus -i 2 m |
| many | multi -ae -a |
| march | contendo -ere contendi 3 |
| market-place | forum -i 2 n |
| master | dominus -i 2 m |
| master (sch) | * magister -ri 2 m |
| me | me |
| meal | cena -ae 1 f |
| meanwhile | interea |
| meet | convenio 4 |
| merchant | mercator -is 3 m |
| message | nuntius -i 2 m |
| messenger | nuntius -i 2 m |
| middle | medius -a -um |
| mind | animus -i 2 m |
| miserable | miser -a -um |
| mistress | domina -ae 1 f |
| money | pecunia -ae 1 f |
| more | magis |
| mother | mater matris 3 f |
| mountain | mons montis 3 m |
| move | moveo -ere movi motum 2 |
| much | multo |
| much | multus -a -um |
| must | debeo -ere debui 2 |
| my | meus -a -um |
| name | nomen nominis 3 n |
| narrate | narro 1 |
| near | prope (+acc.) |
| nearest | proximus -a -um |
| nearly | paene |
| neither | nec, neque |
| never | numquam |
| new | novus -a -um |
| news | nuntius -i 2 m |
| next | deinde |
| next to | prope (+acc.) |
| night | nox noctis 3 f |
| nine | novem |
| nineteen | * undeviginti |
| ninth | * nonus -a -um |
| no | minime |
| noble | * nobilis -e |
| nobody | nemo gen. nullius |
| noise | clamor -is 3 m |
| no one | nemo gen. nullius |
| nor | nec, neque |
| not | non |
| not know | nescio -ire nescivi nescitum 4 |
| not want | nollo nolle nolui |
| nothing | nihil |
| notice | sentio -ire sensi sensum 4, conspicio -ere conspexi conspectum 3½ |
| now | nunc, iam |
| now | iam, nunc |
| o! | o |
| offer | offero offerre obtuli oblatum |
| often | saepe |
| old man | senex senis 3 m |
| on account of | propter (+acc.) |
| on the next day | postridie |
| once u. a time | olim |
| one | unus -a -um, quidam |
| only | solus -a -um |
| order | iubeo -ere iussi iussum 2 |
| other | alius alia aliud, alter |
| others | ceteri -ae -a, alii -ae -a |
| ought | debeo -ere debui 2 |

| | | | |
|---|---|---|---|
| our | noster -ra -rum | rest the | ceteri -ae -a |
| out | a, ab (+abl.) | restore | reddo ere reddidi redditum 3 |
| out of | e, ex *(+abl.)* | return | redeo redire redii reditum, regredior -i |
| over | * super *(+acc.)* | | regressus 3½ |
| overcome | supero 1 | reward | praemium -i 2 n |
| overpower | supero 1 | rise | surgo -ere surrexi surrectum 3 |
| overwhelm | opprimo -ere oppressi oppressum 3 | river | flumen -inis 3 n |
| owe | debeo -ere debui 2 | road | via -ae 1 f |
| parent | * parens -tis 3 c | Rome | Roma -ae 1 |
| part | pars partis 3 f | Roman | Romanus -a -um |
| pay penalty | poenas do dare dedi datum 1 | rule | rego -ere rexi rectum 3 |
| people | gens gentis 3 f | rule | imperium -i 2 n |
| perish | pereo perire perii peritum | run | curro -ere cucurri cursum 3 |
| person | homo hominis 3 m/f | run away | fugio -ere fugi fugitum 3½ |
| persuade | persuadeo -ere -suasi -suasum 2 | rush | * ruo -ere rui rutum 3 |
| place | pono -ere posui positum 3 | sacred | sacaer -ra -rum |
| place | locus -i 2 m | sad | miser -a -um |
| plan | consilium -i 2 n | sad | tristis -e, miser |
| play | * ludo - ere lusi lusum 3 | safe | * tutus -a -um |
| pleased be | gaudeo -ere gavisus sum 2 | sail | navigo 1 |
| pleasure | gaudium -i 2 n | sailor | nauta -ae 1 m |
| poet | * poeta -ae 1 m | same | idem eadem idem |
| port | portus -us 4 m | savage | saevus -a -um |
| power | imperium -i 2 n | save | servo 1 |
| praise | laudo 1 | said | inquit |
| pray (to) | precor ari 1 | say | dico -ere dixi dictum 3 |
| prefer | malo malle malui | Says | inquit |
| prepare | paro 1 | scared | sacer -ra -rum |
| present | donum -i 2 n | sea | mare maris 3 n |
| present be | adsum adesse adfui | search for | peto -ere petivi petitum 3, |
| prisoner | captivus -i 2 m | | quaero -ere quaesivi quaesitum 3 |
| prize | praemium -i 2 n | second | secundus -a -um |
| proceed | procedo -ere processi processum 3 | see | video -ere vidi visum2 |
| profit | praemium -i 2 n | seek | peto -ere petivi petitum 3 |
| promise | fides -ei 5 | seem | videor |
| protect | servo 1 | seize | * occupo 1, rapio |
| proud | superbus -a -um | self | ipse ipsa ipsum |
| punish | punio 4 | sell | vendo -ere vendidi venditum 3 |
| punishment | poena -ae 1 f | senator | senator -is 3 m |
| pupil | discipulus -i 2 m | send | mitto -ere misi missum 3 |
| put (up) | pono -ere posui positum 3 | serious | gravis -e |
| queen | regina -ae I f | set fire to | incendo -ere incendi incensum 3 |
| question | -ne? | set free | libero 1 |
| quick | celer -is -e | set out | proficiscor -i profectus 3 |
| quickly | celeriter | seven | septem |
| quiet be | taceo -ere tacui 2 | seventeen | * septendecim |
| race | gens gentis 3 f | seventh | septimus -a -um |
| raise | tollo -ere sustuli sublatum 3 | several | nonnulli -ae -a |
| reach | pervenio -ire perveni perventum 4 | she | illa, ea, haec |
| read | lego -ere legi lectum 3 | shield | * scutum -i 2 n |
| real | verus -a -um | ship | navis -is 3 f |
| realize | intellego -ere intellegi intellectum 3 | shop | taberna -ae 1 f |
| receive | accipio -ere accepi acceptum3 ½ | short | brevis -e |
| refuse | nolo nolle noluui | should | debeo -ere debui 2 |
| rejoice | gaudeo -ere gavisus sum 2 | shout | clamo 1 |
| remain | maneo -ere mansi mansum 2 | shouting | clamor -is 3 m |
| reply | respondeo -ere -i responsum 2 | shout | clamor -is 3 m, vox vocis 3 f |
| report | nuntio 1 | show | ostendo ere -i ostentum 3 |
| resist | resisto -ere restiti *(+dat.)* | sign | signum -i 2 n |

| | | | |
|---|---|---|---|
| signal | signum -i 2 n | than | quam |
| silent be | taceo -ere tacui 2 | that | ille illa illud |
| since | cum | that ... not | ne |
| sing | * canto 1 | the rest of | ceteri -ae -a |
| sister | * soror sororis 3 f | their (own) | suus -a -um |
| sit | sedeo -ere sedi sessum 2 | themselves | se |
| six | sex | then | deinde |
| sixteen | * sedecim | there | ibi |
| sixth | * sextus -a -um | therefore | igitur |
| skill | ars artis 3 f | the same | idem eadem idem |
| sky | caelum -i 2 n | these | hi hae haec |
| slave | servus -i 2 m | thing | res rei 5 f |
| slave-girl | ancilla -ae 1 f | think | puto 1, cogito 1 |
| sleep | dormio 4 | third | tertius -a -um |
| slow | lentus -a -um | thirteen | tredecim |
| slowly | lente | this | hic haec hoc |
| small | parvus -a -um | those | illi illae illa |
| smile | rideo -ere risi risum 2 | three | tres tria |
| so | tam | through | per (+acc.) |
| so great | tantus | throw | iacio -ere ieci iactum3 ½ |
| so greatly | adeo | thus | sic |
| so many | tot | time | tempus temporis 3 n |
| so much | adeo | tired | * fessus -a –um |
| so that | ut | to | ad (+acc.) |
| soldier | miles militis 3 c | to such an extent | adeo |
| some | nonnulli, quidam | to where | quo |
| some time ago | olim | today | hodie |
| son | filius -i 2 m | tomorrow | cras |
| soon | mox | too | etiam |
| soul | animus -i 2 m | top (of) | summus -a -um |
| speak | loquor -i locutus 3 | towards | ad (+acc.) |
| spear | * hasta -ae 1 f | town | * oppidum -i 2 n, urbs |
| spirit | animus -i 2 m | tribe | gens gentis 3 f |
| stand | sto -are steti statum1 | troops | copiae copiarum 1 f pl. |
| standard | signum -i 2 n | true | verus -a -um |
| stand up | surgo -ere surrexi surrectum 3 | trust | credo -ere credidi creditum 3 |
| stay | maneo -ere mansi mansum 2 | try | conor 1 |
| steal | aufero auferre abstuli ablatum | turn | verto -ere verti versum 3 |
| storm | tempestas tempestatis 3 f | twelve | duodecim |
| street | via -ae 1 f | twenty | * viginti |
| strong | validus -a -um | two | duo duae |
| stupid | stultus -a -um | unhappy | tristis -e |
| such | talis | under | sub (+abl.) |
| uch a great | tantus | unless | nisi |
| suddenly | subito | unlucky | infelix infelicis |
| suffer | patior pati passus 3½ | understand | intellego -ere intellexi intellectum 3 |
| support | faveo | until | dum |
| surely not? | num? | urge | hortor 1 |
| surely? | nonne | vain, in | frustra |
| sword | gladius -i 2 m | very greatly | maxime |
| take | capio -ere cepi captum 3½ , | very little | minime |
| | duco -ere duxi ductum 3 | victorious be | vinco -ere vici victum 3 |
| take away | aufero auferre abstuli ablatum | victory | victoria -ae 1 f |
| take in | accipio -ere accepi acceptum 3½ | villa | villa -ae l f |
| task | opus operis 3 n. | virtue | virtus virtutis 3 f |
| teach | doceo -ere docui doctum 2 | voice | vox vocis 3 f |
| teacher | * magister -ri 2 | violently | vehementer |
| tell | narro 1, refero | wage war | bellum gero -ere gessi gestum 3 |
| temple | templum -i 2 n | wait for | exspecto 1 |
| ten | decem | walk | ambulo 1 |
| tenth | * decimus -a -um | wall | murus -i 2 m |
| terrified | perterritus -a -um | | |

| | | | |
|---|---|---|---|
| wander | * erro 1 | wine | vinum -i 2 n |
| want | cupio -ere cupivi cupitum3 ½ | wife | uxor -is 3 f |
| war | bellum -i 2 n | willingly | libenter |
| warn | moneo -ere monui monitum2 | win | vinco -ere vici victum 3 |
| watch | specto 1 | wise | sapiens sapientis |
| water | aqua -ae 1 f | with | cum *(+abl.)* |
| wave | * unda -ae 1 f | without | sine *(+abl.)* |
| way | modus -i 2 m , via -ae 1 f | woman | femina -ae 1 f |
| we, us | nos | woman | mulier mulieris 3 f |
| wear | * gero -ere gessi gestum 3 | wonder at | miror 1 |
| wear out | conficio -ere confeci confectum 3½ | wood | silva -ae 1 f |
| weapons | arma -orum 2 n pl | word | verbum -i 2 n |
| weather | tempestas -atis 3 f | work n | labor laboris 3 m |
| weep | lacrimo 1 | work v | laboro 1 |
| well | bene | worry | cura -ae 1 f |
| well-known | * notus -a -um | worse | peior peius |
| what? | quid? | worst | pessimus -a -um |
| what sort of? | qualis -e? | wound | vulnus vulneris 3 n |
| when | ubi, cum | wound | vulnero 1 |
| when? | quando? | wound | vulnus vulneris 3 n |
| where? | ubi? | wretched | miser -a -um |
| whether | num | write | scribo -ere scripsi scriptum3 |
| which | qui quae quod | year | annus -i 2 m |
| while | dum | yesterday | heri |
| who? | quis? | you | tu *(nom. sing)* |
| who | qui quae qoud | you | te *(acc. sing.)* |
| whole | totus -a -um | you | vos *pl.* |
| why? | cur? | young person | iuvenis iuvenis 3 c |
| wicked | malus -a -um, scelestus -a -um | your (sing.) | tuus -a -um |
| wife | uxor uxoris 3 f | your (pl.) | vester -ra -rum |
| wind | * ventus -i 2 m | | |